People are talking about…

"Father Joseph G. Donders offers here an interesting thesis. He says that the gospel readings of the weekday liturgies present to us the working Jesus 'evangelizing, healing, and reordering the world,' and that we are invited to join him in completing this work. His reflections are sensitive to individual human emotions, strivings, failings, and sensitive, too, to the need for transformation of our world. Through vignettes about life, reminders of our personal stories, attention to details in the Scriptural text, apt quotations and poetry, Fr. Donders deftly draws us into Jesus' story, and with a clear social justice consciousness, he prophetically prods us to respond by doing the work Jesus did. Each reflection is brief and should help worshippers internalize the gospel more fully, whether read individually or used by pastors to frame their homilies."

Zeni Fox, Ph.D.
Associate Professor
Director of Lay Ministry
Immaculate Conception Seminary

"This is an excellent tool for homilists and for anyone looking for a brief, yet substantial reflection for each weekday of the liturgical year. Fr. Donders chooses a line from the gospel of the day (and on occasion from the first reading), which he illustrates with a story or an experience. He then applies it to everyday life, bringing to his commentary solid Biblical knowledge and pastoral sensitivity that both inform and challenge the reader. This is a wonderful book, one that you will want to carry with you all year long."

Rev. Anthony J. Ciorra
Director, Center for Theological
and Spiritual Development
College of St. Elizabeth
Morristown, NJ

"Reflecting on the weekday liturgical readings throughout the year, Rev. Joseph Donders highlights the routine tasks and conversations that Jesus had with the men and women of his day. Effectively selecting a phrase from each day's reading, he uses contemporary experiences to help the reader relate to the message. Short, concise and pregnant with inspiration, each reflection nurtures a daily connection with Jesus of Nazareth. This is a book not to be overlooked by anyone wishing to become and remain Jesus' companion."

Loretta Girzaitis
Author, Adult Educator, Spiritual Director

"With a deft touch, Fr. Donders reminds us through these commentaries that we must change our ways of thinking about the many little worlds we inhabit. And we must also change the unjust and oppressive systems that make it so difficult—if not impossible—to live the golden rule. From Matthew's story of the wedding feast at Cana, for example, he draws the message that while transforming ourselves and the world is a serious task, we should also enjoy life, celebrating with dancing and singing, eating and drinking, loving and making merry.

"I also appreciate the inclusiveness and contemporary tone of Fr. Donders' writings, which are easy to enjoy on several levels. These reflections should enrich those who deliver homilies as well as those who are active in small Christian communities or Bible study groups. There is a wealth of new ideas here for discussion around the dinner table. After all, Jesus did much of his storytelling at the table."

William V. D'Antonio
Adjunct Research Professor
The Catholic University of America

"Let's face it. It's virtually impossible for a harried parish priest to prepare a prime-cut daily homily. Most need all the help they can get. In *With Hearts on Fire*, Joseph Donders reflects on the weekday readings by looking at Jesus' day-to-day work of healing, teaching, and evangelizing. His commentaries are unvarnished, unfiltered stuff—and proof positive that you can illustrate moving truths in under three minutes. There is no need for the harried pastor to 'wing it.' He has these gospel companions to enlighten the Scripture readings. This is a high level homily helper."

Tim Unsworth
Columnist,
National Catholic Reporter

JOSEPH G. DONDERS

with Hearts *on* Fire

Reflections on the
Weekday Readings
of the
Liturgical Year

XXIII

TWENTY-THIRD PUBLICATIONS
Mystic, CT 06355

Twenty-Third Publications
185 Willow Street
P.O. Box 180
Mystic, CT 06355
(860) 536-2611
(800) 321-0411

ISBN: 0-89622-974-2
Library of Congress Catalog Card Number: 98-61777
Printed in the U.S.A.

Table of Contents

with HEARTS *on* FIRE

Introduction

Many books offer reflections on the Sunday readings, and there are many books with a Bible reflection for each day of the year. None of those books, however, are a great help to the reader or pastor interested in a reflection on the readings of the weekday celebrations of the Eucharist.

Unlike the three-year cycle of Sunday readings, the weekday readings for Advent, Christmas, Lent, and Easter are the same every year. During Ordinary Time the weekday schedule of gospel readings is the same year to year, but the first readings are arranged in a two-year cycle (while the Sunday lectionary has three readings per Sunday, the weekday arrangement has only two). This book offers reflections on those weekday gospel readings (with the exception of the reflections in Easter time, when I have often reflected on the reading from the Acts of the Apostles).

The lectionary arrangement isn't the only difference between Sundays and weekdays. Sunday is the day we celebrate Jesus Christ's victory, his resurrection, the victorious end to his everyday life and work for justice and love among us. Weekdays are different. In the weekday readings we see Jesus busy evangelizing, healing, and reordering the world around him. On Sunday we are invited to celebrate his victory with him. During weekdays we are asked to join him in completing his work.

As I wrote these weekday reflections I realized better than ever before how the weekday readings guide us through the gospels and the Acts of the Apostles. These reflections want to be a companion to the readers of those texts, nothing more but also nothing less!

These reflections might help us to accompany Jesus and his first disciples—women and men—at his and their daily task as described by Matthew, Mark, Luke, and John.

Most of this book was written on the verandah of the Marist Brothers home in Melbourne, Australia. Their hospitality is, I hope, gratefully reflected in these reflections!

Advent
Christmas

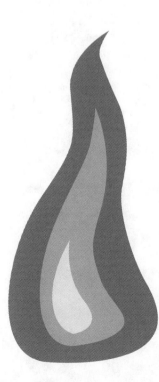

Monday of the First Week of Advent

MATTHEW 8:5–11

A New Beginning

"Many will come from East and West..."

For ages God's people have been singing psalms about the final outcome of our human history. They sang of how God would be a canopy, a tent, a shade, a refuge, and a shelter for all. It would be a new beginning. Prophets foretold how all the nations would together climb the Holy Mountain of God.

In today's gospel Jesus, too, speaks about this new beginning. "People will come from east and west." He turns the scene into a feast, the final feast, the great everlasting get-together of the whole human family at the banquet table in the reign of heaven.

This get-together started at the birth of Jesus. Think of the stories that surrounded that event. God broke the news by sending angels to alert the shepherds nearby, and by lighting a star to attract people from afar. The family from Nazareth was exposed to sights and sounds they had never known in Joseph's carpenter shop: the visit of shepherds and their sheep; the gifts of spices, incense, and perfume; and the gaze of camels and kings who had traveled a long way.

It was the beginning of a gathering around Jesus as foreseen by psalms and prophets, a rally that never stopped.

According to John's gospel, it even has to do with Jesus' death on the cross. John wrote that Jesus was going to give his life "to gather into one the scattered children of God" (John 11:52). If that was a reason Jesus was willing to die, it should be a reason for us to do our part in bringing together the whole human family.

Tuesday of the First Week of Advent

LUKE 10:21-24

The Child Jesus

"...revealing them to little children...."

There is something touching about a newborn child. Children have their own way of relating to the world around them. They were so one with the womb of their mother; they are so one with her breast. They relate to the world around them with that sense of oneness. It is as if the whole world is their friend.

You can see it sometimes in the way they play, step through puddles, and seem to trust humans and animals alike. You have to be careful when you visit a zoo with small children. Without hesitation they would walk up to a lion to pat its shoulder. Of course, that would be impossible in a zoo since fences and moats give sufficient protection. When a child meets a dog in the street, however, the danger is more real. The dog might not be as friendly as expected, and it might give a sharp growl. But children are fearless. They really embrace all life around them. They sit down in the most dangerous places. They eat mud and try to catch the sun and the moon. They trust everyone they meet.

Jesus must have noticed this attitude. It touched him. For him, it was a picture of the ideal world, a world without danger and fear. He said that we should relate to each other as children. He knew from bitter experience that this was often impossible, but he asked us to strive after it.

This is why he invited us to be like small children in order to be ready for him and God's reign among us.

At Christmas he presents himself as a child. Soon, as a young man, he will explain what he comes to do among us, what his intentions are. He wants to introduce a new world, a period of grace, the paradise children carry with them in their eyes, hearts, heads, and dreams.

Wednesday of the First Week of Advent

MATTHEW 15:29-37

Nothing to Eat

"I don't want to send them away hungry."

When Isaiah describes the world in today's first reading, he is very somber. It is, he writes, as if a dark veil is thrown over all people, a web cast over the nations. The world is stuck in the dark and cannot wrestle itself free. It isn't a nice picture The world is in a shameful state. Yet, in a way, it is this somberness that gives Isaiah hope. God cannot leave us like this. People today ask the question, "How can God want famine and hunger in this world?" The answer is that God does not want these things. That is why Isaiah was so sure that a new child was going to be born among us, a savior who would show us the way.

Jesus is this savior. Today's gospel says that when he looked at the hungry crowd, he felt sorry for all those people. They had nothing to eat, and he didn't want to send them away hungry. Jesus gave them the food they needed, using a few loaves and fishes. But he worked through his disciples, who distributed the food to the crowd.

Liam Hickey, an Irish priest, tells this story: "A young man was angry with God because of all the hunger and famine in the world. That night he had a dream. God spoke to him and said. 'I have done great things for the poor and hungry.' The young man said, 'Like what?' God said, 'I sent you!'"

Yet, you can't solve this problem on your own. Jesus didn't. The first thing he did was to look for some company. Maybe there is a committee trying to solve this problem in your parish or locality. Or you might join an organization that tries to overcome the hunger in our world.

Thursday of the First Week of Advent

MATTHEW 7:21, 24-27

Committees

"...the person who does the will of my Father in heaven."

One pitfall we all know about is the trap of the committee and the sub-committee. Of course there should be meetings. There should be committees, studies, and reports. Yet if we remain in the realm of words, Jesus says we are not sensible. We are building our work on sand, which will be blown over at the slightest turbulence.

We establish ourselves in this world through concrete activities. To say "Lord, Lord" isn't sufficient. Neither is writing your plans and good intentions on sheets of paper, or feeding them into a computer.

To be with Jesus means to take over his sentiments, to live with the same single-mindedness he had, to be like he was and is. Jesus makes it clear that anyone who listens to him and doesn't draw these conclusions is foolish. Such a person is as foolish as someone who builds a house on surface soil, without any foundation.

The foundation of our faith is the living of the life of Jesus, no less and no more. If we don't intend to live that kind of life we are deceiving ourselves and others when we say that we are "his."

Everyone knows how easy it is to talk about what should be done for the poor, the homeless, the orphaned, the drug users, and even society in general. We all know how comforting it is to be counseled about problems with your loved ones, your children, your parents, your past, and your addictions. But at a certain point the talking has to give way to action. To say only "Lord, Lord!" is really not sufficient.

Friday of the First Week of Advent

MATTHEW 9:27-31

On God's Love

"Have pity on us!"

The two who followed Jesus shouted that they could not see. They followed him to the front door of the house where he was staying. It was then that he turned to them. Again they told him that they couldn't see. He touched their eyes, and their sight returned.

Those two were helpless and in need. They trusted Jesus, not because they had something to offer, but because they knew about his goodness. At the other extreme, we often think that it is our prayers and good deeds that make us lovable in God's eyes. God loves us in weakness, failure, warts, blindness, and all. It is always God's own loving kindness that takes the initiative.

This is the kind of love that is sometimes mirrored in our own human love. Once when I visited a prison in Kenya, the guards told me that many of the criminals were visited regularly by their mothers, sometimes for years on end. When I asked why, they told me: "Mothers say: whatever my child did, he or she remains my child."

It is good to remember this. We are on very shaky ground if we think that our deeds are the reason God loves us. We are often blind to the real reason. It has nothing to do with what we offer God; it has everything to do with God's unconditional love.

One of the readings of today is Psalm 27. It is a beautiful psalm. In it the psalmist prays: "I am sure I will see the Lord's goodness!" That is what those two blind people were sure of when they met Jesus.

Saturday of the First Week of Advent

MATTHEW 9:35—10:1, 6-8

Give without Charging

"You received without charge, give without charge."

The family arrived very late in a foreign country, and they were very hungry, so hungry that the children probably wouldn't be able to sleep. The hotel restaurant was closed. They would have to find food elsewhere, they were told. Stopping a taxi, they asked to be taken to a restaurant.

The cab driver told them that everything was closed so late in the evening. Then he added: "I know one place, the best in town." They got in the cab, and they were very surprised when they didn't stop at a restaurant but at a house. It was the home of the driver, who, together with his wife, prepared a meal that was—considering the circumstances—terrific.

The driver then took the family back to their hotel. They had to pay for the ride, but the rest was free! Later, when they told friends this story, they added, "Now we know what the Eucharist is all about!"

A dream world? No, this really did happen. And things like this happen all the time! The world depends on those small gifts we give one another! Jesus would smile and say: "You received without charge, give without charge."

Today, at least once, why not take Jesus' words literally? Render at least one service just for free, even it costs you something. Do it for someone who would least expect you to do so. Just say, "You don't owe me anything. It's free."

Monday of the Second Week of Advent

LUKE 5:17-26

Solidarity

"And now some men appeared, bringing on a bed a paralyzed man."

Jesus was teaching in a packed house. A larger group of men and women were standing in front of the entrance to the house. When some persons came with their paralyzed friend on a stretcher they couldn't enter. Nobody gave way. Nobody was willing to give up their place. It wasn't even fair to expect that they would.

The newcomers climbed on the roof and managed to push and pull the roofing aside and make a hole big enough to lower the stretcher through. It dangled for some moments rather dangerously in the air. But then it came down just in front of Jesus.

"Seeing *their* faith he said: 'My friend, your sins are forgiven you.'" There's that little word "their" in this gospel story from Luke. Jesus forgave and healed the crippled man because he saw *their* faith. He saw the faith of the paralyzed man together with the faith of his friends who brought him and who were so insistent on having something done for their disabled friend that they didn't hesitate to break through the roof above Jesus' head.

Jesus must have been amazed at what he saw. It must have been another sign of hope to him. He saw signs of a greater justice, a growing human solidarity everywhere.

He often healed persons who were brought by others. Even more often, he healed persons who were introduced to him by others. In today's text he explicitly forgives and heals because of the faith of those who brought him the paralyzed man.

To Jesus it was a sign that conversion is possible, that differences can be overcome, that forgiveness can be granted. It was their togetherness, their solidarity, that prompted Jesus to forgive and heal.

Tuesday of the Second Week of Advent

MATTHEW 18:12–14

The Greater Joy

"Will he not leave the ninety-nine in search of the stray?"

Jesus' story about the good shepherd is about God and God's love for each of us. It is also an extraordinary story about Jesus himself. It is a tale about a certain preference, a predilection for compassion and forgiveness.

Someone told me another story that parallels what happens in the good shepherd story. An old rabbi had two sons. One behaved well and was the pride of his parents. The second one was a disgrace and ended up badly. When the rabbi did all that he could to help the second son out of his misery, someone asked him why he bothered. After all, this was his stray son. "Shouldn't you be more interested in your successful son?" He answered, "My stray boy needs my love even more than the other one."

This is the lesson Jesus would like us to draw from his tale about the good shepherd. That shepherd leaves the rest of his flock to look for the one who has strayed. It is this kind of love that Jesus wants us to share with one another.

This kind of love is compassionate and forgiving. It should be our first priority in life. It is our way of being in line with the love that comes from God.

Wednesday of the Second Week of Advent

MATTHEW 11:28–30

Rest

"Come to me, and I will give you rest."

Finding our way through life is tiring. All kinds of things happen at the most unexpected times. You thought you were settled; then something happens and everything changes.

Mary and Joseph knew about this better than most. Angels kept flying in and out. What those angels said wasn't even always consistent. Take the case of their return from Egypt. First an angel came to tell them that they could leave Egypt, that the danger was over. So they packed, walked, got tired, and finally came to the last bit of the journey to Bethlehem.

Then, during one of the last nights before they arrived there, the angel returned. They weren't supposed to go to Bethlehem. The danger wasn't over. They had to go to Nazareth. This was enough to make anyone impatient, to say the least!

Joseph and Mary had a way out of all these problems. Their lives revolved around Jesus. They were willing to change at every new signal from heaven because of their child.

Jesus was their center. This is something we often find in the lives of mothers and fathers around us. A mother works almost day and night to earn college tuition for her son; a father takes on a double job to help his daughter finish an internship. Their children are the center, and even the explanation, of their lives.

We find it in the lives of many others as well. A friend helps a friend through the greatest difficulty of all, that of facing death after a lingering and devastating disease like AIDS. The lives of millions turn around the lives of others in life and death.

Jesus said that if we take anyone as the center of our lives in such a way, we center around him. He promised that he will never forget it. Just as we will be with him, he will be with us, and our weariness will be taken away. He will give us rest!

Thursday of the Second Week of Advent

ISAIAH 41:13-20

God Loves the Poor

"The poor and needy...I, the Lord, will not abandon them."

If you look through the Bible to find evidence of God's concern for the poor, you will discover that ours is a compassionate God. God provides for the poor (Ps 68:10), delivers the poor (Ps 72:12), secures justice for the poor (Ps 140:12), hears the poor (Job 34:28), does not discriminate against the poor (Job 34:19), protects the poor (Is 41:10), will not forsake the poor (Is 41:17), and gives food to the poor (Ps 146:7). We read in the prophet Jeremiah that King Josiah "defended the cause of the poor and needy...," and the prophet adds (speaking for God): "Is that not what it means to know me?"

In the gospel of Matthew Jesus says, "Blessed are the poor in spirit, for theirs is the reign of heaven" (Mt 5:3). He also says, "Give to everyone in need, and do not refuse them" (Mt 5:42). If this is the God we serve, we should enter into the spirit of comforting and serving those in poverty.

Being kind to the poor is equivalent to lending to the Lord (Prov 19:17). At the end of his gospel Matthew tells us about the last and final judgment. The judge will be Jesus telling us that he always identified himself with those in need. "Whatever you did for these least ones, you did for me" (Mt 25:40). It is a rather unsettling picture, when you come to think of it.

Friday of the Second Week of Advent

MATTHEW 11:16-19

Depressed

"We played the flute for you and you did not dance....sang dirges, and you did not weep!"

I have heard mothers say something similar when their children said they were bored and didn't know what to do. Mothers aren't the only ones. It is something you hear over and over again: "I did everything I could, what more could I do? You never seem to be satisfied. Whatever I do is wrong."

It is good to know that even Jesus was struck by this mood so familiar to parents, educators, pastors, and managers.

Jesus adds another remark we all know and have often used: "Whatever you do is wrong. When you eat and drink they say of you, 'Look at that drunkard and glutton,' and when you don't eat and drink, they say, 'Look at that miser.'"

You can't win. Pope John Paul II suffered this kind of blues when he recently complained: "...activity is waning... difficulties both internal and external have weakened the missionary thrust...a fact which must arouse concern...a lessening that [always is seen] as a sign of a crisis of faith" (*Missio Redemptoris*, #2).

Many a priest and many a parish member might suffer this kind of inner turmoil when they think about their parish community, or even about their own personal life.

How did Jesus blow these blues away? How should we get rid of them? By putting things back in real perspective. By opening ourselves up to the larger mission and to the larger picture. All those smaller tensions fall away when we realize the task that is waiting to be done.

Saturday of the Second Week of Advent

MATTHEW 17:10–13

Peace Challenge

"Everything is once more as it should be."

When I was a child, my country was at war. We considered the occupying troops our enemies. As boys we would pester them all the time. We would walk behind them as near as we could, trip them, and run away as fast as possible. We would deflate the tires of their cars and consider ourselves to be great heroes.

We would never dream of being friendly to them. When they asked directions, we would send them the wrong way. We would never take candy from them, though they sometimes offered us sweets. We would steal all we could from them. We would never think of eating with them. We thought we were obliged to hate them with all our hearts. Things between them and us were not as they should be.

There was one exception that I remember well. One Christmas night the military commander of the town lifted the curfew so that we all could go to the midnight Mass. We did. It had snowed that night; you could see your footsteps in the fallen snow behind you.

At the beginning of Mass there was some noise in the back of the church, a noise we knew only too well, the sound of the heavy hob-nailed boots of the occupying troops. The soldiers remained in the back of the church with their guns. They came up for communion. They knelt next to us, and at that moment we were as we should be.

In their pastoral letter *The Challenge of Peace*, the American bishops wrote: "Nowhere is the Church's urgent plea for peace more evident in the liturgy than in the Communion rite." How right they are!

Note to the user:
There are special Advent Masses from December 17-24. For the reflections on the readings of those days turn to page 22.

Monday of the Third Week of Advent

MATTHEW 21:23-27

What Authority?

"What authority have you for acting like this?"

I once heard that question when I was regularly helping out in a parish on Sundays. It was a nice parish with a very kind community. Every Sunday we had the usual prayers for the faithful after the homily and the creed. Those prayers were well made, they covered a lot of human needs, and every week there was a prayer for peace.

One day a letter came to the priest in charge. The letter protested that those prayers were too political. "On what authority were those prayers said? All prayers for peace should stop, otherwise...." The letter wasn't signed. At the end it read: "Some worried Christians."

This isn't the only story of its kind. There are many like it. When they wrote their pastoral letter on war and peace the bishops of the United States felt from the very beginning that they had to defend themselves against that sort of objection.

They didn't write for a political reason. They wrote with the authority given to them as church leaders by Jesus Christ himself. They stated: "Peacemaking is not an optional commitment. It is a requirement of our faith. We are called to be peacemakers, not by some movement of the moment, but by our Lord Jesus. The content and context of our peacemaking is not set by some political agenda or ideological program, but by the teaching of his Church" (*The Challenge of Peace*, Summary).

Tuesday of the Third Week of Advent

MATTHEW 21:28-32

Prostitutes

"Prostitutes are making their way into the reign of God."

He was a parish priest in good standing. All his life he had been interested in social work. Lately he had been struck by the plight of the homeless. He decided to find out what it meant to be like that. One day he put on some shabby clothing and a knapsack. After some days he had a shaggy stubble of a beard and nobody recognized him any more.

He told me his story afterwards. He could hardly ever reach those better off to get some help. Their homes were unapproachable; he was chased away from their lawns by dogs. He went to the presbytery of one of his friends. He was not recognized. His friend's housekeeper had pity on him and let him in the kitchen. While he was sitting there, in a place he knew very well, his priest colleague and friend came in. He was told to leave immediately. He did.

He began to notice that the only ones who helped him were those not too well off. It was the kind of experience Mary and Joseph had when they looked for a place for Mary to give birth to Jesus. The innkeepers had no place for them, but someone must have shown them the shed where Mary brought Jesus into this world. And if the shepherds didn't show or lend that shed to Mary and Joseph, they definitely didn't chase them away from it.

Those shepherds—in that region and time ranked with prostitutes and sinners—allowed them to use their stable and welcomed them. They respected their plight and human dignity.

Afterwards Jesus would tell the people around him: "I tell you solemnly, tax collectors and prostitutes are making their way into the reign of God before you." A hard saying, but as my friend experienced, a very true one.

Wednesday of the Third Week of Advent

L U K E 7 : 1 8 – 2 3

Patience

"The good news is proclaimed to the poor...."

John the Baptizer was in prison. He had been arrested because Herod didn't like what John had said about his behavior. John had announced a total change. He had said: "The ax is at the root of the tree. God is going to intervene with power and might. All will be different."

John had been enthusiastic when he saw Jesus coming from Nazareth. With his own eyes he had seen Jesus, the one who was going to bring the change he had announced. Now he was in this horrible dungeon, and Jesus was walking about. Why didn't Jesus do something? What about the change?

We know the answer: "Go back and tell John what you have seen and heard: the blind see again, the lame walk, lepers are cleansed, and the deaf hear, the dead are raised to new life, the good news is proclaimed to the poor and happy is the person who does not lose faith in me."

Jesus spoke about the people around him who were healed in his presence. He wasn't speaking about himself healing and changing. He was speaking about them being changed and healed, and walking around as they had never done before.

The change was greater than even John had guessed, and different from what he expected. No brimstone and fire, but a gradual healing process that slowly but surely would heal us in our everyday activities.

This change would ask for great patience from John, and from all of us. This patience will bring forth its fruit, because in the end we will be able to say, together with Jesus Christ, "we" did it. We got through to the reign that will last forever and ever. The signs of its coming are visible all around us, for the blind see again, the deaf hear.... Patience!

Thursday of the Third Week of Advent

LUKE 7:24-30

Forerunner

"No one greater than John."

All of us know stories about parents who sacrificed their whole lives to ensure a better life for their children. Maybe it is your own story. There have been periods in human history when a whole generation did that. Isn't it really the heroic story of so many immigrant families? People dedicated their lives to a future they wouldn't even see. It is the tale of an old grandmother or grandfather planting a fruit tree for their grandchildren when they don't expect to eat from that tree themselves.

John was that type of prophet. He was there to announce something that he wasn't really part of. He was a forerunner. Once he had seen Jesus he knew that he should get smaller and smaller to give place to the new future in Jesus.

Jesus admired him for that. He said: "There is no greater one than John," but he added, "yet the least in the reign of God is greater than he is." John was willing to put his whole life at the service of a newness that he himself wouldn't live to see. That was John's greatness. He remains an example for us who struggle for a peaceful and a just society in the future. Some years ago the bishops of the United States wrote: "Let us have the courage to believe in the bright future and in God who wills it for us—not a perfect world, but a better one. The perfect world, we Christians believe, is beyond the horizon, in an endless eternity where God will be all in all. But a better world is here for human hands and hearts and minds to make" (*The Challenge of Peace*, #337).

Friday of the Third Week of Advent

JOHN 5:33–36

For All The Peoples

"The works my Father has given me to carry out."

Today's gospel reading has to do with the justice and integrity, the togetherness and blessing, for which Anna and Simeon, Elizabeth, Zechariah, and John the Baptizer waited. They all lived in occupied zones with freedom fighters in the hills. People were divided into oppressors and oppressed. They yearned for a more beautiful and just tomorrow. It is against that background that Jesus said he had come to do something, referring to "the works my Father has given me to carry out."

In the reading from Isaiah today, Isaiah explains that assignment in terms that Jesus would make his own. Isaiah said in the name of God: "...My house will be called a house of prayer for all the peoples." And he added: "Let no foreigner say: 'The Lord will exclude me from his people.'"

God recognizes no outcasts, foreigners, aliens, or "others." Neither should we. In the human family, in God's family, all are welcome. We belong together; it is only together that we form humanity, that we reach our full potential. When the wise men from the East came to visit Jesus and his mother, that prophecy began to be fulfilled.

The final day will be a glorious day. All nations and religions will have their own gifts to offer, just as they began to do in Bethlehem with their gold, myrrh, and frankincense. We are a rainbow in our colors, a symphony in our languages and poetry, one living body in Jesus Christ.

December 17

MATTHEW 1:1-17

His Days

"And Jacob fathered Joseph the husband of Mary; of her was born Jesus who is called Christ."

Just before Jesus' genealogy is triumphantly announced in Matthew's gospel today, the responsorial psalm in between the first and second reading announces: "In his days justice shall flourish and peace till the moon fails" (Ps 72:7).

This is the world and time Mary and Joseph, Simeon and Anna, and so many others dreamed of, a world of human dignity where everyone is a shepherd of creation. An earth where all children play, run, dance, shout, and sing, not die of malnutrition, where young people look forward to a life everyone shares and no one is marginalized, where old people see visions and young people dream dreams, where all people are cherished and no one is abandoned, where swords are hammered into plowshares, the lion lies with the lamb, and a little child leads them—and there is no preparation for war.

Is this merely a naive dream? Isn't it Jesus' dream? It is God's dream, God dreaming the world and we dreaming with God!

When Stephen Naidoo, the Catholic Archbishop of Capetown in South Africa, was arrested on an anti-apartheid mission years ago he said: "You can kill the dreamer but you cannot kill the dream! The dream is freedom and the dream is alive—and no amount of force is going to change that."

December 18

MATTHEW 1:18-24

This Is How

"This is how Jesus was born."

"This is how Jesus Christ came to be born," Matthew writes. He then describes in a very matter of fact way how everything started in the modest home of a Nazareth family, and how it led almost immediately to serious, but very homey, problems.

There is something consoling about this. We are often struck by a feeling of helplessness when we become aware of the problems in our world. Often our lack of attention to them is caused by our fear of that very frustration. How would we be able to change the world, we ask.

Mary did it by giving birth to a child, Joseph by changing his mind and bringing Mary into his home.

This is the only way things really get done in this world. We might dream about a just society, wonder about a "green" environment, or hope for peace the world over. But all these issues are determined by what is done and realized at home, where we live and make decisions. What we are asked to do is not the impossible, but the beginning of a new life at the level where we live. Think globally, act locally.

December 19

God Intervenes

"Elizabeth was barren."

The readings today tell the same story about two women. They were both barren. One was the mother of Samson. Her name is not even mentioned, though we are told that God sent an angel to her!

The other woman is Elizabeth, the mother of John the Baptizer. We are told that the villagers humiliated her because she was childless. In the lives of both women God intervenes, taking what the world considered worthless to show God's glory.

In Sacred Scripture God often intervenes in this way. Just consider that our creator didn't use gold, uranium, diamonds, or pearls when making the human body, but just dust.

God didn't speak to Moses from a mighty cedar, but from a low-growing bush. God picked David to be king, though David's father hadn't even bothered to call his son in from the field.

Jesus followed the same divine pattern when working his miracles. Consider how a few pieces of loaves and some fishes were multiplied to feed a crowd of thousands.

However humble and domestic our life stories might be, we are deeply valued in the eyes of our maker, created as we are in God's image. All of us have our own role to play in God's mighty work.

December 20

LUKE 1:26-38

You Are Special

"Rejoice, so highly favored! The Lord is with you."

The woman received a beautiful string of pearls in the mail. She could guess who had sent this gift, but she almost burst into tears when she didn't find any message with the gift. She went through the package three times, but there was no note, no word attached, only those pearls. What she really wanted was a card that said "I love you!" That message would have been more valuable to her than the most expensive gift.

When the archangel from God greets Mary in Luke's gospel, the first thing Mary hears is: "Rejoice, you are special, precious. You are loved!" God doesn't leave out the important words. All further blessings in Mary's life followed from that greeting.

Words of affirmation and love are blessings for us. They are the kind of words that bring people together. They make the connections needed to turn this world into a civilization of love!

Still today, God greets us as Mary was greeted. Each one of us is unique, precious, and loved in God's eyes. Each one of us has a special role to play! God calls each one of us by name.

Draw your lesson from the way God greets us! Pay attention to your own greetings today! Greet someone whom you would normally not have greeted. Watch his or her pleasant surprise. Do your part weaving the world around you together in kindness and love.

December 21

LUKE 1:39-45

Mary's Privileged Place

"Of all women you are the most blessed...."

Pope John Paul II can't write a letter without mentioning the Blessed Virgin Mary. Theologians can't stop speaking about her. Millions of faithful visit her shrines in Lourdes, Fatima, and Medjugorje. The well-known priest/sociologist/novelist Andrew Greeley holds that Mary is a central figure in the Roman Catholic religious imagination.

No wonder that you seem to touch a sensitive nerve when you speak about Mary in Catholic circles. Such was the case even during the Second Vatican Council, when the council members had to decide whether to dedicate a special document to the Blessed Virgin or whether she should be included in the document on the church. It proved to be the closest vote of the whole council.

While in almost all council votes the majority was about ninety-four percent, in this case the decision to include Mary in the document on the church carried by only seventeen votes. Mary was not going to get a special document dedicated to her. Instead, she would be given her own chapter in the document about the people of God. The idea was to give her a special place among the faithful, among us.

Somewhere in Australia near Perth, a parish council expressed this intention in a beautiful way. They had a new statue of Mary made. The statue was made so that it could be placed in the front pew in the church. This was a perceptive way of expressing about Mary what Elizabeth said of her when the two met after the annunciation: "Blessed are you among all women, and blessed is the fruit of your womb." Mary is called blessed because she is the only one who could say of Jesus: "He is of my body, he is of my blood!"

December 22

LUKE 1:46-56

Mary's Song

"He has...raised high the lowly."

Mary's song expresses her feelings. She doesn't mince words; she makes it clear what she expects her son to do. She must have sung this song to him often when he was a baby, and even when he was older, explaining to him why she had agreed to accept him as her child.

It is not a violent song. It is a song about peaceful change. We are not incited to take up arms or anything like that. The song describes how God will take care of all those who cannot come into their rights, how God will work the original plan of creation when all were considered to be good and equals without preference or discrimination.

Mary had suffered much discrimination as a Jewish woman, living in an occupied country, taxed and administered by strangers. Her son was going to restore the old *shalom*. That is what he did when he broke bread with everybody. Mary was his earliest inspiration when she gave him bread and wine at home.

Children hear the gospel message first from the lips of their parents who consciously introduce them to the issues of justice and peace, who introduce them into the practice of love, and who help their children to solve their conflicts in nonviolent ways, enabling them to grow up as peacemakers.

December 23

LUKE 1:57-66

The Power of Speech

"His power of speech returned and he praised God."

The President of the Theological Union recently presented a gift to the school's receptionist. He said that the first contact people have with this establishment is through her, and that she is really its ambassador.

He might have added something else, something that applies to all of us. Speaking to and with others is something divine!

To be able to express our thoughts and emotions is part of being created in the "image of God." The book of Genesis tells us about the power of speech. God said: "Let there be light," and there was light. God pronounced the names "Adam" and "Eve" and they stood before God in all their glory.

At Christmas we celebrate how God's Word is born among us. This emphasis on the "Word" teaches us that our words and gestures are also meant to communicate God's Word.

We do this when our words offer life, joy, comfort, consolation, and peace to others. The lesson of Advent and Christmas is this: our words should echo God's Word and Spirit. We are ambassadors for Christ.

December 24

LUKE 1:67-79

Tender Mercy

"By the tender mercy of God."

Zechariah was standing with his little son in his large hands. He was a priest; his hands had carried many offerings to the altar of God. He understood what his son's role would be. He must have foreseen his son's martyrdom, his unavoidable end in this world.

Yet, Zechariah speaks about God's tenderness and love. That little baby in his hands makes him speak of God's mercy and goodness. So often you hear that someone changes when he holds a baby in his hands.

We have been preparing for Christmas. There are many ways to do that. Jesus came to bring the peoples of the earth together. He came to undo sins. He came to die for us. He came to restore God's peace, a peace that implies a right relationship with God, bringing with it forgiveness, reconciliation, and union.

Yet, we should not forget that many theologians and saints thought that God would have been born among us as a human being even if we hadn't sinned and weren't in need of redemption. God would have done that in God's love. God would have come to us because, as our Mother and Father, God wants to be with us.

So don't be afraid! God visits us out of love. God would have come to be with us anyway. Doesn't that say something about God? In one translation of Luke's gospels it is put so nicely: "By the tender mercy of our God, who from on high will bring the Rising Sun to visit us."

December 25

LUKE 2:1–14

Christmas

"You will find a baby wrapped in swaddling clothes."

Jesus was never alone
in what he did in this world.
Born from Mary
and protected by Joseph,
shepherds and magi surrounded him
from his very beginning.

Born and reared in a small village
he followed its customs,
relating to God in an unheard of and special way
and yet within the context
of one human culture.

He surrounded himself
with women and men wherever he went,
entrusting them with his own mission,
undoing evil,
atoning for the past,
healing the world,
announcing the good news,
breaking bread and sharing wine,
building a body
in this world.

Christmas is the beginning.
Christmas will also be the end,
when the Spirit of Christ
is brought to life
through the changes
we make in this world. Amen.

December 26

MATTHEW 10:17-22

The First Martyr, Stephen

"The Spirit of your Father will be speaking in you."

It is the day after Christmas, and the scene is violence. Violence used against the first deacon, Stephen. Why did this happen? Was it because of the theological discussions he had with the people from Cyrene and Alexandria? Or was it because of the role he was asked to play in the conflict that led to the institution of the diaconate? Was it because he had been successful in that role?

We know about the conflict: a difficulty arose in what we would call a soup kitchen, the food distribution system among the poor organized by the Jerusalem Christian community. That distribution had begun to treat the Hebrew-Christian widows differently from the Gentile-Christian ones. It was a question of discrimination. You might even call it racism. The Judeo-Christians got preferential treatment. They got the best of the soup. They went in through the back door, while the others were waiting at the front door.

Peter himself had been asked to intervene. He had appointed Stephen to reorganize the proceedings and to restore equity in the community. Stephen had been able to do that. What Jesus had called "the Spirit of the Father" had been speaking through him.

Why was Stephen killed? We don't know. But it would put him at the beginning of a line of martyrs who suffered—and suffer—because they witnessed to the oneness of God's family, opposing discrimination and racism.

December 27

JOHN 20:2-8

John, the Loved One

"He saw and he believed."

Her mother told me that she always had kept the room of her thirteen-year-old daughter just as it had been when her daughter had died in a tragic car accident. She insisted on showing me the room. On the bed in the room was a neatly folded T-shirt. She touched the white shirt and said, "She folded that herself, it was one of the last things she did. She always folded them like that." Her eyes filled with tears.

When John saw the cloths in the tomb, one neatly rolled up in a place by itself, he must have recognized Jesus. In his letters he insisted that he knew about Jesus, he had heard him, seen him with his own eyes, and touched him with his own hands (1 John 1:1). He knew about him. He loved him.

Now he found Jesus' burial cloths left behind by him, folded up not to be used any more. It meant that Jesus was alive. It also meant that he was alive again in John. It was like a rebirth of Jesus. A rebirth of God's Spirit in John's presence in him. He saw and believed.

In his letter he wrote that he told us all this so that we might share his love, and his union with Jesus (1 John 1:3). He added that he was writing "to make our own joy complete" (1 John 1:4).

December 28

MATTHEW 2:13-18

Joseph's Plight

"Get up, take the child and his mother with you, and escape...."

We might pray for all kinds of spiritual and material graces, or for peace. Prayer can be deceptive. We might be tempted to leave it all to God. Do you ever catch yourself asking God to do things for you because you're too lazy to do them yourself? Do you ever complain about a situation you could easily solve by yourself?

Joseph might teach us a lesson here. He was sure his Father in heaven would protect Mary, the unborn child, and himself. God did. Every time a danger threatened, God sent an angel to warn them. But that was all the angel did. When they had to flee into Egypt, Joseph had to wake up Mary, and Mary had to wake up the child. They had to pack their bags. They had to dress the child against the cold of the night. They had to walk all the way, while the angel flew off.

Were they not just left alone, like lost sheep in the night? We might think so, but we would be mistaken. We are never left alone.

Mary and Joseph didn't consider themselves lost sheep. They had all they needed to do the things they were asked to do. They weren't lost. They had their common sense, their hands, and their feet, just as we do.

December 29

LUKE 2:22-35

Family Tension

"...and a sword will pierce your soul too..."

As a seminarian I had to prepare a sermon on the Holy Family for our course in preaching. I delivered it to my classmates, not the easiest audience. They liked it. I was proud of my sermon and sent it to my family. That was a mistake. My father read it aloud at the family dinner table. Most of my twelve brothers and sisters were present; so was my mother. When I got their reaction in a letter from my father (the longest one of the very few I ever got from him), I realized that they had laughed a lot. He wrote me that a family as described by me hardly could serve as an example to any existing family. He wondered, he wrote, whether the family in Nazareth was as ideal as I presented it.

Preachers often speak about the Holy Family, projecting their ideas of an ideal family, without asking whether such a projection is realistic.

The tensions in the family in Nazareth must have been great. Practically all we hear about are their problems. A betrothed man who feels jilted; words at the child's presentation in the temple that cause anxiety; a political threat that makes them refugees in a foreign country; a blood bath in Bethlehem after their flight; living in a hideout in Nazareth after their return; a child who runs away in Jerusalem; a mother who has difficulties understanding her son in Cana; a family that declares him out of his mind and tries to get him home; even the strange words Jesus speaks to his mother and to the beloved disciple from the cross.

It is the way they weathered those storms that makes the family in Nazareth a model for our families. There was an underlying bond that kept mother and son together. It was God's reign that kept them together. That it is why we find his mother at the foot of the cross, a great consolation to him, and a pain that she was willing to bear for him.

December 30

LUKE 2:36–40

Affirmation

"She came by just at that moment...."

Some would call it synchronicity, others serendipity, and again others providence. It is about those incidents where unexpected things and events come together in your life. You are looking for the solution to a problem, and the person next to you in the plane or train starts to speak about it. You need an encouraging word, and a car passes you with a bumper sticker saying: "Don't give up!"

The young couple in Jerusalem definitely could do with some affirmation in their situation. Mary herself had been doing something about a support group once she knew she was pregnant. She had left Nazareth and gone to Elizabeth her kinswoman.

But when they went to the temple the affirmation and encouragement they needed seemed to be arranged for them. First they met Simeon, who asked them to be allowed to keep the child in his arms, and then, "just at that moment," the eighty-four-year-old Anna happened to pass by. The story doesn't tell whether she, too, asked to hold the child. She definitely helped Mary to digest what Simeon told her about the sword that was going to pierce her heart. Mary must have been glad to meet a woman in that temple context. A woman who just at that moment came by. Was it synchronicity, serendipity, or providence? Mary surely must have seen it as a sign of God's love, active in her life. Shouldn't we pay greater attention to those "coincidences" in our own existence?

December 31

JOHN 1:1–18

Emmanuel

"The Word became flesh, he lived among us."

This beginning of the gospel of John sounds difficult and abstract. It is like a play of words, beautiful words. Those who study the text and compare it with other texts are convinced that the text is an old hymn, a hymn celebrating the coming of Jesus among us.

For those who composed the text, this celebration had nothing to do with a specific date like December 25th. They commemorated Jesus' birth in a different way. They celebrated the coming of Jesus in the everyday of our human lives.

The Word of God had become one of us. An old promise had been fulfilled. An ancient word had become a deed.

Emmanuel means God-with-us. It is a question of solidarity. It is encouraging news to us living in this world. The goodness of that news can be felt when we compare it with our own human experiences of solidarity—the moments when a friend remains with us in times of sickness, depression, or distress, the times that you yourself decided to be with someone during a troublesome time.

We can discuss the lot of the poor endlessly. It is only when we share their lives that they will be able to say: "Now we know that you are with us!" Words become fact. Now we can speak from our own experience.

In Jesus, God speaks in terms of our own human experience. He is one of us in our joys, trials, struggles, moments of discouragement, and hopes.

Emmanuel, God-with-us, can be personalized by each one of us. Emmanuel is God-with-me, God-with-you, in all the circumstances of our lives, a real presence that shows the passionate way God loves you, the others, and me. Together we form God's offspring, a reality so much greater than just ourselves.

January 1

LUKE 2:16-21

Mary, Mother of God

"..they found Mary and Joseph and the baby lying in the manger."

Chinua Achebe, the well-known Nigerian author, made an interesting remark about men and women in his book *The Anthills of the Savanna.* He tells us how in both our biblical and his African traditions women are blamed for all that went wrong in the world. In our case it is the familiar story of Eve. In Achebe's tradition women were the reason that God, who once lived very near to his human creation, left it. God was so near that the women who were pounding their millet into flour hit God. God warned them against this. They would be careful for some time, but then would start to chat again, forget about the divine presence, and hit God again. Finally, God gave up and left.

In both cases, Achebe writes, men told these stories. They knew that they weren't true stories, and because they felt somewhat guilty about them, they added another story in which they relate that final salvation will come through a woman, different from all other women, who cooperates with God. Achebe warns us to be careful about those stories. They might be told as a patriarchal conspiracy to keep women in a secondary place.

That is why it is good to consider that every woman is invited by God to be like Mary, cooperating with God to give birth to God in themselves and in the world in which they live.

It is what Jesus himself said when a woman in the crowd around him shouted one day: "Blessed the womb that bore you and the breasts that fed you!" He replied: "More blessed still are those who hear the word of God and keep it" (Luke 11:27b–28).

No doubt Mary is the mother of God. She became his mother by doing something all of us can and should do: hear the word of God and keep it.

January 2

J O H N   1 : 1 9 – 2 8

A Real Man

"I am…a voice that cries in the desert, prepare a way for the Lord."

Advertisements all around us attempt to determine our idea of a real man. They display cigarette-smoking individuals often in rough landscapes that look like the desert, or dressed in leather, sitting at a campfire, and using robust types of perfume.

In the gospel description of John the Baptizer some of those characteristics are mentioned, too. He lives in the desert and is dressed in an animal skin.

But they weren't the reason that Jesus once said, "If you want to see a real man, take a look at John the Baptist. Because of all the men born of women, there's never been a greater one than John" (Luke 7:28). Jesus had his own reasons.

When the priests and Levites came to John to ask who he was, his answers were simple. He was neither the Christ, nor Elijah, nor the Prophet. He was the forerunner, a voice in the desert. He described himself in his relation to Jesus and God's reign.

The characteristics that qualified him as a real man can be found in those answers given to the people who had come to harass him: sincerity, simplicity, conviction, courage, vision, and vulnerability (Stuart, *The Men's Devotional Bible*, 1993).

January 3

JOHN 1:29-34

Staying Power

"I saw the Spirit come down on him like a dove from heaven and rest on him."

Reading papers and magazines, you notice some themes that turn up again and again. These themes are the matter of our human story. They inspire ballads and songs. They are broadcast over radio and television. They are the mainstay of country music.

One of those themes is the fragility of human love, lovers jilted by former lovers, children abandoned by their parents, friendships begun in glory fading away.

These complaints are so frequent that one wonders in the end whether there is any human love that really lasts—a question often asked in these songs.

So many things that started full of promise end in utter disappointment. The enchantment is great, but how long will it last? Is it going to be the same with Jesus?

John the Evangelist answers this question by using the Greek verb *menein*, meaning "to remain" or "to stay," more than forty times in his writings. From the beginning he stresses that what appears in Jesus is something definite, something lasting. It is that staying power that made John the Baptizer recognize Jesus, as he said (using the word "remain" twice): "I saw the Spirit come down from heaven as a dove and remain on him. I would not have known him, except that the one who sent me to baptize with water told me, 'The man on whom you see the Spirit come down and remain is he who will baptize with the Holy Spirit.'"

Though human love may fade away, God's Spirit and love never leave Jesus, just as he in turn promised that he will never leave us, whatever happens: "And surely I am with you always, to the very end of time" (Mt 28:20).

January 4

JOHN 1:35-42

Relating to Jesus

"Look, there is the Lamb of God."

Various people will each see the same person differently. This is also true of Jesus. Just read the four gospels, plus Paul's writings, and you get different portraits of Jesus.

Jesus' case is particularly difficult. The gospel authors recognized the divine dimension in him as in no other human being. Jesus is God's offspring. Jesus is the anointed one, the *Christos*, the Christ.

Mark, Matthew, and Luke try to show his divine dimension by describing his everyday life, telling us how he walked through this world.

John has another approach. He stresses the divinity of Jesus from the beginning of his gospel. "In the beginning was the Word, the Word was with God..." (John 1:1). Jesus is immediately recognized as the Messiah (John 1:41). All this seems to be slightly at the cost of Jesus' earthy humanity.

The four gospel authors struggle with an issue we call "Christology." How did Jesus relate to God, and how does he relate to us? This is an important issue that responds to another question: "How do we relate to Jesus?"

When others evaluate us, will they find the Jesus dimension in our lives? The answer will depend not only on their insight into who Jesus is, but also on the way *we* relate to Jesus, the Christ.

January 5

JOHN 1:43-51

Appearances

"From Nazareth? Can anything good come from that place?"

Jesus' story is a human story. Though living two thousand years ago, in a culture different from ours, and in a different region from most of us, his story is our common human story.

Who of us has not suffered discrimination because of our background, family history, education, status, age, profession, class, ethnicity, or simply the color of our skin? Jesus did.

Nathanael disregards him because of the insignificance of where Jesus came from. The religious and secular authorities despised Jesus because of his lack of formal training.

South African Archbishop Desmond Tutu, no stranger to being discriminated against, often tells the story about a girl and a balloon seller in this context. The child is intrigued as she watches the balloon man occasionally release a balloon and let it float into the sky to attract some attention to his wares. Every now and then the balloons go up in the sky—blue balloons, red, green, white, black, and yellow. "Excuse me, sir," says the child. "How come when you let go of the balloons—green balloons, white balloons, red balloons, even black balloons—they always float up into the sky?" The man replies, "Love, it's not the color of the balloon that matters. It's the stuff inside."

It is that inside Jesus spoke about when he said of Nathanael: "Truly, this is one in whom there is no deception!"

January 6 (when Epiphany is celebrated on Sunday)

MARK 1 : 7 – 11

Struggle

"...he saw the heavens torn apart...."

You see it so often in a film, you hear it so often in real life. Someone is struck by disaster and prays to God: "Oh, that you would tear the heavens open and come down!" It is a very human prayer. It is the prayer of the prophet Isaiah (Is 64:1).

A prayer like this was heard when Jesus was baptized by John in the river Jordan. Mark tells us that heaven tore open and a voice was heard.

When we pray that heaven might tear open, we are praying that God will intervene in our need. When heaven tears open above Jesus a voice is heard, a voice that says: "You are my Son, whom I love; with you I am well pleased." Those words refer to old titles and names for the one who is coming to undo the powers that rule the world in order to renew it. Psalm 2 uses them: "You are my son; [the Lord] said to me, this day I become your father; ask of me what you will: I shall give you the nations as your domain, the earth to its farthest ends as your possession. You will break them with a rod of iron..." (Psalm 2:7–10).

By recalling these words Mark intends to dramatize what is happening at the moment of Jesus' baptism. A whole new world is born in the river Jordan. The fight against oppressive powers in the world has started. From now on Jesus is an alien in this old world of ours. He is an outlaw. Mark describes how "at once the Spirit sent him out into the desert.... He was with the wild animals, and angels attended him" (Mark 1:13). At one side "the wild animals" of this world, and at the other side "angels." This kind of symbolism doesn't need any further explanation.

Do you now understand what a struggle we are in for when we join Jesus, the man from Nazareth?

January 7 (when Epiphany is celebrated on Sunday)

J O H N   2 : 1 – 1 2

Cana and Mary's Help

"...and the mother of Jesus said to him, 'They have no wine.'"

What was Mary thinking when she went to Jesus to tell him "They have no wine"? Biblical scholars and theologians have been speculating on that for centuries. Isaiah once used the metaphor of Yahweh being the bridegroom of humanity: "Like a young man marrying a virgin, your rebuilder will wed you, and as the bridegroom rejoices in his bride, so will your God rejoice in you" (Is 62:5). Did Mary think that this final wedding feast between God and humanity was going to start when she saw Jesus arriving at Cana? Is that why Jesus answered her: "My hour has not yet come"?

We don't know. We can only guess. One thing we can be sure of is that God loves us with a love that resembles our most intimate and passionate human love.

Andrew Greeley uses this theme in his numerous novels. He once said that he doesn't write these novels to entertain, educate, or indoctrinate his readers. He writes them to fascinate, thrill, and entice them in such a way that they will understand and feel what the realities and possibilities of God's love for us are if we believe what the prophet Isaiah foretold—a love shown to us by Jesus, who was willing to give his life for the sake of us, his friends.

It is nice to think of the two young folks sitting at their wedding feast in Cana. We don't even know their names. Maybe their names aren't mentioned because they stand for all of us.

When those two were drinking the new wine Jesus made for them, did they realize that they stood as a model for the love that came to us in Jesus?

Monday after Epiphany

MATTHEW 4:12-17, 23-25

Settling In

"...leaving Nazareth he went and settled in Capernaum...."

Once he began his mission, Jesus had to decide where to live, a decision all of us have to make at least once, and probably more often, during our lifetimes. It is a difficult decision. You have to take so many things into account—your family, your work, but also your ideas about what to do with your life.

Jesus was facing the same kind of issue. With what he had to do, where was he going to have his home and his headquarters? Nazareth, Bethlehem, Jerusalem...there were many possibilities.

He chose Capernaum. At first sight this was a strange choice, because Capernaum had a bad reputation. It was a harbor town of sorts, situated in a region known for its cutthroats and pagans. Capernaum was the least Judaic town in the least Judaic province. It was also the most cosmopolitan.

Going to Capernaum didn't mean that he wanted to lie low, or to hide. John was arrested by the same King Herod who ruled over Galilee. By deciding on Capernaum, Jesus settled in the eye of the storm.

He rented, bought, or borrowed a house in a region about which the prophet Isaiah had proclaimed: "Oh, land of Zebulun and Naphtali, Galilee of the Gentiles, the people living in darkness have seen a great light; on those who lived in a land as dark as death a light has dawned" (Is 8:22—9:1).

According to Isaiah, Jesus came to liberate God's people, "to break the yoke that burdened them, the rod laid over their shoulders...for his title will be Wonderful Counselor, Mighty Hero, Eternal Father, Prince of Peace" (Is 9:4, 6b). Jesus settled in Capernaum in view of his task and intention to establish God's reign in this world.

This is an indication that we should take that reign into account when *we* have to decide where to settle.

Tuesday after Epiphany

MARK 6:34-44

Compassion

"He took pity on them."

When Jesus saw the large crowd waiting at the shore, he took pity on them because they were like sheep without a shepherd. They must have looked lost, just like people disembarking from a commuter train or plane often look forlorn and lost. They all hurry along with briefcases hanging from their hands, or clenched under their arms, looking in front of them. Nobody looks around. Hardly anyone speaks. No one laughs. A long file of women and men in their gray business clothes on their way to their work. Have you been one of them?

Jesus took pity on the crowd when he saw them. He began to do what they expected him to do. He healed, told them of his vision, and made them feel great in his company. If he hadn't done things like that they wouldn't have stayed so long with him.

Before they realized it, it was evening and "very late." It's what happens when you are totally taken up by what you hear. What did he tell them? We don't know. But we can guess. G.K. Chesterton once said that the great person is the one who makes the people around him feel great. He added that he thought that consequently Jesus was the greatest of all.

It was in the company of Jesus, listening to him, that they discovered or better understood their divine origin, their connectedness, their human rights, and their potentiality. He unveiled to them their greatness! He had a way to make a person his or her most shining self.

It was the sustenance they needed as much as, and maybe even more than, the bread and fish he gave them afterwards. And so do we!

Wednesday after Epiphany

MARK 6:45-52

Another Epiphany

"He was going to pass them by...."

Jesus noticed, after having finished his prayers in the hills, that his disciples were having a hard time getting across the lake. They had the wind against them and had to row. At about the fourth watch of the night (which could have been at three AM) Jesus came toward them walking on the sea. And then follows that strange remark: "He was going to pass them by," or in other translations: "He wished to pass them by."

He didn't have to rescue them. They weren't caught in a storm or any danger like that. They simply had the wind against them. The only fear they had was that they thought they saw a ghost walking on the water. Why did Jesus wish to appear like that, wishing "to pass them by"?

The term "passing by" is used more often in sacred Scripture to describe what one calls a theophany. They are the moments that God manifests God-self.

It is what Jesus does, revealing himself in all his divine majesty and power by his dominion over wind and sea to those disciples of his, mainly fishermen who ought to know all about water and wind. He acts towards them as Yahweh did in former times.

It is another epiphany, or appearance of Jesus, who makes that point by telling them, "Do not be afraid, it is I." He then enters the boat, and water and wind die down in his presence.

Mark notes that those in the boat were "utterly and completely dumbfounded." He mentions that to let us know that we should react differently to Jesus' presence among us!

Thursday after Epiphany

LUKE 4:14-22

Jubilee Celebration

"He has sent me...to proclaim a year of favor from the Lord."

In Nazareth the people had heard about Jesus' baptism by John the Baptizer. They must also have heard about the miracles he had already worked in Capernaum. It is understandable that they were slightly upset. So would we be, if we had been living in Nazareth then. Why hadn't he immediately returned to Nazareth to heal the sick there?

They all came to the synagogue the weekend he was home. They expected him there because, as Luke notes, it was his custom to come there for the Sabbath celebrations.

As the moment for the reading came, Jesus stood up to read. They handed him the scroll of the prophet Isaiah. All eyes in the synagogue were fixed on him. Unrolling the scroll he read how the prophet foretold that the year of favor, the year of the jubilee, would start. He rolled the scroll up, returned it, and said, "This text is being fulfilled today."

To understand what happened, we must know something more about that year of the jubilee. Every fiftieth year priests were to sound a horn, called a *jobel*, to begin the jubilee year. Slaves should be freed, debts forgiven, and all property—especially land—would be redivided. The intention was to avoid an ever-growing gap between the rich and the poor, and to promote the reorganization of a just equity.

It is not certain whether the Jewish people ever practiced that divine directive. That is why prophets like Isaiah foretold that one day Yahweh would start a jubilee year, a year of grace.

No wonder the people in Nazareth grew excited when they heard that justice and equity finally were going to be restored. It would be quite something even today. In fact, it is what Pope John Paul II has asked for several times, advising us not to forget that the goods of this world are meant for all.

Friday after Epiphany

LUKE 5:12-16

His Prayer

"He would go off to some deserted place and pray."

Luke's gospel speaks more about prayer than any other gospel. He has a reason for this. It has something to do with how he discovered Jesus' presence in his world. Luke was a traveling medical doctor. He journeyed from one patient to another. Traveling around in the decadent Middle East of his time he discovered some rays of hope in the midst of that chaos. He found some communities in Jerusalem who owned everything they had in common, and who had started a food distribution system to help the poor. And in Joppa he noticed a kind of thrift shop that provided the naked with clothing. His amazement made him inquire why they did the things they did, and their answer had been that they were aware of God's Spirit in them. That Spirit spurred them on to act as they did. Once they gave that Spirit in them another name: they called it the Spirit of Jesus (Acts 16:7).

Luke's next question must have been, "How do you get into contact with that Spirit in yourselves?" Their answer had been, again and again: "In prayer."

Luke built his gospel around this discovery. Just remember how he tells about what happened at Jesus' baptism. The other gospels tell how the Holy Spirit revealed herself at the moment the water flowed over Jesus' head.

In Luke's report nothing extraordinary happens at that instant. It is when Jesus is out of the river on the riverbank praying that heaven opens and the Spirit is seen!

Saturday after Epiphany

JOHN 3:22-30

Glory to Whom Glory is Due

"No one can have anything except what is given them from heaven."

According to the story we read today both John and Jesus were baptizing at the same time; Jesus in Judea and John at Aenon, near Salim. It looked like competition. No wonder that a discussion arose on how the two were relating to each other, especially because more and more people were joining Jesus.

Interviewed about this issue John explained once more his role: "I am the one who has been sent to go in front of him." He added: "No one can have anything except what is given him from heaven." This is a spiritual version of the saying, "No one can give what one does not have."

There is an old Hasidic Jewish story about Abraham and Sarah that puts it in another way. One evening a guest had joined them for a meal. After he had eaten and wiped his mouth, he stood up to thank Abraham, but Abraham replied, "Was the food that you have eaten mine? You have partaken of the bounty of the God of the universe. Now praise, glorify, and bless the One who spoke the word 'world,' and the world was." Glory should be given to whom that glory is due. John did so without hesitation.

Lent
Triduum
Easter

Ash Wednesday

JOEL 2: 12-18

Sharing

"Rend your hearts, not your garments, and return to the Lord your God."

About the year 128, a journalist named Aristides was called to the imperial court of the emperor Hadrian, who wanted some information about Christians. Aristides told his amazed audience: "When someone is poor among them who has need of help, they fast for two or three days, and they have the custom of sending the hungry person the food they prepared for themselves."

An old Christian custom recommended by Saint Augustine when he wrote about fasting and mortification notes: "Don't believe that fasting suffices. Fasting punishes you, but it does not restore your brother! Your fasting will be fruitful if you provide for the needs of another. How many poor people could be nourished by the meal you did not take today?" He echoed Isaiah who, in the name of God, once said: "Is not this the sort of fasting that pleases me—to share your bread with the hungry...?" (Is 58:6-7).

This is an idea that Christians have never lost. In 1961, in order to promote a Family Fast Day, the British bishops stated: "What we save thereby can be offered for the hungry and the starving. Such a sacrifice would be very much in the spirit of Lent, for it would touch both palate and purse."

The bishops of the United States made the same kind of suggestion, not restricting it to Lent, but suggesting it for every single Friday of the year. They did that when they wrote a letter to all of us on the need to reconsider our economic structures, recommendations that rarely seem to be followed. If we did, we would not only be organizing our own lives and priorities, but even society itself. The needs of others would find a new place in our "new agenda." And all of us would be happier because of it.

Thursday after Ash Wednesday

LUKE 9:22-25

Dignity

"...anyone who wants to save his life will lose it, but anyone who loses his life for my sake will save it."

Jesus speaks about the possibility of losing yourself. According to him it is the worst thing that can happen to you. He says that you can't compensate for that loss by winning the whole world. Some people know this from experience. They once made hundreds, thousands, maybe even millions of dollars, and then one day discovered that they had lost themselves in the process. One day this truth suddenly dawned upon them, changing them completely.

Francis of Assisi is one of the more famous cases. He was a romantic young man, son of a rich merchant, fashionably dressed and eager to ride his horse into battle. Coming home defeated, having lost that battle, he suddenly realized that what he was doing had little or no meaning. His life was empty. He had lost himself in glamour and vain snobbery.

He changed his way of life, leaving his father's shop and wealth, to regain his real human dignity. He succeeded, and what a joy he has been to the whole world ever since.

Others redirect their lives in less romantic and dramatic ways. They change jobs to be more themselves; they alter their policies; they become more critical and reflective; they join self-awareness programs, church communities, or support groups to regain their heart, soul, and humanity along with their dignity.

It isn't always possible to do it the way Francis of Assisi did it. It is almost always possible, however, to redirect the work we do, to shift our interests from merely making money to more human matters that are of God. In that way we will really find ourselves.

Friday after Ash Wednesday

MATTHEW 9:14–15

On Fasting

"...then they will fast."

In 1981 a university chaplain, Father Thomas Ryan, published a book that he called *Fasting Rediscovered: A Guide to Health and Wholeness for Your Body-Spirit.* He included a whole set of testimonies from people who had rediscovered fasting. "I fast to pull the loose ends together in my life." "I used to do a lot of things that were at cross-purposes with my own health and well-being." "Fasting introduced me to a more genuinely life-supporting way to live."

All kinds of people are fasting again. Athletes, boxers, musicians, dancers, astronauts, medical professionals, students, teachers, designers, writers, secretaries, bus drivers, store managers, homemakers, people from all backgrounds and in all professions are doing it.

We are surrounded by people who stopped smoking, restrained their drinking, or became vegetarians, people who overcame their addiction to caffeine, sugar, chocolate, alcohol, nicotine, and drugs.

They shop in health shops, drink soya milk, eat lean food, and watch their weight and calories. As Father Ryan noted, most times these changes all have something to do with what one might call body-ecology. For almost all of these people fasting is a conscious option for a healthier life and a clearer mind. Even for those whose religious faith can't motivate them to do it, fasting seems worth doing.

Others don't fast only for their own sake. They do it also for the sake of others, for the sake of the earth, and for God's sake. They restrict their over-consumption so that they can support others who haven't enough to consume and to live with. They do it opting for life—their own life and the lives of others.

Saturday after Ash Wednesday

LUKE 5:27-32

Healing

"It is not those who are well who need a doctor..."

Luke was a doctor seeing the world from a physician's point of view. He even looks at Jesus from a medical viewpoint. In fact, he makes Jesus into a doctor. In Luke's gospel, when Jesus introduces himself in the synagogue of his hometown, Nazareth, he tells them: "No doubt you will quote me the saying: 'Physician, heal yourself'" (Lk 4:23). Jesus here called himself a doctor. It wasn't the only time in the gospel of Luke that he did this. He also did it when he was accused of eating and drinking with sinners. He answered his accusers: "It is not the healthy that need a doctor, but the sick."

According to Luke, Jesus came to heal a world and a humanity that was sick and needed a doctor. You don't need to be a health expert or a doctor to note that the world around us is sick. Acid rain is killing trees; fish and waterfowl are dying in polluted rivers and lakes. Sometimes you can hardly breath without doing damage to your lungs, and you even have to be careful when you take a shower, because the water you use might be full of chemicals. We all need a doctor; we all need to be healed, not only we, but also the plants, animals, rivers, seas, forests, and deserts.

Something has to be done; you always have to take some steps to regain your health. Jesus suggests *repentance*. A doctor won't use that word when recommending a diet or discontinuing one or another habit in order to restore your health. What he or she recommends, however, often comes to the same thing: you have to change your life to make up for what went wrong in the past.

The healing we need also requires more than a personal and individual transformation. It asks for a structural revision of our society and of the world, a change we have to be interested in if we want to be touched by the healing power of that physician Jesus!

Monday of the First Week of Lent

MATTHEW 25:31–46

Royal

".. he will take his seat on his throne of glory...."

The time of kings and queens is over. It even becomes difficult to speak about the reign of God in a world with more and more republics.

There are two ways to look at the disappearance of queens and kings. They disappeared because we no longer tolerate that others not elected are put over us in any way. Or, you might say that they vanished because all of us proved to be of royal stock and dignity.

The Old Testament uses the word "king" more than 2500 times. It expects much of a king. Psalm 72 is one of the texts that outlines those expectations:

God, endow the king with your own justice, his royal person with your righteousness
that he may rule your people rightly
and deal justly with the oppressed ones (1–2).
For he will rescue the needy who appeal for help, the distressed who have no protector.
He will have pity on the poor and the needy, and deliver the needy from death.
He will redeem them from oppression and violence
and their blood will be precious in his eyes (12–14).

When, at the end of Matthew's gospel, Jesus appears on the clouds at the end of time, he appears sitting on a throne as a king. In that description all of us will be standing before him. He will ask us some questions about our lives. You know the questions: did you feed the hungry, did you help the oppressed, did you have pity on the poor and the needy? He will ask us whether we did what a king or queen is supposed to do according to Psalm 72.

Jesus Christ is king, but all of us are called to be royal as he was, is, and shall be.

Tuesday of the First Week of Lent

MATTHEW 6 : 7 – 15

Cleansing

"And forgive us our debts, as we have forgiven those...."

A parish youth group met for a retreat on a winter evening in Melbourne, Australia. They had to decide how to organize their day. Soon ideas began to fall into place. The first thing they decided to do was have each person write down anything from the past that might hinder the group from having a fruitful retreat. They did this, and then, one by one, burned those papers to ashes. There was silence during this whole solemn exercise.

It was Christmas time in Dublin, Ireland, at another youth retreat. In the middle of the conference room was a large undecorated Christmas tree. Under the tree was a high pile of yellow and purple pieces of ribbon. The participants were asked to remember any person they had not forgiven, write that person's name on a ribbon, and put it on the tree if they could forgive them now. By evening time the tree was full of ribbons.

It isn't only the things that clutter up our kitchen shelves, cupboards and wardrobes, desk drawers, attics, basements, and garages that hinder us from moving and breathing freely. There are the less tangible, but often more trying, spiritual and moral burdens we carry with us.

Unforgiven offenses, guilt feelings from the past, wrong choices, betrayed loves—they should be burned to ashes, too.

That is difficult. It asks for a lot of discipline. It is all too easy to remain caught in the past, to use the past as an excuse not to do anything at all. It is much easier to continue accusing and complaining.

Forgiving others is difficult; to forgive yourself is sometimes even more difficult. Yet, it is a step we have to take before we can proceed much further.

Wednesday of the First Week of Lent

LUKE 11:29-32

Signs

"This is an evil generation; it is asking for a sign."

Jesus told the crowd that they had to change their ways. He said: "This is a wicked generation; it is asking for a sign." They didn't believe him. They asked him to give them a sign that he was right about their situation. Jesus was upset about that. Why would they need a sign? Wasn't it obvious that things would fall apart if they didn't change their ways?

Not only prophets, but even concerned scientists in our day often have the same difficulty as Jesus. Economists tell us that the world will run out of resources if we continue to exploit the earth as we are currently doing. Biologists speak about the disastrous effects of our waste of energy, of the destruction of the rain forests, of the pollution of the atmosphere, of the dumping of radioactive waste, of using materials like plastics that are not biodegradable. Physicians warn us that we're eating too much fatty stuff, that many drink too much, that we should drive our cars less and use our feet and bodies more. Sociologists warn that families are falling apart, that children are not well educated, and that there are too many homeless people in our streets.

Too few listen. Those who don't listen often say that they want clearer signs, more proof, stronger evidence, while all around us forests die, fish rot, air and water are polluted, and human beings suffer.

We don't need more signs. We need changes. Of course, it would be impossible to change everything at the same time. But we all can begin and enter the process. Today you might change one of your consumer habits. Take a mug or cup with you to work instead of using paper or styrofoam cups.

Thursday of the First Week of Lent

MATTHEW 7:7–12

Asking and Receiving

"Everyone who asks receives; everyone who searches finds; everyone who knocks will have the door opened."

You know the story. You've heard it so often. He didn't look well. That's what everybody who cared for him told him. He himself had some vague worries about his health. He sometimes had those strange pains. He felt so deadly tired even before the day was half over. His friends told him to go to a doctor. He didn't want to do that: he might have to change his life-style. In a way he acted like a child who doesn't want to know the truth. His fear stifled him, made him deny everything. It would pass, he told himself; he had had something like this before. He delayed and delayed. He didn't dare to ask questions. He didn't want to find out.

We often accuse ostriches of this kind of practice. They are supposed to stick their heads in the desert sand when danger approaches, so that they won't see the danger. That is only a legend. Ostriches are wiser. They organize themselves better than that.

Jesus, too, asks us to question and to search what went wrong, or what our situation is.

That isn't easy. When you start to question yourself about some event or situation, you might gain some awareness of things you never knew before. The one who asks always receives. If you have no questions, you won't be answered. And in the end you risk mistaking a stone for bread, a snake for fish, and your sickness for health.

Friday of the First Week of Lent

MATTHEW 5:20-26

Taking Life

"You have heard how it was said to our ancestors, You shall not kill."

He was a theologian speaking in an African students' community. The subject was "You must not kill." During the talk the topic of abortion came up. The discussion afterwards was mainly on that issue. All went well until one student asked a question the speaker couldn't answer: "Why is it that the church leadership pays so much attention to voluntary abortion and not to spontaneous abortions that are due to the fact that in slum areas so many pregnant women abort spontaneously because of their poverty, their misery, their sickness, and their hunger?"

When the answer didn't come, the student who asked the question gave the answer himself: "It is, I think, because in that case you would have to do something about the economic order, and you aren't willing to do that, are you?"

The remark may not have been a fair one, but it definitely pointed at something: there is a whole infrastructure of unhealthy and even sinful circumstances that are killing human life.

Other theologians and bishops do address this issue when they speak about the "seamless garment." They state that human life is woven in one piece, just like the garment Jesus was wearing when he was stripped to be put on the cross. The seamless garment of human life shouldn't be rent into pieces. It shouldn't be divided against itself.

If we want to do justice to Jesus' words, we have to tackle the circumstances that make this world a killer of so many people.

Saturday of the First Week of Lent

Enemy

"But I say this to you: love your enemies and pray for those who persecute you."

Jesus' love is inclusive. So is his logic. He doesn't exclude anyone. He knows he has enemies. He feels that others have broken with him, judged him unjustly, and treated him accordingly. But he refuses to break with *them.* He advises us: "Do not resist those who wrong you! Love your enemies and pray for your persecutors." According to Jesus, even if they betray us, we, fueled with Jesus' love, simply can't do the same.

From the earliest days there have been Christians who radically lived his love and logic. Did you ever hear the story of Maximilian? It was March 12 in the year 295. Conscripted as a soldier, he refused to serve. He was brought into the court of Dion, the proconsul. The first to speak was the attorney, Pomeianus: "As Maximilian is liable for military service, I request that his height be measured." When the proconsul asked his name, Maximilian answered: "Why do you want to know my name? I am not allowed to be a soldier, I am a Christian." He was measured: five feet and ten inches. Dion then said: "Put the military badge on him." Maximilian protested: "I refuse, I cannot serve." "Be a soldier, otherwise you must die." "I will not be a soldier. You can cut my head off, but I will not be a soldier of this world. I already bear the sign of Christ my God." The dialogue went on until Dion said, "Strike his name off." Then he said to Maximilian, "Since you have refused to serve in the army, you shall suffer the penalty of the law. You are condemned to die by the sword!" Maximilian said, "God be praised." He was twenty-one years, three months, and eighteen days old. He wasn't the only one to stand firm in the radical love of Jesus. But the impact of his story is still felt as a kind of promise to be fulfilled.

Monday of the Second Week of Lent

LUKE 6:36-38

Ecology

"Be compassionate just as your Father is compassionate."

Yesterday as I passed a bush I caught myself picking off a tip of one of its branches. I don't know why I did that. I walked away with a twig, something I often catch myself doing.

An old Indian saint said once that you should never just pick a leaf or a branch from a plant when you are passing it. He must have noticed that many of us do that almost automatically. We should have respect for those plants. We should have compassion and empathy for all forms of life around us.

This is not something new, discovered in our "environmental" days! Old biblical rules asked pity for the animals that work for you. It is even one of the reasons given for the seventh day of rest: "So that your ox, your donkey, or any of your cattle may rest as you do" (Exodus 23:12). Even the earth was respected and not overtaxed. The land should lie fallow in the seventh year to recuperate and come to itself. People should respect their workers, and give a rest even to their slaves. They should not overwork themselves, either.

These biblical suggestions give a new meaning to the remainder of the gospel text of today: "Give and there will be gifts for you: a full measure pressed down, shaken together, and running over, will be poured into your lap."

We need these suggestions to survive in a world where we are depleting the soil and causing massive erosion. It is estimated that forty-seven billion tons of soil are lost every year because we don't care for trees and plants as we should. Our love should extend to the piece of land we might own, even if it is just a small plot around our house. Take care to protect it against pollution and destruction as well as you can. Plant a tree in it to help the oxygenation of your environment.

Tuesday of the Second Week of Lent

MATTHEW 23:1–12

New Order

"The greatest among you must be your servant."

A "new order" is something we are all looking forward to. Politicians know this. They often display those very words on their banners. So do the millions and millions of people who have been demonstrating recently—and all through the history of democracy—through the streets and squares of the world.

We often see the word "new" used when things have changed, or when improvements are promised—for example, a gas station that has a sign reading "Under New Management," or even a detergent that promises new cleansing power.

The phrase "new order" is often abused. When the phrase appeared in the program of a convention of the Association of Mission Studies in Rome, some older European participants wanted it scrapped. The words reminded them of the Hitler Nazi regime. Hitler, too, had spoken about a new order of things, in which one ethnic group was going to rule the whole world. The discussion was long and sometimes fierce. In the end it was pointed out that even Jesus used the term, speaking about "the world that is to be" (*paligennesia*; Mt 19:28).

It is an order where no one can be called father or master or teacher, a world where we will be sisters and brothers who are friends, without discrimination, a world in which we are servants to each other in our daily relationships. It is a world where no one puts herself or himself above or below another, where each person is a gift, God's gift, to the others.

Wednesday of the Second Week of Lent

MATTHEW 20:17-28

Raising Children

"Anyone who wants to be great amongst you must be your servant...."

At a parish meeting without much of a focus, the conversation soon turned to the topic of this world and its sad state. Something should be done. All kinds of action programs were thought of. Then a homemaker, a mother of young children, said something that put everything in a new perspective: "I think that the best contribution to the betterment of the world that I can make is the careful raising of my children." While she said that, she put her hand on the head of her cute youngster.

"Childrearing is almost always an invitation to asceticism," wrote Elizabeth Dreyer. "In our society the raising of children is perhaps the ascetic opportunity par excellence."

Parenting isn't something we spontaneously think of when speaking about mortification. Too often we imagine people like Father Damian, the hero of Molokai, Mother Teresa of Calcutta, Dorothy Day, or great saints from the past when using those words.

"A full night's sleep, time to oneself, the freedom to come and go as one pleases," says Dreyer, "all this must be given up in a way that is quite different from a monk who chooses to rise once or twice during the night to recite his prayers.... Huge chunks of life are laid down at the behest of infants."

As Jesus' saying goes: "As you did to the least of my sisters and brothers you did to me."

Besides, Jesus himself seems to have lived for thirty years in the circle of his family in the modest conditions of Nazareth, preparing himself, his family, and the people around for God's reign.

Thursday of the Second Week of Lent

LUKE 16:19–31

Aid

"There was a rich man who used to dress in purple and fine linen and feast magnificently every day."

The poor of the world are lying at the gates of the rich. "This is a situation that is particularly embarrassing for Christians. The 1.5 billion followers of him who had no place to lay his head now control two-thirds of the earth's resources and, on average, are three times better off than their non-Christian neighbors," wrote Father Sean McDonagh, an Irish missionary priest in the Philippines (*To Care for the Earth*, 1987).

The distance between the poor and rich has been growing ever since colonial times. The gap has never been so large.

Jesus tells the story about the rich man eating and drinking to his stomach's content, dressed in silk and purple, with poor, hungry, and sick Lazarus at his door. It is only when they both die that the rich man discovers that the gulf between the two has become so wide they cannot help each other any more.

Fortunately there are signs that things are changing. Christians in the "developed" world are becoming more and more aware of this gulf separating rich from poor. They are becoming better informed about the poverty "at home," too.

We are becoming more aware of the legacy of a history of colonialism and exploitation. A new challenge is felt. Many people feel helpless when thinking of the consequences. How to be faithful to Jesus' words? It is difficult to do that just on one's own. It is obvious that it is a task we can only tackle together. That is why aid organizations and networks like Bread for the World and Catholic Relief Services are growing, a development that should be promoted and joined by all of good will.

Friday of the Second Week of Lent

MATTHEW 21:33-43, 45-46

Fruitfulness

"...the reign of God...will be given to a people who will produce its fruit."

It is still a bit early in the year, but in a few weeks' time a great silent activity will begin in gardens and fields. Buds will swell and unfold. Some of them will blossom, turning into fruits. Soon the fields will be full with wheat, rye, barley, corn, and oats. The branches of the trees will hang loaded with a bounty of apples, pears, and plums.

The whole of nature will be groaning, giving birth to new life. In the vision of a sane, safe world, with the reign of God in our midst, mother earth produces her fruits, her boundless and endless life.

We are taken up in that life-giving process. We belong to that groaning nature. We should be participating in this life-giving process, not only individually, but also communally in the nations we belong to. Do we bring forth those fruits?

In the United States alone the money earned by the export of arms from 1968 to 1982 escalated from $1 billion to $21 billion. Fifty percent of the world's one million scientists are involved with the military in one way or another. There are two-and-one-half times as many military personnel as health workers.

It is a pity that so much effort and money is spent on war and preparation for war. It is an even greater pity that the livelihood of so many depends on the production and servicing of arms. Their effort and money, too, would be such an asset in improving our common lot in this world.

How do we change this? How can we be fruitful in view of the reign of God, that reign of justice and peace? Peace and justice start at home; they begin in your heart. Let us begin there!

Saturday of the Second Week of Lent

LUKE 15:1-3, 11-32

Prodigal Son

"He ran to the boy, clasped him in his arms, and kissed him."

In 1988, people in Washington, D.C., voted on the mandatory introduction of returnable bottles. As long as people don't get anything back for their empties, they throw them away. When they are paid something for them, they usually return them.

The new law was voted down. The big bottlers had been campaigning against it. It would have cost them too much money, they said. So bottles are still thrown away.

So much is thrown away in our society: paper, plastics, clothing, food, and all kinds of unnecessary packing material.

Like the lost and prodigal son, those who have the money to buy squander the resources of the earth.

Many people in First World countries have developed a lifestyle and consumption pattern way beyond what mother earth can support. They can only be maintained by exploiting the vast majority of the world's resources and population.

You might object that this has nothing to with a Bible reflection. If you think that way, it might be helpful to reflect on what Arthur Simon said as the Executive Director of Bread for the World: "The urgent need is not for churches as churches to enter the political fray (although they must take a moral stand), but for Christians as citizens to exercise their renewed consciences and contact decision makers."

It is no use trying to put the blame for the sorry state of the world on others. It is no good to think that we are so much better than the others, like the older brother did when the prodigal son returned to his father. We are a mixed bag, all of us. We all have to change our ways if we want to avoid sitting at the end of our days on top of a polluted world. We all need to say, "Father, I have sinned." We all need the arms of our creator, Abba, Father, around us again.

Monday of the Third Week of Lent

LUKE 4:24-30

Prophet

"No prophet is ever accepted in his own country."

When Jesus faced his family, acquaintances, and villagers in the Nazareth synagogue, he told them: "No prophet is ever accepted in his own country." If what Jesus says is true, then no country is able to be saved on its own. Whole countries would never find the help they need. The prophets who would be able to help them would have to come from elsewhere.

Jesus illustrates his point by telling the story of a woman and the story of a man who didn't find solutions to their problems with their compatriots, but had to go for help to someone alien to them. Zarephath, a Sidonian woman, and Naaman, a Syrian army commander, didn't belong to the Jewish people. They needed to be rescued, Zarephath from a drought and Naaman from his leprosy. They needed a prophet and a healer. They couldn't find one among their own. They had to look outside their own circle. They couldn't help themselves in isolation.

Nowadays there isn't a single human group that would be able to assure a solution to the problems of humanity. There isn't even a single human group of religious believers that would be able to do that.

Many religious leaders in the world know this. That is why Pope John Paul II called religious leaders of all convictions together in Assisi a few years ago. That is why the Catholic and Protestant churches in Europe called together a special Ecumenical Assembly in 1989 in Switzerland, to discuss the issue of the healing of our planet, and to secure the assurance of justice and peace.

One of the difficulties those leaders have is the same one Jesus had in Nazareth. The people who listened to him were too provincial, too bigoted to understand his universal vision. They didn't want to hear of it. They even preferred to kill him.

Tuesday of the Third Week of Lent

MATTHEW 18:21–35

Debt

"I cancelled all that debt of yours."

Poor countries owe enormous debts to the rich ones. Many African and Latin American countries haven't been able to pay even the interest on the loans. The money was borrowed mainly in the 1970s, but by 1990 Africa's debt was almost double what it had been in 1980. In certain cases the repayments already made are greater than the amounts originally borrowed.

Jesus spoke about borrowing and lending "Do not refuse him who would borrow from you" (Luke 6:34). He added: "If you lend to those from whom you hope to receive what credit is that for you? Even sinners lend to sinners to receive as much again" (Matthew 5:42).

He extended to everyone the old command: "If you lend money to any of my people who are poor, you shall not be as a creditor, and you shall not exact interest from them" (Exodus 22:25).

Many countries cannot pay, except at the cost of the lives of their citizens. The only way out is renegotiating those debts as Pope Paul VI suggested in his encyclical *On the Development of Peoples* over 25 years ago: "All nations must initiate...a dialogue, between those who contribute aid and those who receive it.... What is needed is mutual co-operation among nations" (54).

It might be good to remain closer at home as well! Consider the difficulties credit cards, mortgages, and debts play in people's lives. Are you able to do something about the difficulties others have with their debts?

Wednesday of the Third Week of Lent

MATTHEW 5:17–19

Law's Purpose

"...not one dot, not one little stroke, is to disappear from the law until all its purpose is achieved."

Children often have difficulty with the things they are supposed to do, like washing their hands before meals or brushing their teeth afterward. It is very difficult to convince them that you don't ask them to do those things just to annoy them, but because they are good for them.

When those children grow older they sometimes have the same difficulty with the Ten Commandments, not realizing what Moses said: "Observe them, that you may have life."

It would be difficult to imagine a society that would be able to survive without a set of fundamental principles like those expressed in the Ten Commandments. Most, if not all, of the commandments are about the organization of human society. Without them life really would be brutish and short, as we all know from periods in our history when they were overlooked.

No wonder Moses added: "Tell them to your children and to your children's children." No wonder Jesus said that he didn't even think of abolishing them: "Do not imagine that I came to abolish the Law or the Prophets."

It would be the end of human society, and that would be the end of human life. The Ten Commandments protect human life and human society. The same is true of so many of our human laws that are derived from them.

Think of the laws that oblige us to keep to one side of the street, that restrict us to a maximum speed, that forbid us to drive while intoxicated. They not only make driving safer, they make driving possible.

God's laws are our lifeline. They deserve our esteem and appreciation.

Thursday of the Third Week of Lent

LUKE 11:14–23

Gathering In

"...anyone who does not gather in with me throws away."

Jesus describes his work among us more than once as a bringing together, a gathering. He speaks in terms of a common table, a common home with many rooms, fish that are gathered together in a net, a harvest that is brought in, a party to be started.

He uses the same images when he describes the mission he left to his disciples. They were the ones sent out to bring the guests together. They were going to be the fishers of men and women, the harvesters who would bring the crops and the fruits together. We too are called to participate in that bringing together.

Missionaries are those among us who go out to other societies to tell them about God's desire to gather all human nations together in one body, under the influence of one Spirit. They are the ones who remind us of all that binds humanity together, and also of our cultural, social, and religious differences. They help us to understand how we may complement each other in the different ways we develop and approach our common world.

Today, this task shows dimensions that were never seen before. The whole world is coming together through communication and travel, while at the same time religious, political, racial, and economic conflicts are tearing us apart.

The need for this togetherness is more strongly felt than ever before. We are unable to save ourselves, either individually or communally, without it. Jesus' words, "He who does not gather with me scatters," are more significant than ever. They are not only significant in a vague and abstract way. They are true for each of us. If we aren't willing to gather together, we are scattered, harming our common human fabric.

Friday of the Third Week of Lent

MARK 12:28-34

Justice and Peace

"You must love your neighbor as yourself."

We can use words like smoke screens to hide behind. Simple issues we don't want to tackle become extremely complicated ones, as we try to convince ourselves that we would never be able to handle them.

You can organize conferences that study justice and peace; you can read or write books on such topics; you can study their theological implications almost forever and obtain academic degrees in them, all without much actually being accomplished. And then it sometimes happens that suddenly one simple statement clarifies all, in an uncompromising way. 'Love your neighbor as yourself' is such a statement. Your love of the neighbor should be based on a healthy love for yourself:

"You created my inmost self, knit me together in my mother's womb. For so many marvels I thank you; a wonder am I, and all your works are wonders" (Ps 139:13).

Such a prayer applies not only to you. Your neighbor is knit together in the very same way. No wonder the Book of Proverbs says: "The one who oppresses a poor person insults that person's maker" (Proverbs 14:31). Statements like this are so simple and true because they form the foundation of our society. Let the verse from Psalm 139 accompany you all during the day, loving your neighbor as yourself.

Saturday of the Third Week of Lent

LUKE 18:9-14

Prayer, Fasting, Doing Good

"...anyone who humbles himself will be raised up."

In the time of Jesus Jews fasted twice a week, on Monday and Thursday. Whoever wished to fast did so on those two days, though there was no general command for it.

The self-righteous Pharisee who prayed in the temple, "I thank you, God...I fast twice a week," did fast those two days. He thanked God for that. He even did some other, extra things besides paying a prescribed temple tax. The people around him might have thought him a good person. Yet something had gone wrong. The man in question fasted to please God. But why would God be pleased by anyone who is fasting? Didn't that person fast only as a kind of spiritual self-indulgence, so that he would be able to brag about it to himself, and in a way now even to God?

The early Christians didn't fast that way, but in another context. Some spiritual authors call it the Big Three: (1) Prayer, (2) Fasting, and (3) Doing good to others. They practiced the Big Three especially when they had to discern the Holy Spirit, when they wanted to find out where God wanted to lead them.

To give you one example from the Acts of the Apostles: before Paul and Barnabas set off on a special mission to bring the good news of Jesus Christ to others, the prophets, teachers, and the whole community fasted and prayed. And "after they had fasted and prayed, they imposed hands on them and sent them off" (Acts 13:2–3; 14:23).

Fasting should not be done in view of self-righteousness, righteousness in the eyes of others, or even righteousness in the eyes of God. Fasting should be done to clear your body and mind, to take away what stands between you and God in your innermost self.

Monday of the Fourth Week of Lent

J O H N   4 : 4 3 - 5 4

Journey in Faith

"The man believed what Jesus had said and went on his way home."

The official's son was sick. He went to Jesus and asked him to heal his son. Jesus gave him his promise: "Your son will live." He believed Jesus, petitioned Jesus no longer, and started the long journey home. As John writes in his gospel: "The man believed what Jesus had said and started on his way."

For part of the journey he traveled in pure faith and confidence. He had no further proof that anything had happened at home. There was no sign of healing, no news. It was during that time that the healing process of his son began, because while the official was on his way they came to tell him that his boy was alive.

All of us are on a journey. We are on our way. We have the promise of Jesus, and of the prophets before him, that the whole of humankind will be healed, that there will be wholesomeness, peace, and harmony. It is under the protection of that confidence that we should continue our journey home. It is in that light that we find the courage to give life to children in this world and that we can educate them, sharing our hope with them.

There often seem to be good reasons to give up on the good outcome of our journey. Yet, we believe that Jesus is walking with us toward that goal.

We are not traveling alone with Jesus. We should help one another to continue our journey, not giving up, not asking for special signs, doing whatever we can to help others along the way, and being assured of the final human and divine outcome.

Tuesday of the Fourth Week of Lent

JOHN 5:1-3, 5-16

Initiative

"Get up, pick up your sleeping mat, and walk around!"

Jesus must have been participating in the life around him during the thirty years when we hardly hear anything about him. In the evenings he must have sat down with his family, friends, and acquaintances and talked about the world in which they lived. That talk was not very much different from the talk we are accustomed to hear in our evening hours, though it was in another time, in another country, in another set of difficulties. There must have been complaints about the political, economic, and religious leadership, laments about prices and exploitation, horror stories about injustice, discrimination, and oppression. We can find all those themes in the things Jesus would say once he appeared on the public scene.

Jesus did what the other talkers and lamenters did not do. He not only complained, he not only asked why others didn't do something; he left Nazareth, his sleepy hometown, and took an active part in bringing about change. He didn't wait for others. He took the initiative. He picked himself up and walked.

He asked others to do the same. Don't just sit there and lament. Don't wonder all the time why others, why the leadership isn't doing things. Take the initiative. Start yourself. It is what Jesus suggested to the man who complained that he had no one to put him into the pool to be healed when the water was disturbed. "Jesus answered: 'Stand up, take your bed and walk.' The man recovered instantly; he took up his bed, and began to walk."

It might be good to listen carefully to our own complaints about ourselves, others, working conditions, or whatever—there is indeed no end to our grievances—and decide to take the initiative toward remedying some of them.

Wednesday of the Fourth Week of Lent

JOHN 5:17–30

Gardener

"My Father still goes on working, and I am at work, too."

Jesus not only says that his Father is working, he compares the work God does to that of a farmer or a gardener. Our world started as a garden. It is that garden of God that made human life possible.

Even nowadays the tropical forests are among the richest life systems in the world. They contain millions of plants, animals, insects, and birds. They produce most of the oxygen all living beings need.

Tropical forests are intimately bound up with the quality of our air and water: they preserve soil, they moderate climate, they affect water distribution, they break down carbon dioxide. The rain forests are God's most abundant nurseries, supplying the raw material for the plants that feed and heal us.

Even a common medicine like aspirin was originally the product of a tree. Experts agree that there is probably a plant for every human disease.

Yet this life system is being destroyed during our lifetime. An area the size of England, Scotland, and Wales is being destroyed each year. Obviously this is leading to complete extinction of those life systems. In some countries the day of reckoning has already arrived. God's garden entrusted to us is often in very poor hands indeed.

These are alarming thoughts. Thoughts that might lead us to try to do something about it, yet thoughts that may also help us in another way. It may help us to be good gardeners ourselves. It may help us to instill in our family a deep respect for anything that is alive, and for the earth itself, a respect so well developed by some of the best gardeners and farmers, like the Amish people in Pennsylvania and Ohio—a respect that is the reason for their success.

Thursday of the Fourth Week of Lent

JOHN 5:31–47

Co-Responsibility

"How can you believe since you look at each other for glory?"

It struck the priest for the first time years ago while hearing confessions. The woman on the other side of the screen said: "I confess my responsibility for the drug war in the streets of my city." He wasn't only struck, he didn't understand. Confession had almost always been about individual personal sins and about interpersonal behavior. Much less thought, if any, was given to group behavior. Later on the priest understood the shift. He understood better and better how much of the evil in the world is due to group behavior.

This is not a new idea as far as the Bible is concerned. It is an experience that is brought out so well in the words of Jesus: "How can you believe; since you look to one another for approval?" We approve of things because all of us do them. We look at each other to see that others are doing it, so we can go ahead.

This is also true in less important things. We speed on the interstate because everyone is doing it, even though we know that the police don't accept our reasoning. We are dishonest in small things at work because everyone is, and we take it for granted. We are often too lazy to reflect upon what we are doing, and just follow what others do, who in their turn do what they do because they see us doing it. "How can you believe, since you look to one another for approval," and Jesus adds, "and not to the approval that comes from God?"

We have to come to ourselves; we have to enter into the inner sanctuary of our own conscience. It is true that it is difficult to remain on one's own even in this. We really are all in this together. That is the reason that more and more Christians are beginning to share their faith experiences, forming groups or communities that are standing up in this world with a new sense of responsibility, seeking the approval of God together.

Friday of the Fourth Week of Lent

JOHN 7:1-2, 10, 25-30

Outlaw

"They wanted to arrest him then...."

It is not impossible that what happened to Jesus could happen today. In fact, this is a story that repeats itself all the time. Oscar Romero, a bishop who championed the rights of the poor, was shot to death while celebrating the Eucharist. Reverend Martin Luther King, Jr., pleaded for equal rights and was assassinated.

Any believer who takes the side of justice and peace as Jesus did will be treated as Jesus was. Didn't he say that his followers would be persecuted as he himself was? They wrote him off; they will write off his followers.

Indeed, how can we escape from that wrath of the enemies of God's reign, if we are really and actively faithful to what Pope Paul VI asked us to do: "For the church it is a question not only of preaching the gospel...but also of affecting and as it were upsetting, through the power of the Gospel, humankind's criteria of judgment, determining values, points of interest, lines of thought, sources of inspiration, and models of life, which are in contrast with the Word of God and the plan of salvation" (*Evangelii Nuntiandi*, #19).

As followers of Jesus, we are engaged in the process he introduced in this world, a nonviolent struggle against all that is sinful and evil. Those engaged in that struggle will have to carry the cross that goes with it, a cross that is to be their glory and pride. Oscar Romero and Martin Luther King, Jr., are not the only ones. There are many others, such as the Maryknoll Sisters, the Jesuit fathers, and their helpers who were murdered in Central America, but also the people in our own neighborhood, and maybe we ourselves, suffering for the sake of justice.

Let us, too, reach out our hands to Jesus and be ready to walk in his ways together with all those of good will.

Saturday of the Fourth Week of Lent

JOHN 7:40-53

The Jesus Prayer

"He is indeed the prophet...he is the Christ."

It is a temptation to think that piety, virtue, and care are for weaklings. This is a serious error in judgment. It is simply not true. There is a quality in a genuinely virtuous person that fascinates, invites, attracts, and challenges.

Jesus was not a weak and unattractive human being for being virtuous and pious. He brought all his human powers and capacities to fulfillment as the Spirit prompted him. He was fully alive, an admired and loved human being because he was loving, just, courageous, and unpretentious. His spiritual vibrations were immediately felt by all. He changed everyone at the first contact; some loved him intensely, others hated him fiercely.

That is why those poor guards sent to arrest him came back without him. According to the gospel of John they reported to their commanding officer: "There has never been anybody who has spoken like him!" They were completely taken with him.

Our own spiritual leaders sometimes have the same effect. Years ago, when then-Vice President Mondale said good-bye to John Paul II at the airport, Mondale said: "You have unleashed the best and most generous sentiments within us, and given us courage to go forward."

There is an old way to get into contact with the good vibrations that go out from Jesus. It is called the Jesus prayer. It is simple. Just sit down in a relaxed way, get control of your breathing, and say the name "Jesus" slowly while breathing in and breathing out.

It is a gentle way of picking up his wavelength and starting to resonate with him. It is a very effective way of tuning in to his spirit. It is a practice that has changed the life of millions.

Monday of the Fifth Week of Lent

J O H N   8 : 1 – 1 1

Taking Sides

"Go away, and from this moment sin no more."

One day they almost forced Jesus to take sides against someone, the woman caught in adultery. He refused to take sides against anyone. What he did was express his belief in her inner goodness. He told her not only to go home, but to change her life.

He did what the prophet Isaiah once foretold God would do: "No need to remember past events, no need to think about what was done before. Look, I am doing something new, now it emerges; can't you see it?" (Is 43:18–19).

It isn't only the woman who goes home a better person when he tells her: "Neither do I condemn you; go away, and from this moment sin no more." Her accusers and molesters, who didn't throw their stones, also go home better persons. Jesus healed all of them by awakening something in them that was greater than they were.

Jesus refuses to discriminate between the "good" and the "bad" in the story. He refuses to take sides in that way. The side he chooses is that of unity and cohesion, and of the ultimate goodness hiding in each one's life. It is a choice that is against anything that tears human life apart, makes it impossible, or kills it. Jesus did what he helped the woman and her accusers to do: "Don't condemn. Go home, and don't sin."

It is an invitation, a piece of advice, or, better, a command we should apply in our own lives. It is no good condemning ourselves or others. It is better to get away from the past and change our lives.

Tuesday of the Fifth Week of Lent

J O H N   8 : 2 1 – 3 0

Universe

"He who sent me is with me, and has not left me to myself."

God is not only the Father of humanity, but of all creation. Jesus didn't come to save only the human community. He came to save the world. Paul expressed this best when he wrote: "Through him God chose to reconcile the whole universe to himself, making peace through the shedding of his blood upon the cross reconciling all things, whether on earth or in heaven, through him alone" (Col 1:20).

We should extend God's embrace not only to the whole of humanity, relating to all human beings as sisters and brothers; we should extend it to the whole of creation. As long as we think that the world is here to be used by human beings, doomed to pass away in the future, pollution and the extinction of animal and plant life do not matter.

No wonder the whole of creation is eagerly waiting for the moment that we will be revealed as the daughters and sons of the Father who created all of us and put us as shepherds and guardians over the rest of creation. It is then that we will do what pleases the Father as Jesus did. It is then that we will be able to pray as he did. "God has not left me to myself, for I always do what pleases him."

A meditation like this one should not remain a mere pious thought. A lot of information is available on what is detrimental to our environment. You can find out how and whether you are contributing to the ozone breakdown, the pollution of the air, and the destruction of your environment.

Let us ask our almighty Father to help us live the life we were created for, a life that depends on the air we breathe, the things we eat, the water we drink, and the earth we walk on. Let us respect those relations now that they are threatened by our waste and abuse of them.

Wednesday of the Fifth Week of Lent

J O H N   8 : 3 1 – 4 2

Truth

"You will learn the truth and the truth will set you free."

We are inclined to say what Pilate said to Jesus, when Jesus used the word "truth" as he stood in front of that Roman governor. Pilate cynically asked: "What is truth?"

Jesus didn't speak about truth in an abstract way, as Pilate did. His words and deeds explained that truth about us. We find it expressed in our prayers. Listen to this part from the preface in the Mass for Justice in the Roman Missal: "Father, you have given all peoples one common origin, and your will is to gather them as one family in yourself. Fill the hearts of all with the fire of your love, and the desire to ensure justice for all their brothers and sisters. By sharing the good things you give us, may we secure justice and equality for every human being, an end to all division, and a human society built on love and peace. Amen."

The truth is that we have one common origin. We belong together. The truth is that we form one family.

In 1987 John Paul II wrote an encyclical letter, *On Social Concerns*. He stresses several times in that letter that we belong together and that the goods of creation are not meant for only a few, but for all. He explains that it is a shame that we speak with the greatest ease about the First World, the Second World, the Third World, and even about the Fourth World, because the use of those names indicates that we do not live in the truth. They indicate that things are not going well, that our unity is compromised. We live a lie.

Because of this lack of unity we have to arm ourselves against one another. The rich have to protect themselves against the poor. And the poor have to protect themselves against the ever-growing greed of the rich. Only the truth about ourselves can save us.

Thursday of the Fifth Week of Lent

J O H N   8 : 5 1 – 5 9

Holy Shroud

"...in fact my glory is conferred by the Father...."

The holy shroud in Italy is believed by many to be the linen in which Jesus was buried. For that reason it is considered very sacred. Splinters of the wood of the cross on which Jesus died are venerated in crosses and reliquaries all over the world. They are considered sanctified by Jesus' touch. The holy places in Bethlehem and Nazareth, in Jerusalem, and at the Sea of Galilee are visited by thousands of pilgrims because Jesus sanctified those places with his presence.

Many restrict their devotion to these special relics and localities. That is a pity, because this whole world is a sanctuary in a way, because Jesus walked with us. He walked on the same earth we are walking on; he breathed the same air we are breathing. The molecules and atoms he was using when eating his food and quenching his thirst are still with us. They are all around us. He sanctified the whole of creation because of his presence.

Life would never have been able to exist if there hadn't been the trees and plants that made human life possible. The whole of the earth was in a way his holy vestment and shroud!

In him all things are united. In him all things come together. John wrote in the beginning of his gospel that all things are created in him, who said of himself (and of us): "My glory is conferred by the Father, by the one of whom you say 'He is our God.'" This union makes us live in fellowship with the whole of creation, the heavenly and earthly host.

All this is reason for us Christians to love and cherish the earth and to find the divine therein, to develop a respect based on the living unity of all in Christ.

Friday of the Fifth Week of Lent

JOHN 10:31-42

You Are Gods

"Is it not written in your Law: I said you are gods?"

Not so long ago, a married couple was visiting one of the husband's friends, who happened to be an important clergyman. The clergyman only addressed the husband; he spoke not a single direct word to the wife. Anything he wanted to tell her was directed to the husband. She considered his behavior rude and offensive. By not speaking to her, the clergyman showed her that she was a mere nothing in his eyes.

It is the same story you hear from people who are disabled and sitting in a wheelchair, helped by a friend or parent: people often don't address the disabled person directly.

Jesus says all those who are addressed by God should be called gods! "It is those to whom God's words came who are called gods" (John 10:35). We should appreciate ourselves as daughters and sons of God because we are all addressed by God. Holy Scripture used the word "gods" of those to whom the word of God was directed.

How could anyone look down upon people whom the Bible considers daughters and sons of God? How could anyone not think them worthy to be addressed by us, if God considers them worthy of being so addressed?

That is easy to say but not easy to do.

At the moment a wave of new immigrants is trying to find a place for themselves in North America. Many of them are Hispanic Catholics who sometimes complain that they are not well received in some of our settled Catholic communities, that people look down on them. It is as if they are not taken seriously as people as much willed and loved by God as are the others who are having difficulties receiving them. Jesus uses the word "gods" for all those God addressed; we are God's own daughters and sons, all of us.

Saturday of the Fifth Week of Lent

J O H N   1 1 : 4 5 – 5 6

Fullness of Christ

"Jesus was to die not for the nation only, but also to gather together into one the scattered children of God."

It was late in the evening. The chief priests had come together to discuss the latest events in the country. The main topic of discussion was Jesus, especially his resurrecting of Lazarus. That worried them. They were afraid that things would get out of hand, that there would be a popular uprising with all its consequences. "The Roman troops will come in," one of them said, "and it will be our end, the end of the temple and the end of the nation." Caiaphas spoke up. He was the high priest that year and the chairman of the meeting. He said that Jesus had to die: "It is to our advantage that one man should die for the people, than that the whole nation should perish."

At this point in the story John the evangelist takes over. He notes: "He did not speak in his own person, but as high priest that year he was prophesying that Jesus was to die for the nation—not for the nation only, but also to gather into one the scattered children of God."

Jesus died for all, to bring all of us together in God's homestead. This truth is the foundation of our mission outreach to all others in the world. Pope Paul VI somewhat paraphrased the words of Caiaphas when he wrote: "Your vocation is to bring not just some people, but all people together as brothers and sisters. Christians know full well that when they unite themselves with the expiatory sacrifice of the divine savior, they help build the body of Christ, to assemble the people of God into the fullness of Christ" (*Populorum Progressio*, #78-79).

Monday of Holy Week

JOHN 12:1–11

Scent and Perfume

"...the house was filled with the scent of the ointment."

Mary must have loved Jesus very much. Love often makes lovers intuit each other's feelings. When Mary anoints Jesus' feet, Jesus sees this as a gesture having something to do with his death. Mary comes to embalm him before he dies. She comes to tell him that she loves him, that she knows that he is going to give himself up to death for the life of the world, but that she doesn't believe in the finality of his death.

Her gesture makes her different from all the others. They could have known what he was going to do. They, too, could have known that he was not only going to risk his life, but that he was even going to give it. He had told them often enough. They don't believe. They avert their gaze. They don't pay attention. Mary does.

There must have been an intimate understanding between the two while she anointed his feet and he spoke about his burial. When Judas protested, "Could not this perfume have been sold for three hundred denarii, and the money given to the poor?" Jesus said, "Leave her alone; it was the intention that she should save this perfume for the day of my burial."

She was affirming him, and he was affirming her. He, intent on giving himself up for her and for all of us, and she, sealing her willingness to be with him until the end that would be a new beginning. She was not embalming a friend who was going to remain dead; she was anointing one who was going to rise from death. She understood. Maybe she wouldn't have been able to say it in so many words. That is why she came with her oils and scent, to express it in deeds. He understood her intent. No wonder he appeared to her first after his resurrection.

Tuesday in Holy Week

JOHN 13:21-33, 36-38

Betrayal

"As soon as Judas had taken the piece of bread he went out. It was night."

The darkness of night falls over us after each betrayal. It is when we take our own piece of bread and leave others behind, thinking only about how to get more out of our situation. Did you ever leave others behind in that dark of night?

People built their lives on your promises and you never kept them. They waited for your return, and you never came back. Were you ever left in the dark by others who betrayed you?

This kind of betrayal is not something we only do as individuals toward the persons around us. It is something we often do with others as a community.

We rarely see how all are bound together. We fail to see ourselves and others as part of the universe, as part of all that is created in Christ. We look too seldom at long-range efforts and pursuits. We are out for a quick gain. We squander energy, we cut down trees irresponsibly, we consume irreplaceable goods, we let whole species of animals and plants just die off.

We, the current dwellers of this earth, are impoverishing and betraying our offspring. We took our piece of bread, and so much more than that, and we often thought of nothing else.

Night will be falling over the whole of the earth. It will be falling over all of us if we don't change our ways.

Wednesday of Holy Week

MATTHEW 26:14-25

Dying

"When evening came he was at table with the twelve."

He was sitting at table, eating with those who were going to betray him. He even went so far as to wash their feet. This is Jesus' way of handling opposition, violence, and betrayal. Not only Judas would run away from his arrest and death. In the end only John would return, brought by Jesus' mother, Mary.

Jesus took the road of nonviolence, of consistent love, a road taken by the best of his followers even in our days. Listen to what one of them, Martin Luther King, Jr., said:

> To our most bitter opponents we say: we shall match your capacity to inflict suffering by our capacity to endure suffering. We shall meet your physical force with soul force. Do to us what you will, and we shall continue to love you. Throw us in jail, and we shall still love you. Bomb our homes and threaten our children, and we shall still love you. Send your hooded perpetrators of violence into our communities at the midnight hour and beat us and leave us half dead, and we shall still love you. But be ye assured that we will wear you down by our capacity to suffer. One day we shall win our freedom, but not only for ourselves. We shall appeal to your heart and conscience that we shall win you in the process, and our victory will be a double victory.

Another great mind and heart in this country, Father John L. McKenzie, summed it up in his own poignant way. "If Jesus taught us anything it was how to die, not how to kill!" These are words worth reflecting upon in the violence and harshness of our days.

Thursday of Holy Week

JOHN 13:1–15

Intimacy

"Jesus, knowing that his hour had come...loved them to the end."

The life of everyone is colored and directed (you might even say consecrated) by some private moments—the moment your mother really spoke to you, heart to heart, the moment your father kept a promise, or your friend gave you a piece of advice.

It was the same with Jesus' apostles that evening. He was alone with them in that upper room. He had invited them, they had eaten, drunk, broken bread, and shared wine, just as we do. For them, however, that evening had been much more private, much more personal, especially when he had washed their feet.

Having your feet washed is something very private, very personal, and very powerful. After a tiring trip have your feet ever been washed by someone who loved you? Did you ever wash and massage the feet of someone you loved? Do it once, and you, too, will know what I am talking about.

He had washed their feet, he had dried them—in a way he had consecrated them. And it was at that moment that he had said to them: "I am sending you, you have to go, if you want to be faithful to me." And though they were very ambitious, very shallow, very consumer-minded, very competitive, and very contentious, they never forgot that moment.

Moments like that kept them together with him and with one another. It is those private moments with someone we love and respect that keep us together, that keep us faithful at unexpected moments in our lives.

Don't you remember a happening, an event, a private moment that determined and still determines your life's direction?

Good Friday

JOHN 18:1 — 19:42

Foolishness of the Cross

"Put your sword back in your scabbard."

They killed Jesus. That killing was their last resort against him, just as it remains the means of those who are willing to use weapons against others. That same willingness is the taproot of violence in our society today.

It sounds like a terrible indictment, but our intent, or at least our consent, to use nuclear weapons or even to wage war against others makes the violence in our streets and parks, trains and buses, comprehensible and defensible.

If you have children and buy a gun, even to defend yourself, your children will think that violence is the way to live.

Standing before Pilate, Jesus told him that he could have used violence, that he could have resorted to legions and legions of angels, to the whole of the heavenly host and their precision armaments, but that he chose not to do so. He continued choosing life, even in that ultimate moment of distress.

The cycle of violence can only be broken the way he did it, by simply refusing to enter it.

The sun darkened. The curtains in the temple ripped apart. The earth shook in vehemence when it received his body. When they left him hanging on the cross, allowing some of his friends to take him off and bury him, his opponents must have thought they had made a fool of him. When he rose from the death they had inflicted upon him, he proved them wrong. He was killed, but the cycle of violence was broken. Foolishness? Foolishness in the eyes of the wise of this world, the foolishness of the cross.

Holy Saturday

(There is no liturgical text today)

He had been like a beautiful dream,
living a life
that would have changed
the whole of this world...
Oh yes,
they agreed on that.
          Yet, in the end,
          they had shaken their heads,
          the life he had lived
          was too good
          to be true.
"Let us be logical,
business is business,
let us not lose our heads,"
and they gave up on him,
          though the best ones among them
          did it with great regret.
No wonder that the sun
stopped shining
          at the scene of his death.
          From now on
          darkness was going to be
          the fate of all.
But then,
the cries and shouts of
women running early in the morning:
          a tomb cracked,
          life overcame death;
          "He is risen,"
               light undoing the dark.
Finally, he himself was found
by a friend,
in a garden!
Alleluia, praise the Lord.

Easter Monday

ACTS 2:14, 22-32

Unshaken

"...for with him at my right hand nothing can shake me."

After studying at one of the best theological schools in the country, a priest chose to minister to a poor rural community somewhere in the Andes mountains. After some years there he returned for a well-deserved leave. His former school invited him to speak to the students and the faculty about his experiences.

He was grateful for all he had learned. "Yet," he said, "I would like to make one observation. The theology I learned here was based on the resurrection. And rightly so, but that theology was of little help to the people I was with. They had trouble identifying with the risen Lord. They suffered so much that they preferred to identify with the suffering Jesus. This was most obvious during the Holy Week celebrations. They came in great numbers to the Good Friday celebration, while there was less interest in the Easter service. On Good Friday many came with a ball of cotton wool soaked in olive oil, which they used to 'cleanse' Jesus' wounds on the cross. Some even swallowed the cotton afterwards."

He suggested in a friendly way that the school should pay more attention to the reality of human suffering in the Christian (and all other) communities of this world.

In those Christian communities in the Andes and all over our suffering world, Jesus remains with people at their right hand, just as God remained with Jesus. "I saw the Lord before me always, for with him at my right hand nothing can shake me."

Easter Tuesday

ACTS 2:14, 36-41

Resident Alien

"Save yourselves from this perverse generation."

The first thing that struck the people in Jerusalem was the joy of those who experienced the life and spirit of Jesus in them. They thought that joy unrealistic, utopian, and crazy. Sometimes they even thought that the Christians' behavior was due to drugs. "They have been drinking," they said to each other. "This is not for real, they are nuts!" It was what his critics (and his own family!) had been saying of Jesus. Those first Christians were laughed at and considered naïve.

Today, when we feel embarrassed to be identified as Christians, or when we hesitate to confess ourselves as such, we ourselves can feel that we are victims of that same kind of sneering.

When we do confess to be followers of Jesus Christ, we might feel like "aliens" in the world as it is now. In a way, we should. Who can really feel at home in the world as it is?

Not everyone thought that Jesus' disciples were out of their minds. Many were dissatisfied with the way they were living their lives. Others were very upset about the situation of the world in which they lived. For too long they had been on the lookout for a change, for something new. When they saw the joy of those first Christians they came to them and asked. "What must we do? Can we join? We would like to put aside the lives we have been living."

Their question may put our doubts to rest. Yes, it is a good thing to be a kind of "resident alien" in the world as it is. If no one felt himself or herself alien and uncomfortable with the world, there would be no desire or hope of changing it. We must turn things and ourselves around, change the world, and live the gift of our new life.

Easter Wednesday

LUKE 24:13-35

Recognizing Jesus

"...they had recognized him at the breaking of bread."

If Jesus appeared again, how would you recognize him? It is an intriguing question. When Father Joseph F. Girzone wrote a book about it, he called it *Joshua*. At first publishers thought it wouldn't sell. Who would read a book about Jesus returning as a woodworker to an American town? They must have laughed at the idea.

Their question was answered. Girzone published the book himself, and thousands of people read it. You can meet people who have read it a dozen times over. The book became a bestseller. A big publishing house acquired the publishing rights, and hundreds of thousands of copies have been sold.

How do the people in the book recognize Jesus? It is in fact an old story. The first time the story was told it involved Cleopas and his companion walking with Jesus. Who is that companion? Luke, who tells the story, doesn't give a name. Was it Cleopas's wife? We don't know.

We do know that the two are upset. They went to Jerusalem expecting to see a victorious Jesus. Instead, they come home with the story of his death. They have heard a rumor about his resurrection, but obviously that wasn't what they had been hoping for.

Then Jesus "comes up" and walks with them. They talk and argue. Jesus explains to them "everything in scripture that refers to him, starting from Moses and all the prophets." They don't recognize him. They have no clue! His words do not reveal him.

They arrive in Emmaus. They persuade him to stay. They sit down at table. "He takes bread, says the blessing, and breaks it."

Then they recognize him, and he disappears, leaving them with their bread in their hands. He leaves them with a clue about how to recognize him, and how to make themselves recognizable as his disciples, breaking in their turn the bread he left them.

Easter Thursday

LUKE 24:35–48

Wounds

"See by my hands and my feet that it is I myself...."

When the risen Jesus appears to his followers he often shows them his wounds. "Look at my hands and my feet; yes, it is I, indeed. Touch me and see for yourselves; a ghost has no flesh and bones as you can see I have."

The risen Lord is showing his wounds. Jesus keeps the two—wounds and resurrection—together. "It is written that the Christ would suffer and on the third day rise from the dead. This is what I meant when I said, while I was still with you, that everything written about me in the Law of Moses, in the prophets, and in the Psalms had to be fulfilled."

His wounds would not make sense if they were not connected to his resurrection. Suffering never makes any sense without that connection. That is not only true for him, it is true for us. There are moments in life when we can't escape suffering and pain. Like Jesus, we will be wounded, too. If we live in this world the way he did, we are going to be wounded. That is unavoidable. Jesus' way of life goes against the grain of this world. It is a life that wants to go against the grain of this world in order to realize the alternative: a better world.

The relation between this world and the world to come made Jesus' life possible. To remember only his suffering is one-sided. To remind ourselves only of his resurrection is also one-sided. We have to keep the two together in our lives, as he did.

Easter Friday

J O H N   2 1 : 1 – 1 4

Jesus' Last Breakfast

"...there was some bread there and a charcoal fire with fish cooking on it."

Every Christian is able to tell what the last supper was about. It is an unforgettable meal, one that is commemorated in most Christian communities in one way or another. We very rarely hear, however, about another meal that Jesus had with his disciples after his resurrection, his last breakfast with them.

Evening meals are generally nice. The day is over, the work done. Breakfast is a different issue. It is at the beginning of the day; the work has to be started, organized, and divided. When people come together for breakfast, it is often for a working breakfast.

That is what happened that day. Peter and some others had gone out fishing. They hadn't caught anything. When they approached the lake shore they saw a man who asked them for some fish. When they told him that they hadn't caught anything, he suggested they throw the net out once more. They did, and caught 153 big fish. By that time they had recognized Jesus, and they were surprised to be invited to a breakfast for which he had already baked the bread and some fish. It was after that breakfast that he asked Peter, "Do you love me?"

After that breakfast they got to hear with Peter what loving Jesus would mean—going out to the whole wide world taking care of his sheep and his lambs.

On the shore was that strange number of fish—153. Experts have puzzled over that number. It probably represented the different varieties of fish observed in that region at the time. If so, Peter and company must have understood that the number symbolized their mission to the world. Plenty for them, and us, to do!

Easter Saturday

ACTS 4:13-21

Lay Women and Men

"They were astonished at the fearlessness shown by Peter and John."

It wasn't only the new life of the first Christians that amazed the leaders in Jerusalem; the self-assurance of the Christians was another reason for their consternation. They had been surprised in the case of Jesus because he came from Nazareth, an insignificant town. Now they were surprised by his followers, whom they called uneducated lay women and men. Luke puts it in a striking way: "The rulers, elders, and scribes were astonished at the assurance shown by Peter and John, considering they were uneducated lay women and men." God was not supposed to act like that. It would upset their whole order of things. This type of lay theology didn't fit in with their schemes. No wonder Peter asked them to believe what they saw and heard.

Later when the community grew, Peter would have the same difficulty. Often he couldn't believe his own eyes and ears. How was it possible that others, even aliens, were under the influence of God's Spirit?

Bishops sometimes have the same difficulty with "their" pastors, pastors with "their" faithful, and parents with their children. It is difficult enough to accept the spirit of Jesus alive in your own heart and mind. It is even more difficult to accept that presence in those persons with whom you live.

God's Spirit doesn't dwell in a precious few. God's Spirit dwells in all of us.

Monday of the Second Week of Easter

ACTS 4:23-31

Grace

"...help your servants to proclaim your message with fearlessness...."

"On their release Peter and John went back to their own people. [Together with them] they raised their voices in prayer!"

Dismissed from court, Peter and John hurried back to their community, to their support group. They began to pray, not as you would expect, that they would be spared from further persecution or difficulties, but for courage and grace.

They prayed to be able to heal the world and spread the good news. They prayed for the spirit of Jesus. They prayed to be able to witness to him with boldness.

It is the grace Christian communities need, because our world needs the message of Jesus so badly. Many priests change a prayer in the canon of the Mass just after the community has prayed the Our Father together. The text reads "deliver us from all anxiety," but some add a word to that "anxiety" and pray: "free us from all needless anxiety."

There is a certain type of anxiety that is absolutely necessary—the anxiety that helps us to spread God's truth about humanity and this world. Pope John Paul II, in his encyclical on our mission, wrote that the world has a right to hear the good news from us.

We have to pray for the grace needed to advance that news. And then will happen to us what happened to them: "When they ended their prayer, the building where they were assembled rocked, and all were filled with the Holy Spirit and spoke God's word with boldness."

Tuesday of the Second Week of Easter

ACTS 4:32-37

Communality

"...everything they owned was held in common...."

In those early days being one in spirit and heart was not only a question of praying together. The early Christian community assisted one another materially. We might be struck by the radicalism of their approach: "The whole company of believers was united heart and soul. No one claimed any of the possessions as his or her own; everything was held in common...there was no needy person among them."

Wondering about the way they organized themselves, we might overlook the point Luke is making. His point is not so much how they organized their communal welfare, but the fact that they felt socially responsible for one another. In this way they set a model for all communities to come.

Luke describes different ways that they organized this mutual assistance. In one instance they shared all they owned in common. In another case they sold everything they had and then distributed the proceeds according to their needs.

Luke doesn't describe one set way for all time to come; there are many ways of organizing social responsibility. But they did organize it! In a recent essay Larry Woiwode made a remark regarding our Christian mutual responsibility that might make us reflect: "Surely it's at least partly the failure of the contemporary church to provide for its own that has caused its members to turn to the government as benefactor."

Wednesday of the Second Week of Easter

JOHN 3:16–21

Dancing Our Life

"...so that everyone who believes...may have eternal life."

The late president of Kenya, Jomo Kenyatta, liked to invite the ambassadors to his country to the celebration of Kenyan national feast days. They would sit for hours watching people dance their traditional dances. One of the ambassadors once complained to the president of this use of their time. The president replied that the core of African culture is the celebration of life, and that you can't do that better than by dancing.

You don't have to be African to like dancing. Dancing is so much part of our human nature, we might ask ourselves if it is inborn. Haven't you seen small children dance around their very serious-looking mothers on their way to kindergarten?

The Bible says. "God created the human being in God's own image; male and female God created them!" If it is so natural to us to dance, is it in God's nature to dance? Has it to do with our promised eternal life?

From ancient times Christian mystics and theologians have been trying to understand the life in God's Holy Trinity. How do those three relate to each other? A difficult question. All kinds of technical Greek terms were used to answer it. One of the terms used was *perichoresis*. Maybe you recognize something in that word. Some common English words find their root in it: choir or chorus, choral, carol, caroling (which originally meant to dance in a circle).

Ancient mystics described God's inner life as a dance, *perichoresis*, a circle dance. They thought (and felt) that the persons in the Blessed Trinity are celebrating their divine life, dancing together! It is a dance to which all of us are invited. The dancing around us is a sign of our final vocation. We should take our dancing more seriously. Once Jesus complained, "We piped for you and you would not dance" (Luke 7:32).

Thursday of the Second Week of Easter

ACTS 5:27-33

Identity

"We are witnesses to this, we and the Holy Spirit...."

The conversation at a party turned to religion. Many gave their opinion on a whole series of contemporary issues. One person kept silent. Then one of the guests asked him: "By the way, what are you?" In the context it was clear that he was asked what religion he was affiliated with. He said: "Oh, I happen to be a Christian!" You could tell by the way he said it that either he didn't take his religious conviction seriously, or he didn't want to admit it if he did.

How different from those Christians in Acts! They had no difficulty in describing or defining themselves; they had no identity problems. They would say things like: "We are witnesses to all this, we and the Holy Spirit whom God has given to those who listen" (Acts 5:32).

They didn't just "happen to be" Christians. They *were* Christians, by conscious choice and commitment. They knew why they were. They had opened their hearts and minds to the presence of the spirit of Jesus.

They not only witnessed to Jesus by professing what had happened to him; they witnessed to Jesus by living as he lived. They lived in a way that attracted many others.

Friday of the Second Week of Easter

JOHN 6 : 1 – 15

Apartheid

"Jesus, as he realized they were about...to make him king, fled back to the hills alone."

Albert Nolan is a South African priest, a Dominican. He interprets the gospels from the point of view of the difficulties in his own country in the book *Jesus Before Christianity*. He is especially interested in what happens when the oppressed people around Jesus want to make him their king. Jesus refuses, and when they want to seize him, he gets away from them into the mountains.

Nolan explains how the different reports of this incident in the gospels remind him of developments in South Africa. He wonders why in the gospel story so many people came together in an isolated place on the same day. Who had organized this? The reason, Nolan thinks, can only have been a secret political rally.

Jesus controls the throng by asking them to sit down in groups. It is easier to deal with sitting people in smaller groups than with a large, uproarious, standing crowd. Fearing that the crowd would want to make him king, Jesus withdrew.

The disciples themselves are another problem for Jesus. They don't mind him becoming king. They like it. They are already dividing the jobs in his reign among themselves! Jesus sends them away before he gradually dismisses the crowd. He is not going to be their king, either.

He would be king of one group against another group. Being the offspring of God who sends his sunshine and rain for all, Jesus simply cannot do that. Making such a choice is not divine, it cannot be divine. Jesus' divine policy is to gather people together. They belong to the same human-divine family. What God has united no one should pull asunder!

Saturday of the Second Week of Easter

ACTS 6:1-7

Soup Kitchen

"...the Hellenists made a complaint against the Hebrews...."

The first communities wouldn't be much of an example to us if they hadn't had their problems. One problem was the distribution of food to the widows of the community. They started what we would call a soup kitchen. Followers of Jesus have always been organizing them, and they are still doing so. The soup kitchens of our Christian organizations go far back in Christian history, down to those first days.

Parishes that don't organize soup kitchens as such will organize their food care for the poor in other ways. Hardly any parish worth its salt is without that outreach in one way or another. They organize "loaves and fishes" Sundays when food and money are collected to feed those who are hungry.

The name "loaves and fishes" explains where the dynamic to do this comes from. It comes from Jesus. He began this process by feeding the hungry around him and by identifying with them, telling us that even a cup of water given to someone who needs it will be considered by him as given to himself.

The difficulty that crept in was discrimination. "The Hellenists made a complaint against the Hebrews; in the daily distribution their own widows were overlooked." The Hebrew widows got the best of the food, while the Greek widows got the leftovers.

This is an issue that often hits at the very heart of our communities today. How does your parish receive strangers, especially if they are poor immigrant refugees who don't speak our language? Is your Christian family community ready to welcome them as warmly as they welcome others?

They appointed Stephen as director to settle this intolerable discrimination. They chose him because he was full of the Holy Spirit. It led to his death!

Monday of the Third Week of Easter

ACTS 6:8-15

Peacemaker Stephen

"You are always resisting the Holy Spirit, just like your ancestors used to do."

Stephen did what he was asked to do. He stopped the discrimination against the Greek widows. It was a great thing to do. A miracle! Stephen worked great miracles, indeed.

We are often impressed by physical miracles. When we speak about miracles, we frequently think about healed and restored organs and limbs. We often overlook moral miracles, such as conversion, reconciliation, and making peace. Stephen's task was to work such a moral miracle, to bring people together, to overcome racial strife.

It is a miracle we need in our midst: bringing one another together, breaking ethnic barriers, undoing racism, forming a world where all feel at home with God and one another, where we are all sisters and brothers who are friends.

Some people didn't like what Stephen did, even some members of his community disliked it. They betrayed him. People were paid to give false witness against him. He was arrested.

It's an old story—the story of Jesus himself. Isn't it a story we all know from the world in which we live?

Though Stephen might have escaped his persecutors, he would not accommodate them. He had been asked to end the discrimination and to bring people together in the name of Jesus. He wouldn't change his course or give in to their ways. Doing so would mean "resisting the Holy Spirit." That's what he himself accuses his accusers of. They resisted the Holy Spirit.

When he accused them of this, they must have known that he was right, otherwise they wouldn't have become so angry. In their anger they stoned Stephen, our first martyr.

Tuesday of the Third Week of Easter

J O H N   6 : 3 0 - 3 5

Bread

"I am the bread of life. No one who comes to me will ever hunger; no one who believes in me will ever thirst."

As an old Chinese saying puts it, when you want to help feed people, don't give them a fish, teach them how to fish. Anyone who ever has been engaged in a food distribution organization will acknowledge the truth of that. If you offer only food, the food line will form itself every day again and again for the simple reason that filled stomachs will again get empty.

When the crowd comes to Jesus because they got all the bread they wanted from him the day before and were looking for more, he makes the same remark. He tells them that the bread he has been giving them is of no lasting use. He explains to them that the giving and receiving of that bread and fish will not solve their problems, or the problems of the world. He tells them to be interested in something that will help them more definitively, and he suggests they take *him* as their food and drink. He asks them to make him and his way of living their "bread and butter" in daily life.

We should eat "him." These words are true in the most literal sense. If we would accept his life-style and adopt it in this world, no child would ever again die of hunger, and no senior citizen of loneliness. We would be attentive to each other, using the gifts we are to each other. We would be washing each other's feet and serving at the table of the world. We would have to start soup kitchens in many places, but we would organize them as temporary measures, not as lasting solutions. We would be interested in a reorganization of our world. We would die but not remain dead, because we would have eaten of the bread of life. We would be like he was, is, and ever will be!

Wednesday of the Third Week of Easter

A C T S   8 : 1 – 8

Lay Apostles

"Once they had scattered, they went from place to place preaching the good news."

People who move because of their employment sometimes end up in a spot miles and miles away from a church. This situation can be a blessing in disguise. From the beginning this has been the way that Christian communities spread. When a great persecution broke out against the church at Jerusalem after the execution of Stephen, all except the apostles were scattered over the countryside of Judea and Samaria. "Those who were scattered preached the word wherever they went" (Acts 8:4).

It seems a reversal of roles—the apostles at home and the others in the mission field—but it happens all the time. Some people of the same denomination come together and begin to worship in a home, a coffee house, or some other place. Preaching the word takes place in our everyday life at home.

It happens in Africa. The adults I have baptized heard the Word from others who witnessed to Jesus. When they came to ask for baptism, it was because someone had told them about Jesus, who had changed their lives. Have you ever preached the Word that way?

It can happen at the roadside, in a plane or train. It happened just that way to that Ethiopian two thousand years ago who was in his chariot reading a prophecy from Isaiah that referred to Jesus. He wondered what it was all about and complained, "How can I understand unless someone explains it to me?"

How many people pass us every day who have never received a relevant explanation of God's Word? I don't mean the self-serving Bible-pushing of a fanatic out of touch with the reality of our world. I mean the good news of the risen life as it should be lived in this world.

Thursday of the Third Week of Easter

JOHN 6:44–51

Drawing Power

"No one can come to me unless drawn by the Father...."

Jesus speaks of a mysterious power penetrating this whole world. It is so mysterious that we cannot see, smell, touch, hear, or taste it directly. It is everywhere.

There are more of those hidden energy fields. Early in the morning there is silence, no sound. Yet, the room is full of frequencies, waves, vibrations, and electric power fields. Pressing a button on your radio brings those frequencies to life, monks singing their plainchant in a monastery, hard rock from a group in London, a symphony orchestra in Cleveland, and voices from all over the world. Switching on television, you tap into another energy field that connects you with events in Beijing and Moscow, Pago Pago and Brussels.

All that energy was there without being visible, without being noticed. Enormous forces are hiding in nature, seeds that grow into trees, plants that turn the whole day following the sun, insects that crawl around, animals looking for a nest to perpetuate their lives, people embracing each other—even the clouds are chasing each other in the wide, blue sky.

Jesus speaks about another power, a drawing power that influences all of creation, especially the whole of humanity. It is a kind of attraction, a divine attraction. God draws all of us through Jesus toward our original and final home, an energy that draws us to God and also to one another. Protestants and Catholics, Muslims and Jews, Americans and Russians, Asians and Europeans, Christians and Hindus, aren't we all dialoguing with each other more than ever before in our world? Although we often fight with each other, the idea that we all belong to the same human family is growing among us every day.

Indeed, a power is at work among and in us. Almighty God is drawing us to where we all are coming from!

Friday of the Third Week of Easter

JOHN 6:52-59

Eucharist

"Whoever eats my flesh and drinks my blood lives in me and I live in that person."

What happened at the last supper is not difficult to understand. It was some hours before Jesus' arrest. They had been partaking of the meal during which Jews remember their Exodus. The meal was over. Jesus wanted to express how much he loved them.

He is in a situation you know from personal experience. It is the evening of a departure. You are not going to see each other for some time. You would like to express your feelings and your love, but how do you do it? Every gesture falls short.

Some bread and wine remain on the table. They are looking at him. Though they do not know what is at stake, they have some idea. They know that something drastic is going to happen. He takes the bread and wine and says: "This is my body that will be broken for you; this is my blood that will be shed for you." The bread is passed around. So is the wine. They eat and drink themselves into the same body, the same spirit. He adds: "Do this when you want to commemorate me."

That is what we do, commemorate him, when we celebrate the Eucharist. Or do we? Was that commemoration of him the only thing he asked of them that evening? Did he come to be worshiped by us? Is that the mission he left to you and me?

When Jesus takes the bread and the wine he is thinking, as he himself says, about what is going to happen to him, about what he is willing to do. He is giving himself in view of the healing of this wounded world, reconnecting creation to its creator. He is not only hungering and thirsting for the reign of God, he is putting his person and life on the line for that reign. Commemorating him is not only breaking his bread and sharing his wine; it means partaking of his life and his mission.

Saturday of the Third Week of Easter

JOHN 6:60-69

Technology and Spirit

"It is the spirit that gives life, the flesh has nothing to offer."

We live in a computer era. Not everyone in the world does, but we do. Even if you have no computer at home on your desk, small computers are hidden in so many things we use. Those computers can do wonderful things. They can handle all kinds of problems and issues. They are very logical in their solutions to those problems, much more so than we are ourselves. They are also fast. In a few fractions of a second they can work out problems that would take a human being months. They remain dependent on our input, but once they have it, they seem to be much more rational than we are.

That is their strength. It is also their weakness. They have nothing but that rationality. That is why they are not human. When we humans say to each other, "Now let's be logical," we all know that something is going to happen that shouldn't happen. A child is sent away, a marriage is broken, a business is closed, even if it causes a lot of heartbreak to those involved.

Love is different from rationality. The flesh is different from the spirit. Technique is different from the heart. Jesus says, "The flesh has nothing to offer; it is the spirit that gives life!" He doesn't want to condemn either our body or our technique. Nor does he want to separate them. On the contrary, he wants us to keep the two together. Without the spirit that gives life, the flesh is dead. Technique on its own is dangerous and can be deadly. It should be accompanied by love. A mere technical or even rational consideration is never sufficient. It has led to endless disasters. Ancient Greek philosophers defined the human being as a "rational" animal. We are more than that. Our rationality is accompanied, directed, and humanized by our human spirit. It should be directed by Jesus' living spirit of love.

Monday of the Fourth Week of Easter

J O H N   1 0 : 1 – 1 0

Named

"...one by one he calls his own sheep and leads them out."

Jesus is a shepherd who knows the names of all his sheep. I once met a shepherd who knew the names of his sheep. He didn't have so many, but they all had names. When he called a name, one would look up, and he would say, "You see, they know me, they know their names."

Knowing the name of someone can be important. We all have been in a situation where we know we should remember the name of someone we meet, and we don't. Some people are quite brazen about that—they just use a name that comes to mind, so they can be corrected and thereby learn the name they forgot. When you are not so daring you have to ask for the name, and you can see the disappointment on the face of the other. You forgot this person's name, how could you?

It must also have happened to you that someone prominent in your eyes, someone whom you don't meet too often, nevertheless—to your great surprise—remembers your name.

To be called by your name by a friend always gives you a warm feeling. Your uttered name touches something in you like nothing else.

Jesus says of himself that he knows us by name. In the Hebrew Scriptures we are told how God inscribed the name of his people on the palm of God's hand. Jesus reveals to us the personal love of God for each one of us. God knows you by name. God knows me by name. It is a love that resembles the love the Father has for Jesus, and Jesus for the Father. It is a love that not only relates us to God, but also to each other. It makes us belong to the same family, or, to use the image of Jesus, it makes us members of the same flock.

Tuesday of the Fourth Week of Easter

J O H N   1 0 : 2 2 – 3 0

Messianic Secret

"If you are the Christ tell us openly."

It is a cold morning, John writes, when they come again to ask him whether he is the messiah. "How much longer are you going to keep us in suspense? If you are the Christ tell us openly" (John 10:24).

In the original text their question sounds like a threat, and it is. They suspect he is the messiah. They are right, but they have their own idea of what the messiah should do. According to them, as messiah Jesus should be for them and against others. That was not Jesus' idea.

If he had said, "Yes, I am the Messiah, the one you are expecting," it would only aggravate the confusion. He wanted to keep it a secret for the time being, until they grew in insight.

He didn't come to divide, he came to bring together. He didn't come to scatter, he came to gather.

He answers their question with his parable about the shepherd to whom all the sheep belong, and who has to take care of all of them.

This parable not only says something about him, but about us. If we are with his Spirit, his role in the world is our role, his mission our mission. As he told his disciples after his resurrection and before he left them: "As the Father sent me, so I am sending you."

The secret of his identity is out. There should be no secret about who we are and what our intentions are, either. He entrusts us with his "Good Shepherd's Project."

Wednesday of the Fourth Week of Easter

JOHN 12:44–50

Self-revelation

"What I speak."

With their headlights on, they followed the funeral procession in their car. A policeman on a motor bike kept the street free of other traffic. One person in the car suddenly said, "She was a very religious person." When no one in the car reacted, he added: "Though she never spoke about it." The driver of the car asked: "So how do you know about it?" He didn't answer.

In John's gospel Jesus speaks frequently in the first person. He doesn't make any secret of his relation to God. He reveals himself in all this without reservation. It is in that way that he doesn't keep us in the dark, and is a light in our world.

It is here, too, that we could and should take him as a model. We know so little of one another's religious experiences, simply because we so often hesitate to talk about them. Spouses often remain spiritual mysteries to each other, children to their parents and parents to their children, students to their teachers, and teachers to their students. And yet, if we would be willing to reveal ourselves to one another, and from time to time to tell one another our experiences, we, too, might be a light to each other in a world that otherwise remains too dark.

Thursday of the Fourth Week of Easter

JOHN 13:16-20

Personally

"I have given you an example so that you may copy what I have done to you."

His name is Hussein. He was a student long ago. I was in charge of the dormitory where he lived. One evening he came home very drunk. Being a Muslim, he had never drunk before. Now he had. He was drunk and sick.

He got in a quarrel with another student. Being out of his mind he pulled a knife and threatened everybody around; he broke a window; he made a mess. Then I came in. I was able to calm him down. I gave him stomach tablets, and he went to bed.

Next morning I called him over and told him what had happened the night before. He didn't remember anything. I took him through the dormitory. I showed him where I had put his knife the night before, I showed him the broken window, and back in my office I told him: "Hussein, now you know what happens when you get drunk. Some get funny when drunk, they start telling jokes; some get very pious, they start to pray or sing hymns; you get nasty and murderous. Now you know. Never drink again."

He never did. I got a letter from him some weeks ago. He wrote that he was doing fine, and he added: "I never forgot what you told me that day in the privacy of your office; that is why I am who I am. Thanks again."

Something like that must have happened to the disciples. Every time they got discouraged, lost their hope, or got depressed, they thought of that evening when Jesus washed their feet and said: "I have given you an example."

He not only said that to them, he said it to us, privately, too. Did he never have such a moment with you? Aren't we sent as they were?

Friday of the Fourth Week of Easter

JOHN 14:1-6

Homestead

"I am going to prepare a place for you, ...I shall return to take you to myself, so that you may be with me where I am."

There is a beautiful Scottish tale about a monastery of pious monks somewhere on the border between Scotland and England. In the monastery nobody ever died; the monks just got older and older. They couldn't even take in new monks because all the places in the chapel were occupied and not a single place ever fell vacant. The monks didn't like it, but no one knew what to do.

Then one night the old abbot had a dream. In that dream he saw the angels ascend and descend day and night between heaven and earth exactly on the spot where the monastery was built. The monastery was almost part of heaven, a kind of bridgehead. The abbot understood: this was the reason no one ever died.

He told his story after morning prayers in the chapel. The monks came together, and that very day they began to evacuate the place where they had been living for so long. They rebuilt their monastery a couple of miles from the old one. And they started their final journey to their heavenly home, one by one, the oldest first. For long enough they had been making the request Philip did: "Lord, show us the Father; we ask no more!"

Jesus told Philip that being in Jesus' presence meant being in the presence of Almighty God. But Jesus added that we have a heavenly home, that he himself was gladly going there, and that he would take care to prepare for us a place. A place that will be ready once our turn comes to go home, having done our part here on earth.

Saturday of the Fourth Week of Easter

ACTS 13:44-52

Joy

"...this message of salvation is meant for you."

We often hear the little word "but." It almost always precedes a real downer. "Everything is all right," someone will say, "but..." and you know that you just heard the good news and that the bad news is coming.

Reading the reports on those first communities of Christians in the early days, the word "but" is also heard, used in another way.

After a description of persecutions, executions, imprisonments, expulsions, and all kind of mishaps and misadventures the reports nevertheless enthusiastically add, "But the disciples were filled with joy and the Holy Spirit" (Acts 13:51). People plotted against them, they were expelled from their homes and persecuted, but they were full of joy.

That joy is an important characteristic. It is as important as keeping our "orthodoxy"! Popes, bishops, priests, and faithful will be up in arms when the orthodox teaching of the church is in danger. They seem to be much less concerned about that other aspect of our Christian life: joy. I agree with the person who once told me, "You are all convinced that you're saved and redeemed, but you don't look like it at all. Why do you look so sad if you believe in your salvation?"

Chesterton once wrote:

"Wherever a Catholic sun does shine,

I always found laughter and good red wine,

at least I always found it so, *Benedicamus Domino*."

Two questions should be asked from time to time in every family and community: Who is safeguarding the faith, and who is taking care of the joy?

Monday of the Fifth Week of Easter

J O H N   1 4 : 2 1 - 2 6

Holy Spirit, In-between God

"... the Paraclete, the Holy Spirit, whom the Father will send in my name, will teach you everything...."

One of the oldest controversies in the Christian community surrounds the Holy Spirit. It is the reason why Eastern and Western Christianity have been torn apart for more than a thousand years. The question is a theological one, and it turns around one word in our Western Creed, *filioque*. The question is how the Holy Spirit originates in God, and how the Holy Spirit is given to us.

Though the question seems to center on a mere detail, it makes all the difference. In the Eastern churches one believes that the Holy Spirit is first given to the community and, consequently, to the individuals. In the Western churches we believe that the Holy Spirit is first given to the individual and consequently to the community. This mere detail points up a difference that is so deeply rooted in the two sides that it betrays itself at the most unexpected moments.

When President Ronald Reagan and Soviet leader Mikhail Gorbachev addressed the world on New Year's Day some years ago, that difference showed up. Reagan, addressing the Russians, stressed his interest in guaranteeing them the individual and personal freedoms and rights Western people take almost for granted, while Gorbachev, speaking to the Americans, emphasized that "we" would have to work together to guarantee world peace. The two opinions belong together; they complement each other.

John gives the Holy Spirit a name, *Paracletos*, a name that means counselor, advocate, consoler, but also mediator. That last translation is perhaps the best one. The Holy Spirit is the "in-between" God, the force and energy that should bind us together, to realize a peace only God can give.

Tuesday of the Fifth Week of Easter

ACTS 14:19-28

Heart of Jesus

"They put fresh heart into the disciples, encouraging them to persevere in the faith...."

The prayer group prayed "to get the heart of Jesus." This is a beautiful prayer, one that fits perfectly well in the context of a Christian community. It is also a delicate prayer. You really have to know what you are praying for, and what you are in for once your prayer is heard. Paul and Barnabas encouraged the first Christians to have a "new" and "fresh" heart: "Barnabas and Paul put fresh heart into the disciples" (Acts 14:22), but they added "We all have to experience many hardships before we enter the reign of God."

The "fresh" or "new" heart the text speaks about is also a good description of the role of a Christian community. That is what we should be: a new heart in the world, to be the heart of Jesus in the world. Charles de Foucauld, the saintly French ex-officer who lived for so long alone in the North African desert, hoped to be the heart of Jesus in that barren place. He carried an image of that heart on his clothes.

The old world has serious problems in accepting the new heart, a new heart in a world that is old and far from ideal. The world often gives signs of rejecting it.

Anyone who has been involved in introducing kindness and a greater concern for justice in any part of this world knows the difficulties this can cause.

We can even experience this in our own lives—how our human nature resists the new heart we know it needs. If you don't believe this, just consider what great effort it takes to get rid of a vice or an addiction.

Wednesday of the Fifth Week of Easter

ACTS 15:1–6

Discrimination

"...after a long argument...it was decided that Paul and Barnabas and others of the church should go up to Jerusalem and discuss the question with the apostles and the elders."

No Christian community has ever been without its problems. One of these derives from the very nature of community. Once you have come together, organized yourself well, and developed some customs and ways of doing things, the risk is that you close the circle to others. The community becomes a group, and often a closed one. Newcomers arrive and are welcomed, but often only up to a certain point. They shouldn't bring in too many new ideas. They shouldn't try to start shifting things around.

What was a Jewish Christian community going to do with those non-Jewish newcomers? What does a white or black middle-class parish do when a number of immigrants would like not only to be welcomed, but to share in the decision making of the group? Should the customs of those who were the first ones to form the community be imposed on the newcomers? One of the issues in Jerusalem was exactly that: how should Christians from different cultures relate to one another? This issue has been with us from the beginning.

The most stifling words in a community context often are "It has always been like that; we have always done things this way!" Do you remember when you last heard those words? Do you remember using them yourself?

The community leaders in Jerusalem made a wise decision. They didn't act as if there were no problem. They didn't suppress the issue. They decided to discuss the problem with the communities involved and their leaders. They made contact, dialogued openly, and came to some wholesome conclusions.

Thursday of the Fifth Week of Easter

ACTS 15:7–21

Equality

"God made no distinction between them and us."

We were sitting in an upper room in Washington, D.C. Many lobbying groups were present. They had all been lobbying in favor of certain sanctions against South Africa. We were waiting for the result of a vote in the House of Representatives. One of the black members of that House was going to come to brief us on the results. We already knew them. Our lobbying efforts had failed. They would succeed later on, but this time they had failed. The one to brief us came and explained what had happened. When he left the room he stopped at the door, turned to us, and said: "If this country learned that a couple of people were killed in the streets of an Eastern European country, we definitely would take measures. Against South Africa we don't. Why? Because the scores of people shot in Africa are not white."

A hard truth. To accept the equality of all was the first internal difficulty the first Christian community met. Remember one group of widows was preferred to another in the distribution of food.

This always has been the difficulty in our communities. There are reports today that some parish council members are reluctant to let Christians from another ethnic background use their facilities.

Not realizing the equality God calls us to can only lead to disaster, as it has so often in church history. Peter, Paul, and James didn't mince words when they came to their final verdict: "God made no distinction between them and us....We believe that we are saved in the same way they are: through the grace of the Lord Jesus."

Friday of the Fifth Week of Easter

ACTS 15:22-31

Discerning the Spirit

"It seems good to the Holy Spirit..."

In a Baltimore parish some parish members came together because they felt the need to take the Holy Spirit into account when making decisions in life. They felt that need not only in their own lives, but also in their community. Should they build a new chapel? How could they solve some recurring problems in the parish school? What about a greater variety in the services offered in the parish? How do you discern the Holy Spirit? Is it sufficient to pray about it by yourself, or in community?

They all agreed on one thing: the Spirit should be discerned to find what decisions are truly of God. The communities in Acts, and the apostles themselves, definitely succeeded in doing this in the early days. They weren't afraid of making statements such as, "It seems good to the Holy Spirit and to ourselves…that we should do this or omit that."

It is a daring and pretentious way of stating things, so daring that we would hardly even care to repeat it. Most probably we would not be able to say it in good faith. We don't relate to the Holy Spirit the way they did. After much prayer, fasting, discussion, and consultation, "the apostles and the elders, with the concurrence of the whole church" came to their decision. Few of us, whether in a leadership position or not, make decisions that way, but it is the only way to make decisions if you want to be sure that the Holy Spirit is in your community and in your own life!

The group in Baltimore decided to delegate some of their members to study discernment more closely. They systematically read all the classical spiritual works on the issue, and they finally came out with a program that helps to form "discerners," people who can introduce persons and groups to tracing the Holy Spirit.

Saturday of the Fifth Week of Easter

JOHN 15:18-21

Creativity

"If the world hates you, you must realize that it hated me before it hated you."

The best way to see your own town, city, or region is to do it with a guest, someone who has never seen it before. The best way to find out how to reorganize your business or routine is to ask someone who is unaccustomed to your way of doing things to check it and to tell you what changes he or she would suggest. The one you invite shouldn't be a total stranger to the situation, but just enough of an outsider to see new possibilities.

It is difficult to be creative in an environment you are totally accustomed to. To be at home and to feel at home is a great thing, but to be totally at home and to feel very comfortable usually doesn't lead to great ideas or creativity.

Jesus is a case in point. He lives in this world, he feels at home up to a point, and yet he has hardly any fixed abode. He is a traveler on his way. He is working with a double frame of reference all the time. Everything he says and does has a kind of doubleness. His home is here and with God. His life is here, and it is there. He sees sickness, health, bread, oil, water, salt, the sky, a sunset, the sea, fish, and especially human beings in a kind of double way. It all reminds him of something else.

Christians should have something of this if they want to be like Jesus, if they want to be as creative as he was in our world. We can't settle in the world as the world is. We have to set it off against something else, the reign of God, the world to come.

We are in this world, but not of this world. We are children of our time, and at the same time we are not. G. K. Chesterton said it well: "The Church is the one thing that saves a person from the degrading servitude of being a child of one's time."

Monday of the Sixth Week of Easter

ACTS 16:11—15

Women's Groups

"We sat down and began to speak to the women who had come to the meeting."

Luke's two books are crowded with women and men, without whom neither Jesus nor his apostles would have been able to survive. It begins with Mary who, as soon as she hears that she is going to be the mother of the Messiah, hastens to Elizabeth. It is when the two meet that the full impact of what happened to them dawns on them, and they both join in song.

All through his gospel Luke speaks of groups of women. Women hail Jesus' birth, they follow him everywhere, they meet him on his way to the cross, they are the last ones to leave that scene, and they are the first ones to visit his tomb, where they learn that he is risen.

Luke continues this trend in Acts. Paul meets a prayer group of women on the riverside in Philippi on a Sabbath day. He speaks to them about Jesus and the good news he is. Lydia, originally from Thyatira, who was in the fashionable purple-dye trade in Philippi, is a member of the group. She is a devout person and reveres God. She opens her heart to accept what Paul is saying. After her baptism, she invites Paul to come to her home. Her household is baptized and soon becomes the support and worship center of Philippi, the community Paul came to love most.

Lydia is only one of the twenty-six women Luke calls by name. Both Luke's gospel and Acts are crowded with women and women's groups—the group that formed itself around Dorcas to make clothing for the needy, for instance.

It is a women's movement that never will stop. Think of the hundreds of congregations of Sisters and the thousands of women's groups throughout the world who really form the heart and the backbone of the church.

Tuesday of the Sixth Week of Easter

ACTS 16:22-34

Laughter

"And the whole family was filled with joy because they had come to believe in God."

Luke cannot stop reporting on the joy of the communities he met, the joy that came from their insight of being "people of the Spirit."

The variety of people Luke describes as exalted in spirit—and consequently confident, realistic, compassionate, loving, and welcoming—is notable. They come from different ethnic groups, from various backgrounds and classes. In the family mentioned above the main persons are a prison warden and his family; in yesterday's reflection the main persons were the well-to-do textile fashioner Lydia and her family.

Luke not only mentions this joy in Acts, he does the same in his gospel. That joy is the difference Jesus makes, according to Luke. In his gospel he mentions twenty-two times in twenty-four chapters that the coming of Jesus brought joy, gladness, praise, and thanksgiving. Life has gained not only meaning, it gained purpose and zest. Luke is the only one who mentions that "we will laugh" (Luke 6:21). Luke offers us scenes of a happy childhood, home, youth, health, gladness, swift feet and burning hearts, music, merrymaking, and dancing (see Luke 15:24–25).

People find their transformation in Jesus and in his Spirit. They see the light. They find meaning. Their eyes light up. Their life changes. And though more often than not they remain doing the same work, they do it in another way, in another spirit, just as they become different persons, enhanced as they are by the Spirit of Jesus!

Wednesday of the Sixth Week of Easter

ACTS 17:15, 22—8:1

Against the Grain

"... and indeed as some of your own writers have said: We are all God's children."

Paul had a difficult time preaching at Athens, the pinnacle of human sophistication. He didn't like the town. Some Athenians didn't react well to his street preaching; they called him a talking bird. But some philosophers invited him over to the Areopagus, their great place of discussion and decision making.

Luke doesn't take kindly to the Athenians, either. About this invitation he notes that they wanted Paul to amuse them. They liked new fads and novel ideas. They were intrigued by Paul's belief in a resurrection.

Paul's main theme, however, was not the resurrection. The God he preached was not the God of one group, tribe, or race, but of all people. He was preaching the God in whom all of us "live and move and exist."

Paul had prepared his speech carefully, for at that point he quoted Aratus, an Athenian philosopher, who had written: "We are all his children." If this is true, Paul explains, then we have quite a lot to repent for. If we are going to be judged according to that norm, our uprightness falls far short. Jesus lived that truth to the full; therefore he was raised from the dead.

At the mention of the resurrection most of his audience burst out laughing. Were they laughing at the idea, or did they laugh because they didn't want to accept the Way of Jesus Christ, a Way that teaches us to love everyone—including our enemies—because we are all in the same way the children of God?

It is a Way that goes against the grain of this world. It is a Way that divides not only those who hear it for the first time, but those of us who are used to it, and who—even when we believe in the resurrection—often have our doubts.

Thursday of the Sixth Week of Easter
(when Ascension is transferred to the Sunday)

JOHN 16:16–20

Joy

"Your sorrow will turn to joy."

When visiting a school I went into the office of the Coordinator of Religious Education. Her office showed all the usual stuff to be expected in such an office—Bibles, books, tapes, CD-ROM disks, maps, candles, and so on. On her desk a computer was running a screen saver. Constantly a text scrolled along like a large banner. It read: "God's presence means joy," and, after a short interval: "Joy means God's presence."

Paul once wrote in his letter to the Galatians that joy is a fruit of the Spirit (5:22), and in John's text of today Jesus promises us this joy. He said he would be separated from his disciples, but when they saw him again, their grief would be replaced by joy. In the same way, our joy is based on seeing God in the middle of our daily lives. We acquire the inward "habit of beholding God" in all the circumstances of our lives. And, as Jesus promised, and so many around us should be able to attest, even our sorrow will turn into joy.

Etty Hillesum, a Dutch Jewish young woman, wrote in her diary *An Interrupted Life* some time before she was put on transport to be gassed, that "listening in" to herself she had found God's presence in herself. On her last postcard, which she threw out of the train that led her to her final destination, she wrote: "We left the camp singing!"

Friday of the Sixth Week of Easter

JOHN 16:20-23

As a Woman Giving Birth

"A woman in birth suffers.... So it is with you."

One of the most powerful images Jesus used to help us understand our situation is that of comparing us and the world in which we live to a woman giving birth. It is a painful metaphor, but it is also a hopeful one.

It is rather obvious that we wouldn't be able to do anything to realize the peace and justice of what Holy Scripture calls the reign of God without paying a large price. The Australian author David J. Tacey wrote in his book *Edge of the Sacred* that "the living too will have to make enormous sacrifices before the spirit can be born," quoting the Australian poet Les Murray who noted: "Sooner or later, I will have to give some blood for dancing here."

We will have to learn that there are limits to growth, to consumption, to earning, to accumulation. We will have to learn that there are no limits to all people having equal access to the benefits we are accustomed to—literacy, education, health care, and even to the more basic benefits—food, adequate sanitation, and clean water.

It will be painful to readjust, to give birth to the new. But once that is done, our hearts will be full of joy, a joy that no one would be able to take from us any more. It is what Jesus pledged, after having put his own life on the line in view of our future.

Saturday of the Sixth Week of Easter

JOHN 16:23-28

Asking

"Ask and you will receive."

Listening to these words of Jesus we run the risk that we reduce the meaning and significance of the verb "ask." Would it be untrue to suggest that most of us hearing this text would immediately think about asking for all kinds of favors?

Isn't this the main reason that candles and devotion lights are lit, that endless prayers are said, that novenas and octaves are held, and that every Eucharist celebrated is for one or another intention? Of course, there is nothing against those prayers of petition. Jesus definitely was referring to them. He even encouraged them. He himself prayed to his Father in heaven.

He, however, never did it to twist God's arm. So often his prayer began by thanking God. He never prayed, "Do it my way." His prayer was always, "God help me doing it your way."

"Asking" is not only about petitioning. Asking can also mean "questioning." In all of the gospels Jesus' mother, Mary, never asks for anything. She never formulates a prayer of petition, but she has many questions. She questions the angel at the annunciation. She wonders (and is that not a kind of questioning?) about the happenings around the birth of Jesus; she asks Jesus whether he never thought about herself and Joseph when he went off to the temple. In that way she tried to find out about God's ways. It is the kind of questioning we should do. And we will find out!

Monday of the Seventh Week of Easter

ACTS 19:1-8

Sign of the Cross

"The moment Paul laid hands on them the Holy Spirit came down on them...."

We should regularly reflect on the real core of our Christian life. The church community reflects on it especially during Easter time, if only because in almost every Christian community new members are baptized at the Easter Vigil.

"I baptize you in the name of the Father, and of the Son, and of the Holy Spirit." We are accustomed to apply all this to God, who, in a mysterious way, is three and at the same time one. But let us not forget that we also apply it to ourselves when we make the sign of the cross, a gesture that covers the whole of our body and person.

The baptismal formula tells us how we relate to God and how God relates to us: the source of our being, the offspring in which we are all created and saved, and the spirit that carries us through life. This is true not only of myself, but of all those I associate with. It shows me how I should relate to others.

Of course, we will fall short of living what we signify when we make the sign of the cross. Christians have been falling short since the very beginning of our communities. But they didn't totally fail. On the contrary, they succeeded. Their kindness has never died. It couldn't die, because it is the kindness of Jesus himself. It is the kindness we should continue to show in Jesus' name until all is fulfilled.

Tuesday of the Seventh Week of Easter

ACTS 20:17-27

Jesus' Way

"And now you see me on my way to Jerusalem in captivity to the Spirit...."

At the end of his life with Jesus Christ, Paul decides to go to Jerusalem. He says: "Compelled by the Holy Spirit I am going to Jerusalem." Paul feels that the Holy Spirit is asking him to go to Jerusalem. He also knows that the Holy Spirit is warning him that if he goes to Jerusalem he will be arrested. He is going Jesus' way. Jesus, too, knew that he had to go to Jerusalem and that he would be arrested there. Jesus' disciples asked Jesus not to go. Paul's friends do the same (Acts 21:12).

Paul's story follows the pattern of Jesus' story. The journey to Jerusalem is the final one. Jesus and Paul both began their journeys reaching into their inner self. Jesus did that before he came out of Nazareth and while he was in the desert after being baptized by John the Baptizer. Saul did it when, being struck by the Lord at Damascus, he turned into the Paul we know. Both Jesus and Paul then continued their journey through life, reaching out to the people they met around them. And both Jesus and Paul decided that going to Jerusalem would be the final part of their journey, bringing all they had experienced and rallying all those they had met. All his life, Jesus was on an inner journey, an outer journey, and a centering journey. So was Paul, following the way of Jesus.

If we are faithful in the world in which we live, our story will be like theirs, perhaps not as dramatic but just as real. Any time we enter into ourselves in prayer we will discover that we are called to reach out and bring the whole world with all its people together in the Lord. This is the way Jesus went, and Paul, and all those who lived the Way before us.

Wednesday of the Seventh Week of Easter

ACTS 20:28-38

Jesus' Affection in Us

"There is more happiness in giving than in receiving."

Paul gives us a glimpse into his own personal dynamic when he says: "I showed you that it is by hard work that we must help the weak, remembering the words Jesus himself said: 'It is more blessed to give than to receive'"—a saying of Jesus that does not occur in any of the gospels.

With those words Paul gives an account of the kindness he showed his friends, of the hard work he did among them. His imitation of Jesus Christ is the key to his life. In all he does he is led by the remembrance of the life and the words of Jesus. In one of his letters he would write even more outspokenly: "God can testify how I long for all of you with the affection of Jesus" (Phil 1:8). This is a mild translation of what Paul wrote to those Philippians. Other translations are more blatant: "I long after you all in the bowels of Jesus Christ!"

We would say, I love you with Jesus' heart, because we think the human heart is the center of emotion. Paul considered one's bowels to be the center of emotion and affection.

We are no different from Paul. We have the same Spirit; we have Jesus' affection in us. We have to tap into these sources of loving concern and kindness. We should be in accord, in harmony, in concert with him—of the same mind and heart. We should ask ourselves: What did Jesus feel and think? What would he feel and think in our situation?

His life vibration should throb in us. His energy should become ours. Our imagination should be plugged into and be charged by his vision. Jesus asked us to follow him. He didn't mean a literal mimicking, but an inner process of being vivified by the same Spirit that enlivened him. It is what Paul did.

Thursday of the Seventh Week of Easter

ACTS 22:30; 23:6-11

Support from Heaven

"Next night, the Lord appeared to him and said, 'Courage!'"

Once in Jerusalem Paul's freedom of movement didn't last long. In no time he was recognized, assaulted, and brought to the military fortress. The guard in charge allowed him to speak to the crowd. They listened to him up to the moment he proclaimed that God's grace is given to the whole of humanity. At that point they started to shout: "Rid the earth of the man! He is not fit to live" (Acts 22:22).

It was the same thing that had happened to him in Athens. The Athenians, too, had been willing to listen up the moment when Paul announced that we all are children of God.

This is almost an exact repeat of what happened to Jesus. When Jesus told those in Nazareth that the year of grace he came to bring was not only for them but for everyone, and when he even gave some examples of graced "pagans" to illustrate this, they jumped up and hustled him out of their synagogue, trying to kill him.

They brought Paul to a military barracks where soldiers must have milled around him. Paul must have been disheartened as he awaited the next turn of events in the prison. The second night there the Lord appeared to him and said: "Take courage! I will be with you!"

It is a promise given not only to Paul but to all of us as well: "I will be with you always." This divine assurance should help us to be the master of all tensions and events, rather than their victim. God's support is always there for us.

Friday of the Seventh Week of Easter

J O H N   2 1 : 1 5 – 1 9

Epilogue

"You are to follow me."

Another day was ending. His disciples were living in that on-and-off period between his absence and his appearance, between resurrection and ascension. They didn't know exactly what to think or do. No wonder Peter said, "I am going fishing." The others replied "We'll come with you." The fishing didn't help. They caught nothing.

When they returned to the shore, Jesus was waiting for them. At first they didn't recognize him. He asked them for some fish, and when they said they hadn't caught anything, he told them to throw out the net once more. They did and caught 153 fish.

Then they saw that it was Jesus. He invited them for breakfast. He had made some bread and there was some fish on the fire. They sat down and had their breakfast with him. As far as we know, this was their first breakfast with him since the resurrection.

We always talk about the last supper, but we hardly ever hear about this first breakfast! And yet, before it was over, the disciples had heard questions like: "Peter do you love me?" And they had heard answers: "You know, Lord, I do." Consequences had been drawn: "If you love me feed my sheep." It was a busy breakfast, a "working" one. Tasks were handed out. They stood up from it at the beginning of a new day, the start of a new era.

Saturday of the Seventh Week of Easter

ACTS 28:16-20, 30-31

Abiding Spirit

"On our arrival in Rome Paul was allowed to stay in lodgings of his own with the soldier who guarded him."

The book of the Acts of the Apostles has no end. The narrative closes with Paul under house arrest. We do know Paul's end, however. He was beheaded. Luke must have known that when he finished writing Acts, but he doesn't mention it. Instead he reports that Paul spent those last two years welcoming "all who came to visit him, proclaiming the reign of God and teaching the truth about the Lord Jesus Christ with complete freedom and without hindrance."

Luke closes, noting with a sense of relief and triumph that the Word was spreading even to Rome. It is strange that he doesn't even mention what happened to Paul. But Paul was not really the topic Luke was interested in. His topic was the continuing activity of the Holy Spirit in the world.

There is really no end to this story! The Acts of the Apostles will be continued forever, until humanity and creation find their fulfillment in Jesus. You and I, all of us, are involved.

What is described in Acts is, in a way, our acts. We live the same risen life as the first Christians did; we live with and by the same Spirit of Jesus. We do this at another time, in a different world. We have to do in our world now what those Christians did then. It is now our turn to witness to the resurrection of the Lord by the lives we live.

Ordinary Time

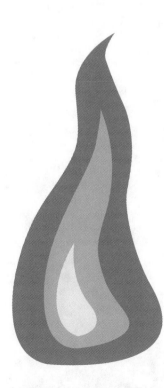

Monday of the First Week

M A R K   1 : 1 4 – 2 0

Fishers of People

"Come after me, and I will make you make fishers of people."

We have heard some of the Bible stories so often we don't pay attention to them anymore. We pay still less attention to their interpretation. We know exactly what the preacher or a book like this one is going to say. We have heard it all before. It is totally predictable. Spiritual books, magazines, and articles often become an utter bore.

The question is whether a commonly accepted understanding is the only one, or even the correct one. Take the text in Mark's gospel where Jesus says: "Come, follow me and I will make you into fishers of people." Most of us probably have the same reaction: that this is a text that applies to missionaries and people like them.

It does, but it can also be read in another biblical context. Prophets had spoken about "fishers" before. Jeremiah wrote: "Watch, and I shall send for many fishermen, Yahweh declares, and these will fish them up" (Jer 16:16). Ezekiel wrote: "I shall put hooks through your jaws, and pull you out of your Nile with all your fish" (Ez 29:4). And Amos prophesied: "The Lord God has sworn by his holiness: Look the days will soon be on you when God will use hooks to drag you away and fish-hooks for the very last of you" (Amos 4:2).

Those texts refer to fishing out the unjust and the oppressors, and to a judgment and a sifting of the world. To introduce the reign of God, people have to change, to convert, and the "old" has to be fished out, caught, and done away with.

Jesus asks Simon and his brother Andrew, and later James, son of Zebedee, and his brother John to leave their type of fishing, to follow him and to get engaged in his work. They leave their nets and follow him at once, ready for a new venture, a different fishing trip.

Tuesday of the First Week

M A R K   1 : 2 1 - 2 8

Authority

"And his teaching made a deep impression on them...
because he taught them with authority."

The people who listened to Jesus that day in Capernaum were struck by his authority. Authority is something we all know about. Many people have exercised their authority in our lives. They influenced us in different ways.

Sometimes people tell us who most influenced them. They will quote their parents or a teacher or someone they grew up with. Sometimes the influence was negative. But as soon as someone says: "As my mother always used to say...," you can be practically sure that what follows is something that influenced the life of the speaker in a positive way. Those are the great ones in our lives, the one who made us feel great, who helped us grow. G. K. Chesterton once said: "Greatness is making others feel great!"

That is what real authority does. It is growth-giving, affirmative, positive, and helpful. The word itself is an indication of this. Its root is a Latin word *augere*, meaning "to make grow."

That is what happened to the people when they were listening to Jesus in their synagogue. Hearing him they began to understand their own possibilities. He gave them a hope the scribes didn't give them. He didn't talk down to them, as the scribes were accustomed to do. He treated them as friends and equals. He didn't flatter them. He told them to be realistic about themselves. In fact, they had to be more realistic about themselves than they had ever been before. They were called by God to greater things than they ever had thought possible.

Listening to Jesus didn't always make life easier, but it definitely made it much more worthwhile! His authority made them do what all authority—our own included—should do: foster growth.

Wednesday of the First Week

MARK 1:29-39

Priorities

"Let us go elsewhere to the neighboring country towns, so that I can proclaim the message there too."

Some mission sisters came all the way from Europe to start a clinic in the heart of an impoverished area in Africa. They built the clinic, opened it to those who needed it, and healed more and more patients. Every morning a long line formed in front of the clinic. It all seemed to work very well, and yet the sisters in the clinic started to worry whether they were doing the right thing. The cases they treated most successfully were children hit by diarrhea. Mothers would bring children dying of dehydration, and the sisters would be able to help them almost overnight.

The sisters began to notice that more and more children and adults were coming back to their clinic, and that often the same people had the same complaints. The sisters came together, discussed the issue, and decided that they had to do something to prevent the recurrence of those sicknesses. It was obvious that there was something wrong with the water the people were drinking, with the available sanitation, and with the whole human environment. They didn't close the clinic, though they thought for some time about that. But they switched their priorities to the causes of the diseases. Some of them started visiting people in their homes and addressing community groups to introduce a whole change of life-style.

When the people come to Jesus to ask him whether he can't continue healing at the house of Peter's mother-in-law, Jesus says that he isn't going to do that. He didn't come only to heal sick people, he came to heal the world. He came to change this place in such a way that sickness would disappear totally. He asks us not to stop healing, but to look at the reasons for so much of the sickness in our society and to change our priorities as he did.

Thursday of the First Week

MARK 1:40-45

Feeling Sorry

"Jesus stretched out his hand and touched him."

A man suffering from a virulent skin disease came to Jesus and asked to be healed. In other translations he is simply called a leper. In other words he was someone not to be touched for reasons of both ritual purity and common health concerns. "Feeling sorry for him," Jesus healed by a word and a touch.

Jesus was compassionate, meaning that he suffered with the man in question out of love. Some old Greek texts even imply that, seeing the state of the sick man, Jesus was upset and in a way angry with his situation.

Christians who meet others in suffering or distress often don't experience this kind of "being with" those who suffer. We might feel some pity or concern. We often lack real compassion. Compassion is more than identifying with someone, or praying about the problem.

Just think of the physicians, dentists, chiropractors, and mental-health specialists who are unwilling to treat anyone with the AIDS virus, and all those others who would reject an offer to open an AIDS hospice—or even a soup kitchen—for the poor and homeless in their neighborhood.

It would, however, be unfair to remember only those among us who fail. Let us also remember all those who, like Jesus, do assist others with word and touch—the word and touch that should be ours as we reach out to all those who turn to us in their worries and distress.

Friday of the First Week

MARK 2 : 1 – 1 2

Just Deserts?

"Jesus said to the paralytic, 'My child, your sins are forgiven.'"

There must have been a connection between the sickness of the paralytic man lowered through the roof in front of Jesus and his life-style. It would explain why the first thing Jesus does is to forgive him his sins. The sick man's actions might have caused his state.

Our human actions have their unavoidable effects. It often is the reason that many show little or no mercy to those struck by diseases supposedly caused by their own behavior. It might even have been the reason that the people in our story, listening to Jesus, didn't give way to his stretcher.

I once overheard a young woman discuss a sermon with her friend. She said, "That wasn't the only time I heard him preach, but his message that time gave me a real spiritual lift. I'll never forget one thing in particular he said."

When her friend asked what the preacher had said, she answered that he spoke about the paralytic who was lowered through the roof. The preacher said, "The world will always say, 'You made your bed, and you must lie on it. But Jesus said, 'Take up your bed and walk. Your sins are forgiven you.'"

When we have met people who got sick through their own fault, how often have we thought—and maybe even said—"They just got what they deserved"?

What would happen to ourselves if that would be the final judgment on us? Wasn't it Jesus who once said, "Do not judge, so that you may not be judged yourself"?

Saturday of the First Week

MARK 2:13-17

At Table with Jesus

"Sinners were also sitting at table with Jesus."

Pope Paul VI once called Simone Weil the most important spiritual woman of his time. She was born into an agnostic Jewish family in France. A story about her as a child might serve as a key to her personality. As a small child she once saw poor children in the cold of winter without any socks on. She asked her mother, "Why are those children without socks in this cold?" Her mother answered that they were too poor to have socks. Simone looked up at her mother and said: "I am never going to wear socks any more until all children have socks."

During a Holy Week celebration that she only attended because she loved old Gregorian chant (which helped her to get rid of her migraines), she experienced herself taken up by Jesus' Spirit. She was utterly amazed, as she had never been interested in anything divine or mystical. A priest friend of hers wrote her that the logical consequence of this experience was to be baptized.

After some reflection she wrote back that she had thought it over, and had decided not to be baptized. She explained her reasons: if she were to be baptized, she would have to be baptized into one or another Christian denominational church. In whatever church she was baptized, she would, in the name of Jesus, have to gather at a table where not everyone was welcome. How would she be able to do that in the name of Jesus? Jesus, who was sitting at table with disciples and sinners alike!

Monday of the Second Week

MARK 2 : 18 - 22

A New Chance

"No! New wine into fresh skins."

The prophet Isaiah foretold the coming of a new world. "See the earlier things have come to pass, new ones I now foretell" (Is 42:9). "Remember not the events of the past...see, I am doing something new!" (Is 43:18–19). "For look, I am going to create new heavens and a new earth" (Is 65:17). All that newness points at the work Jesus came to start among us. He, too, announced a new world!

The new, however, always meets the old. The people of his time were accustomed to their old melodies, and the new noise Jesus made was heard as a threat.

This was something Jesus understood. He told them that the new cannot coexist with the old, the new wine cannot be put in an old wineskin without getting lost.

Giving those examples of the old cloak and old wineskin he was most probably using some popular and well known proverbs, folk wisdom applying to all places and times, and—maybe—applicable to our days in a special way.

Don't we hear and read again and again that we live in a era that is post-modern, post-patriarchal, post-ideological, post-industrial and post-almost anything else? Haven't many among us our doubts about our political, economical, ecological, and social structures? Aren't almost all of us anxious about the growing gap between the rich and the poor?

It seems that in our days the "old," though not exactly over and past, is definitely considered with a greater apprehension than before. Doubting the value of the old wine, shouldn't we be more open to the fresh wine? Doesn't all this offer a chance for the new as never before during our lifetime?

Tuesday of the Second Week

MARK 2:23-28

Son of Man

"...the Son of Man is master even of the Sabbath."

Jesus calls himself "Son of Man" eighty-one times in the gospels. No one else addresses him in that way. They give him other names and titles. The South African Dominican Father Albert Nolan wrote in his book *Jesus Before Christianity* that "there is no evidence that he [Jesus] ever laid claim to any of the exalted titles which the church later attributed to him." According to Nolan this even includes the title Christ, meaning the anointed one. Nolan asserts that the one title Jesus did use, "the Son of Man," was an Aramaic figure of speech meaning much the same as "human being."

Dorothy Day, who died not long ago and whose canonization process has started in Rome, is considered a contemporary American saint by many who knew her. She started the Catholic Worker movement, and opened homes for the homeless, and community farms for the down-and-out. She definitely was a special person. She did extraordinary things. Yet, every time she overheard anyone saying something like that of her, she was indignant. "You say that I am special because you do not want to do what you see me do. You can easily do what I do, but by convincing yourself that I am someone special, you allow yourself to escape from your own responsibility. You can do what I do."

When Jesus uses the title "Son of Man" he changes our relation to him. He changes our expectations. He doesn't change what we can expect from *him*, but what we should expect from *ourselves*. Jesus says it in as many words: "In all truth I tell you whoever believes in me will perform the same works as I do myself and will perform even greater works" (John 14:12).

Wednesday of the Second Week

MARK 3 : 1 – 6

Fearlessness

"He looked angrily round at them…. The Pharisees went out…discussing how to destroy him."

In *Jesus Before Christianity*, Father Nolan makes another remark. He notes that there are "no traces of fear in Jesus." The gospel story of today makes that point. Jesus wasn't afraid of authority, he wasn't afraid of scandal. He challenged the authorities of his time. He wasn't afraid to consort with prostitutes and the unclean. Nor was he abstemious. John the Baptizer fasted, living on insects and walking around in a camel skin. Jesus feasted and complained that the leaders didn't dance while he was playing the flute for them (Mt 11:17). The character Nolan portrays derives his knowledge of the world and people not from set dogmas and laws, but from an intuitive feeling for others, from compassion, from "being with."

It was his fearlessness that made him so dangerous to the authorities around him. If they allowed him to be like that, others might begin to act in the same way. Their power and control would be lost. They couldn't allow him to let his light shine. That possibility might become contagious.

In his inaugural speech as the first African President of South Africa, Nelson Mandela, South Africa's great liberator, expressed a similar message when he said: "It is our light not our darkness that frightens us…. As we let our light shine we unconsciously give other people permission to do the same. As we are liberated from our own fear, our presence automatically liberates others."

Thursday of the Second Week

MARK 3:7-12

Being Crushed

"To keep him from being crushed."

The lives we live can be, and often are, simply crushing. Young children, teenagers, family life, pressure at work, one, two, or three jobs plus some volunteering here and there: often it's simply too much. We are no longer good to ourselves.

Jesus faced being crushed like that. He was surrounded from all sides by a crowd that wanted to touch him. In that crush he wouldn't have been able to really touch anyone in the end. He needed breaks, little treats, silences for himself, and a general "slow down" from time to time. That is why he had asked his friends to have a boat ready for him—to keep him from being crushed.

A parishioner who felt that she had been let down by her pastor—because she hadn't found him home on his weekly day off—told him angrily that "the devil never takes a day off!" "That's right," the pastor replied quietly. "And if I didn't take a day off, I'd be just like him." And he added a bit fastidiously: "Even God took a day off!"

All of us need time to be in touch with ourselves, and to be able to touch others, as Jesus did.

Friday of the Second Week

MARK 3:13-19

His Company

"They were to be his companions."

From the very beginning Jesus decided not to remain alone. He wanted and needed company. When he began to introduce the newness he intended, he did it in and with a group. Walking along the Lake of Galilee he had picked up two couples of brothers, and some others had decided to follow him as well.

Having climbed a mountain he selected his permanent group. He chose a very mixed group. One of the selected ones was Matthew, a tax collector, considered by many to be a traitor to their national cause and an outcast. Another one was Simon, a Zealot, a name that meant he was a fundamentalist, a nationalistic fanatic. They were the two extremes in the politically and religiously polarized society in which Jesus lived.

In our own society and church we would call those extremes the left and the right, or the conservatives and liberals. Extremes have often divided Christian communities, scattering the church over denominational groups. They alienate us from one another in the church community to which we belong.

Perhaps Jesus chose his disciples as he did in order to help show us from the very beginning of his ministry how to deal with these difficulties, insisting that the most diverse people would be able to live together in his presence. It is obvious from the gospel story that he enabled his first group of disciples to do so: they were all living and working together with him, complementing each other. They had a bond and cooperation that should also be present among ourselves.

Saturday of the Second Week

MARK 3:20–21

Family Reaction

"They set out to take charge of him; they said he is out of his mind."

Most of us have had the experience. It was something foretold by Jesus when he said that those following him would have to face the fact that "a person's enemies will be the members of his own household."

In a way it was all well meant. Jesus' family had heard all kinds of rumors about him: how he had surrounded himself with a motley group of strange characters; how he was challenging the religious and secular powers of their day; how he didn't intend to come back home, to do the work he had been accustomed to do; how he didn't even find the time any more to sit down at table to eat a piece of bread.

They were worried about his security, his safety, and his state of mind. They said, "He is out of his mind!" And they weren't only worried about *him*, they were also worried about *themselves*, about their own security and safety, and about what people would be saying about them.

All those who open themselves to Jesus' Spirit in themselves will be facing this problem. The British author H.G. Wells expressed it this way: "For most people the voice of their neighbors is louder than the voice of God!" What will our neighbors say?

Our text doesn't tell us what Jesus said to those who thought of coming to rescue him. It does tell us what he did. He continued the work he had started.

Monday of the Third Week

MARK 3:22–30

Binding Evil

"But no one can make his way into a strong man's house
...unless he has first tied up the strong man."

One day Jesus cannot find the privacy he is looking for. Three groups of people make this impossible: a crowd so numerous that he doesn't even get a chance to get to the table to eat; his family, who wants to get him back home; and a group of scribes from Jerusalem, who want to liquidate him.

The third group, agents from the holy city, accuse him of being possessed by the devil: "It is through the prince of devils," they say, "that he drives devils out." They declare him to be of the devil, an accusation we still hear nowadays.

Jesus overturns the scribes' accusation, saying that if he does what he does in name of the devil, the devil is fighting itself. For that is what he came to do in this world: to fight the devil who is inhabiting our human homestead.

He explains his intention in a fascinating way: "No one can make his way into a strong man's house and steal his property unless he has first tied up the man. Only then can he take his house."

Jesus comes to bind the strong man who terrorizes humanity. He comes to liberate us. He comes as a divine thief in our human night to break through the walls of the existing "order" that keeps us terrorized and imprisoned (Mt 24:43). Binding that strong man is at the same time unbinding us.

Jesus comes to open the door through which we can come to share the spirit and the freedom of the children of God. Being unbound, however, doesn't suffice, nor does opening a door. We have to get up and walk into the freedom assured to the children of God.

Tuesday of the Third Week

MARK 3:31–35

On Being His Mother

"Anyone who does the will of God is...my mother."

Anyone doing the will of God is considered by Jesus as being his mother. A strange saying. It is easy to understand that doing God's will makes you into Jesus' sister or brother. It means that you are living the life God gave you with the same kind of intention and intensity Jesus did. But how would you be able to become his mother?

It was late in the evening somewhere in Africa. A priest told me that he had been invited to visit the family of one of his parishioners. He had been living in Africa as a missionary for more years than he liked to remember, for he had gotten very old in the process. The family had invited him for a kind of farewell. He told me that he had been touched by what they had told him. When I asked him what had touched him most, he thought for a moment and answered: "They called me their ancestor. They told me that I was to them as their father and mother."

Doing God's will is always life-giving. It opens up the divine dimension in ourselves. It gives birth to the Spirit, not only in ourselves, but also in the world of those we touch. We do not only become Jesus' sister and brother and friend, but— as he said—like his mother.

Wednesday of the Third Week

MARK 4 : 1 - 20

Land

"...and some seed fell in rich soil...."

We all know the parables of the sower and the seed. We know them so well that we hardly pay attention to them when we hear them. Heads nod and eyes either close or glaze over, showing that we are dreaming of something else. This is a pity, because we will never discover that those stories are not in the first instance about the sower and the seed, but about something else.

The title "sower and seed" wasn't given by the gospel authors. It comes from our Bible editors, and it is a misnomer. When you pay attention and count the use of the different words in the gospel, you will notice that another word is more often used than those words "sower and seed." The word "land" is mentioned twelve times in the three sower and seed parables of Mark.

The main theme in those stories is the land, that is to say, we are the main issue. It is a story about the enormous powers and potentialities that are conferred on us. They describe how, when we receive the seed of Jesus in ourselves, we are capable of bringing forth fruit a hundredfold!

There is a verb in these stories that is used even more often than the noun "land." It is the word "listening." It is used thirteen times. If we listen to the word and example Jesus sows in us, we will be able to show ourselves and the whole wide world what we are capable of. If we don't listen we won't even know who we really are. On its own the seed can't do a thing. The land without the seed is fruitless.

Jesus' parables are about an interaction. The seed needs to be sown, and the land needs to receive. The reaction to be expected is not so much a conversion, but a revelation, a disclosure. The land will never know its power until someone sows the seed—something we had better take into consideration when communicating with others.

Thursday of the Third Week

MARK 4:21-25

Light to the World

"Is a lamp brought in to be put under a tub or bed?"

At the baptism ceremony a candle is lit from the Easter candle, representing to us Jesus, the light of the world. The lighted candle is then given to the one baptized or, when a baby is baptized, to one of the godparents. Some prayers accompany this rite: "Receive the light of Christ," and "Walk always as a child of the light."

In this way a new light is brought into the world to punch holes in the darkness around us, as Jesus did. Each one of us is such a light. The problem is that the lights we are, often remain hidden. They are screened off. Jesus uses the metaphors of putting one's light under a tub or a bed.

He adds that our lights shouldn't remain hidden. We shouldn't make a secret of ourselves. The lights we are should be disclosed to help others to see.

This disclosure is not a question of words. Lamps do not speak. They shine. They help us to see! Without light the world will remain stumbling in the dark. It is a joy to be able to shine and see!

And if you happen to be a parent or godparent of a child, don't forget that other prayer at the handing over of the light: "Parents and godparents, this light is entrusted to you to be kept burning brightly. This child of yours is enlightened by Christ." You should not only kindle the light but foster it!

Friday of the Third Week

MARK 4:26-34

Sower and Seed

"This is what the reign of God is like. A man scatters seed on land."

"A sower went out to sow his seed." Jesus was that sower. The seed is the word of God. Jesus sowed that seed. He believed in the power and vitality of the seed.

You, too, trust that what you sow has so much power that it will come up without difficulty. You don't sit next to the field to watch the seeds you have sowed, either.

That seed has to grow in us. It will, it *should* grow all through our hearts until we have the feelings of Jesus. It should master us so that we make the decisions Jesus made. It should be the spark in our fingers so that we act, heal, comfort, and nurture as Jesus did. It should even get into our feet and toes so that we walk Jesus' path.

There is another thing to be said. No one would sow only one seed. You can't plant one palm tree, you can't plant one banana plant, you can't grow one stalk of corn or one blade of grass. One plant would never profit from the shadow of others when the sun shines. One plant would never stand up against the storm and the rain. It is only when plants stand together and grow together that they help one another with their shadow and break the power of the sun; that they break the force of the wind together and overcome the beating of the rain.

And so it is with you and with me.

Saturday of the Third Week

MARK 4:35–41

On a Cushion

"But he was in the stern, his head on the cushion, asleep."

Small things often tell more about us than big things. Perhaps that's why people visiting an exhibit about a famous person are often drawn to the knitting needles the person used, or the pencil stub he or she chewed. These are the small things that give them away and show how human they are, and how much they are like us.

"To deprive this man [Jesus] of his humanity," Father Nolan wrote, "is to deprive him of his greatness." A small detail—such as being asleep with his head on the cushion—shows Jesus to be like us in a way that can touch our hearts. We can just picture him adjusting that cushion under his head before falling asleep.

Where did he get that cushion? Was it just a pillow he found in the hold of the boat? Was it a cushion given to him by someone who cared for him, or loved him? And if it was a gift, was there something embroidered on it? However you turn it, that cushion tells us something about his vulnerability as a human person. It puts him on line with us.

At the same time there is that contrasting story about the sheer power of his mere presence. When the frightened disciples woke him up, the storm became a gentle breeze—as it always did and will do even in the storms of our lives in the company of that most human friend of ours.

Monday of the Fourth Week

MARK 5:1–20

The Other Side

"They reached the territory of the Gerasenes on the other side of the lake."

In Mark's gospel Jesus asks his disciples nine times to go to the other side of the lake. Every single time something happens when he is asking them to do so. In fact they don't want to go to the other side of the lake. Why should they go to that other side full of strangers? Wasn't their side good enough?

Gerasa was for them the pits. At the other side they met a madman possessed by a legion of demons. He had been banned by his own people, who had bound him to a tombstone in a cemetery. He had broken his chains and was shouting and hurting himself with stones in the midst of pigs who were grazing nearby.

Mark couldn't have described a person more alien to the disciples than this man. As Jews, faithful to their ritual prescriptions, there were a host of reasons not to be there at all: the madman, the demons, the cemetery, the pigs, the hostile pagan villagers….

The lesson Jesus taught them at that other side of the lake was a difficult one. It was about the inclusiveness of God's reign. No one can be excluded. God is Father of all, and we should be brothers and sisters. All boundaries that divide us from each other should be broken.

Jesus chased the demons out of the man. The healed man asked Jesus to be allowed to stay with him. Jesus told him to go home to his own people to tell his story—the story about God's mercy and love for all, the story that still needs to be told in our homes to offset the demons of racism, sexism, and all forms of exclusivity. They still happen to be "legion."

Tuesday of the Fourth Week

MARK 5:21-43

Initiative

"'My daughter' he said, 'your faith has restored you to health, go in peace....'"

She had been bleeding for twelve years. Mark tells us that she had lost her whole fortune making the rounds of various doctors, without being any better for it; in fact, she was getting worse. (Luke, being a doctor himself, doesn't mention this detail!)

She had heard about Jesus, and thought, "If I can only touch his clothes, I shall be healed." She elbows herself through the crowd. She touches his clothing. She feels a power invading and healing her. He feels a power going out of him.

He wonders what he felt, and asks, "Who touched my clothes?" His disciples laugh at the question. They laugh at him: "How can you ask, did anyone touch me, look at the crowd milling against you!" Their question sounds sarcastic, yet it helps us further.

The disciples were right. Hundreds of people were touching Jesus that day. But nothing happened to them. The touching of Jesus as such doesn't have any effect in itself. It isn't in that way that power goes out of him. That power comes when you do it in faith. It happens at the moment when you share his vision and, consequently, his person and his power.

Faith is not the consequence of the miracle. Faith is its condition. You heal because you believe, because you take the initiative and reach out.

It sounds almost heretical. All seems to depend on your own initiative. But it is Jesus himself who tells her, "My daughter, your faith has restored you to health; go in peace and be free of your complaint."

Wednesday of the Fourth Week

MARK 6:1-6

Dishonored

"Where did the man get all this?"

When he comes home to Nazareth they sneer at him. They wonder where he got it all from, he a carpenter, the son of Mary. That last remark might have been meant as a real insult. In that time people were called after their father. Who was his father? It is not the only time that people around him express their doubts about his legitimacy.

There is another thing in him they might not have liked. He had left his mother to care for herself. He doesn't show too much respect for traditional roles. They don't like his fame. He is just too much for them. Instead of being glad for him, they feel offended by him. They are scandalized by his behavior. They don't believe in him.

He is amazed by their reaction. He didn't expect it, though he says that he knows a prophet is never honored among his own relations and in his own house. He leaves them and, as far as we know, never returns there again. He leaves the old structure that wants to keep him behind in his traditional place.

Though he lays on hands and heals some of his acquaintances, he can't work any great miracle. He is amazed by that, too. They don't have the faith to heal themselves and to break their bonds. The impossibility doesn't come from his side. It is their unbelief that closes them off. He is incapable of convincing them of their own potential.

Not believing in him means not believing in yourself! He always insists, "Your faith has healed you!" The difficulty in Nazareth is not so much that he is not honored as he should have been. The difficulty is that they don't honor themselves as they should! That is why he is so amazed at them.

Thursday of the Fourth Week

MARK 6 : 7 – 13

Pastoral Respect

"Take nothing for the journey except a staff, no bread, no haversack, no coppers for their purses."

Jesus didn't choose his disciples just so they could be with him. It is true that he wanted their company on his mission; he didn't want to be alone. But he had another reason. He wanted to send them out in their turn to announce the good news and to fight evil wherever it is found.

The first time he sends the disciples out he gives them some directives, rules he never withdrew, rules that remain in force. They had to take care of their own travel. Mark says that they had to take a staff and a pair of sandals. For the rest, they are not allowed to take anything, no food, no knapsack, no extra clothing, and no money. The practical consequence of those rules is that they made themselves dependent on the hospitality of those who would receive them.

We don't know whether the apostles obeyed those rules. Because *we* don't always obey them, we know what happens if we don't. When I came to Africa as a missionary, the eucharistic bread we used came from a bakery in the Netherlands. When Pope John Paul II visited Nairobi some years ago, the local church imported large quantities of hosts from that same bakery. The wine came from Cyprus. We didn't depend on the hospitality and resources of the host country.

This lack of trust in others, lack of dependence on others, is important not only when preaching the "good news" in far-off countries. It should concern us when we are in familiar surroundings. Just try to speak to teenagers about Jesus in terms that are not their own! During an instruction on the rite of confirmation, one teenager put up her hand and asked, "Why don't you speak in a way we can understand?" Why don't we?

Friday of the Fourth Week

MARK 6 : 1 4 – 2 9

Wrong Questions

"Herod had heard about him."

Herod must have been an inquisitive and superstitious king. He had a lot of questions after he had heard John the Baptizer. He liked to listen to him and thought him to be a good and upright man, but he remained puzzled by his behavior. Finally, he ended his doubts by cutting off John's head.

That is something we can be sure of, as it is reported Josephus, a historian of that time, though Josephus doesn't mention that it was at one of his birthday parties that Herod decided to have John executed because of Salome's striptease.

When a guilt-ridden Herod heard about Jesus he was again puzzled. He began to ask questions about him. Was he a prophet? Was he Elijah? Was he John who had come back?

Many ask the wrong "religious" questions, that is to say, questions that really don't make any difference to life. "Whom did the children of Adam and Eve marry; did they marry each other?" "Did Jesus have brothers and sisters?" "Did the flood cover even the highest mountains?" "Isn't it impossible that a daughter of the queen behaved like Salome did at Herod's palace?" "How do you explain that Josephus didn't mention Salome when reporting John the Baptizer's execution?"

Questions like these keep us on the fringe of Jesus' message: "God is our source of being, loving all of us notwithstanding our failings." To God, people are first before anything else, including scriptures, churches, and practices. Express God's inclusive care for others in your own lives. Make your world resemble God's realm!

Saturday of the Fourth Week

MARK 6:30-34

Sheep

"...they were like sheep without a shepherd."

The apostles came back from their first mission. They were tired. It had all been new for them. So Jesus said: "Let's get some rest; we'll go to a lonely place and have a good meal and a good sleep." So they went off in a boat to a lonely place. That is what they thought. The crowd had followed them and in no time surrounded them again. They were in for the trouble they had tried to escape from, a situation all of us know too well.

Jesus sent his disciples away to have their rest and took it upon himself to speak to the crowd because he had pity on them, "...since they were like sheep without a shepherd."

How do you listen to such a story? With whom do you identify? With the disciples, with the crowd, or with Jesus?

The temptation to identify ourselves with the sheep might be great. It isn't very flattering, but it is easy. It is nice to be led. Not all of us like to take responsibility for our own lives. Some leaders love to lead "sheep" like that.

Jesus is quite willing to play the role of a shepherd meeting people who behave like sheep. He has nothing against sheep, but he does have something against people who behave as if they are sheep. He wants to change those who behave like sheep into shepherds, who in their turn change others into shepherds, and so on. That is what he does to those who follow him.

In the beginning of this story they came back from a mission he had entrusted to them. They had done things they never thought they could do: heal sick people, change hearts, announce the good news, be full of compassion for others. They hardly recognized themselves. There was nothing sheepish about those newborn men and women around Jesus. (My apologies to all real sheep in the world: they should not be offended; they are perfectly what they are supposed to be.)

Monday of the Fifth Week

MARK 6 : 53 - 56

Touch

"All those who touched him were cured."

We are surrounded by "touch" stories. We have become aware of the healing power of touch. Research shows that patients who are touched by their doctors during their daily visits heal quicker and better than those whose doctors just remain standing at their beds at a distance without touching them.

In a library research project at a college campus, half of a group of uninformed collegians were assisted well by the librarian. She talked to them, answered questions, and helped them find resources. The other half of the group didn't get all that much help, but they were physically touched by the librarian as they left, in a way that seemed accidental.

"As each student left the library, a researcher asked if their time in the library had been positive. The students who had been touched reported a very positive experience. Those who had not been touched (even though they had been helped a great deal) had a more negative response" (Jennie Gordon, *If My Parents Are Getting Divorced, Why Am I the One Who Hurts?*).

Touch has a healing effect on people of any age. Think of reflexology, aromatherapy, and so on. Jesus was a master of touch, and he continued his "practice" in the sacraments, especially in the Eucharist. Let us not only remain in touch with him, but also with all those around us. Did you ever try out your healing power?

Tuesday of the Fifth Week

MARK 7:1-13

Pleading the Fourth

"Hypocrites…. Honor your father and your mother."

Jesus scolds the Pharisees and experts in the law. He calls them names. He calls them hypocrites. He does that to blame them for not taking care of their parents.

Originally the Greek word *hypocrite* just meant "answering." It went on to mean someone answering in a set dialogue, conversation, or theater play—the answer given by an actor. Finally it came to mean someone whose whole life is a piece of acting without any sincerity behind it at all.

Jesus uses the word in a context. The context is filial piety, the care the younger generation takes for the older one. He blames them for not helping their parents because of hypocritical dedication of their money to the temple.

There is something of that hypocrisy in our day and age. According to a Gallup poll in 1994, 85% of Americans think it is the responsibility of adult children to care for their elderly parents. The same percentage said they would consider asking their parents—unable to live alone—to move in with them.

That would mean that only 15% of the elderly would remain without assistance from their children, in one way or another. However, in the same poll 79% of the elderly say they have never received financial help from their children.

Words do not seem to meet deeds. That is what hypocrisy is about. And that is why Jesus' plea for the fourth commandment is still relevant to our time. The commandment reads: "Honor your father and mother." It is in each one's interest to do so!

Wednesday of the Fifth Week

MARK 7:14-23

Internal Hygiene

"Evil things come from within."

Jesus uses a very practical comparison to make his point. He says that things that are taken in from outside don't make us unclean. He gives the reason for that. He says that those things don't go into the heart, but pass through the stomach to be thrown out again into the sewer. He couldn't have been more down-to-earth.

He uses the comparison to insist on our internal hygiene, or the hygiene of our hearts. We have to keep our hearts clean. When we hear about that cleanliness of heart many of us are conditioned to think almost immediately about sex. So does Jesus. In his list of the items to be removed from our hearts he mentions fornication, adultery, and indecency. We should clean those items out, or, even better, avoid them all together, though the latter is difficult in our days. (It is with us in ways totally unknown in Jesus' time, in movies, books, advertisements, and on the Internet.)

Jesus also mentions other uncleanlinesses to be avoided or flushed out. The fifth term on Jesus' list is translated as "avarice" in the Bible version we use.

It can also be translated in another way. The Greek word in the text is *pleonaxia,* meaning "to have more," or "the accursed love of having and wanting to have more."

It is the vice that leads to the wanting and buying of all kinds of things one really doesn't need, and to the renewing and replacing of items that are still very serviceable.

It is a kind of curse that does harm not only to ourselves but also to others who remain deprived of the goods they need because of our lust for having.

Jesus warns, "Flush it out. Get cleansed."

Thursday of the Fifth Week

MARK 7:24–30

Open Door Policy

"For saying this you may go home happy."

"Happy" is the key word in this story, in which Jesus is outside of Jewish territory. He is a stranger in Gentile, or pagan, territory. He didn't wish to be recognized, but his fame had spread too widely. A woman with a teenaged daughter in difficulty recognized him and asked for his help. The first answer she got from him was that the door to such a grace was closed to her.

He told her that others had to be helped first, implying that the others might be helped later. For the time being the door was closed to her. He used the metaphor of a family to explain what he meant. The children of the family should be fed first, and the others afterward. He refers to those "others" by the diminutive form of the word "dogs"—"little dogs," or "puppies." Diminutives take the sting out of a word. Diminutives are often affectionate. Jesus must have been using that term "puppies" with a smile.

The woman immediately saw her chance. She answered: "But those dogs are eating the scraps under the table," implying they belong to the family. The door isn't closed to them. Her faith wouldn't take no for an answer. She responded to his smile with her own.

No wonder commentators later would note that the first Christian communities used this story to tell each other that they always should be open to strangers. It still tells us to keep our doors open to others. There are plenty of them in our world.

Friday of the Fifth Week

MARK 7:31-37

Inculturation

"He put his fingers in the man's ears...touched his tongue with spittle...sighed...."

Inculturation is a new word. You probably won't find it in a dictionary yet. It's a theological term. The popes have been using it only for the last twenty years or so. Inculturation indicates a process in which the Good News is proclaimed and allowed to grow in a culture that never has been confronted with it. It brings the Good News of God's inclusive love in a new context, respecting the ways in which the Spirit had been at work before.

The word might be new, the process might have been rediscovered recently, but its practice is as old as the Good News itself. The gospel of today shows how Jesus brings the new while respecting the old.

Jesus begins by taking the deaf man aside. When they are alone he does all kinds of things he didn't need to do. He could just have said *"Ephphatha"* without any further ado. He doesn't do that. He does what the man expects him to do. He ritualizes the healing process. Maybe he even does what street-healers of his time would have done.

He touches the man's ears, wets the man's tongue with some of his own spittle, and sighs, or, as other versions would translate that sigh, he groans.

The man is healed by the Good News Bringer—Jesus—in his own context. It is a lesson we can learn when we bring the Good News to others, and not only to others in cultures strange to us, but also in our own world, for instance when bringing the Good News to our own offspring, our younger generation!

Saturday of the Fifth Week

MARK 8:1–10

Seven Basketfuls

"They collected seven basketfuls of scraps left over."

The crowd was so large that evening that he had to do some crowd control. He used the same method we still use. He asked them to sit down on the ground. It is easier to handle a sitting crowd than a standing one. Then seven loaves of bread were produced and some sardines, enough for him to organize one of his gigantic picnics.

There is one saint who followed his example in this. History tells that Philip Neri, the founder of the Oratory, did the same in Rome on some feast days, inviting the whole of the population of the city.

That image of everyone eating together is one of Jesus' dreams. We are all invited to the banquet table of the Father. It is a dream dreamt by people like Martin Luther King, Jr., Peter Maurin, Dorothy Day, Mahatma Gandhi, and in fact by anyone organizing, contributing to, or helping in a soup kitchen.

It is a dream older than Christianity itself. A dream at the moment often rudely interrupted by our actual free trade and a globalization that leave so many hungry.

That day Jesus left no one hungry. They all ate as much as they wanted. They even collected seven basketfuls of scraps left over. The number of those "doggy-bags" is significant. The number seven points to all, the universe, the whole of the human family!

Monday of the Sixth Week

MARK 8:11–13

Signs from Heaven

"They demanded of him a sign from heaven."

They came to Jesus for a discussion. They asked him for a sign from heaven. Jesus only sighed and left them. He went to the other side of the lake by boat. He obviously didn't want to waste his time on this kind of discussion. Wasn't he giving them signs left, right, and center? Weren't they surrounded by the signs he was giving them?

One of the questions that recurs again and again in our days is similar to the one asked by those people who wanted to get Jesus into difficulties: "Can you prove to me the presence of God in our midst?"

The signs of God's presence are all around us. The problem isn't the absence of those signs, it's our blindness to them.

I went for a walk last evening. I saw an older woman bent over a low fence by the street to smell a bright yellow rose. I saw some children full of joy licking away at bright green and red cones filled with ice cream. I saw a young man and woman kiss each other. And I saw a child jump with joy when her father came out of a bus.

God's love is at work in men and women minding their children, making a living, bearing the difficulties in life, rendering their professional services as well as possible, being kind, and offering a cup of coffee to people who could do with one.

Indeed, the signs of God are all around us. We don't notice because we are so accustomed to God's presence. They are so common, so ordinary, so uneventful, and so frequent, that we don't notice them. Try to pay attention to them today!

Tuesday of the Sixth Week

MARK 8:14–21

Lack of Understanding

"Do you still not realize?"

In 1991 Pope John Paul II wrote in his encyclical *The Mission of the Redeemer* that we should pay attention to the fact that the gospels are different. They were written by different people, for different people, in different regions, and at different times.

You could add that they are even written in a certain contrast to one another. Luke, for instance, writes in the beginning of his gospel that he is aware that others have been writing their accounts. He then adds, now listen to *my* version!

One of the differences between the gospel of Mark and the one of Matthew is that in Matthew's gospel the disciples practically always understand Jesus, while in Mark's gospel they usually don't understand him at all. Mark's story today illustrates this point. Jesus says almost in desperation—"Do you not understand?"

As a reader of Mark's gospel you might feel that same kind of frustration. Don't those disciples around him see what it is all about? How come?

Commentators who have been studying Mark are of the opinion that it is Mark's intention to provoke in us that feeling of frustration. It is a kind of literary trick. Mark wants us to say: "Good heavens, what a lack of understanding. I would never have acted like that. I would have done much better."

When we read Mark's gospel, we shouldn't spend too much time asking "What does Mark mean?" The question we should ask instead is, what does Mark wants us *to do*? Jesus is asking us, too: "Do you still not realize?"

Wednesday of the Sixth Week

MARK 8:22-26

Step-by-step

"The man who was beginning to see, replied...."

This miracle is unique. It is the only miracle that happens gradually. When Jesus puts spittle on the eyes of the blind man the man begins to see, and Jesus has to repeat the laying of hands before the world around the man falls in focus.

It is a miracle that is not mentioned in the gospels by Matthew and Luke. Mark must have had a special intention to tell it this way.

We might find a key to that riddle by noting the place of this event. Just before this miracle Jesus had asked his disciples: "Do you still not understand?" And immediately after this miracle Jesus asks his disciples, "Who do you say I am?" These questions resemble the question he asks the blind man: "Can you see anything?" His answer is, "Yes, but vaguely."

When Jesus asks his disciples the question "Who do you say I am?" Peter answers, "You are the Christ." But it is only much later that Peter would see the consequences of his answer.

He saw, but vaguely! He needed another application of Jesus' hands. Jesus' work in us is not done just instantaneously either. Let us have the courage to pray that he lays his hands on us again and again, so that we may proceed step-by-step until the reign comes.

Thursday of the Sixth Week

MARK 8:27-33

Dreams and Expectations

"The way you think is not God's way, but man's!"

First Jesus asked them: "Who do people say I am?" That was an easy one. They had their answers ready—a variety of answers: the answers of others that didn't engage them themselves. He then asked them, "But you, who do you say I am?" Peter's answer is, "You are the anointed one!" Peter was right, and he spoke most probably in the name of all the others, because all of them were told "not to tell anyone about him."

They were right, but not completely. They had their own ideas of what the Messiah should do. They dreamt their own dreams, a restoration of their people, a victory over others, joining him in that glorious future.

They weren't the only ones who dreamt those dreams. The Messiah was, in general, expected to be *for* them and *against* the others! Their dream would be like a nightmare to others.

Their Messianic expectations were far from Jesus' intentions. He wanted to keep it a secret for the time being, until they had grown in insight. He wanted to prepare them for the truth about him, and about the price he would have to pay. He wanted to explain to them that they would have to break through their own egoistic and nationalistic expectations.

He was willing to give his life for the sake of all. They—and we—are expected to follow him in that breakthrough.

Friday of the Sixth Week

MARK 8:34 — 9:1

His Cross

"Let them take their cross and follow me."

When Jesus tells them: "If anyone wants to be a follower of mine, let them renounce themselves and take up their cross and follow me," he has not yet been telling his disciples that he is going to be crucified.

He has told them that he is going to be rejected and killed because of his mission, and that he will rise again after three days. He now indicates that the sincere followers of his might have to lay down their lives for the gospel as well.

But there has been—as far as we can know from Mark's text—not a word about his crucifixion. He must have been using the word "cross" in another way at least to their ears.

There is another point that is sometimes overlooked. He doesn't say that we should be carrying his cross. He tells us that we should be as willing to carry our cross as he is willing to carry his.

His sayings put us back into our own lives. He is talking about the life we are living right now—our ways at announcing his Good News in our world. He is speaking about our daily talks, works, walks, ups-and-downs, relations, sorrows, and joys. If we forget that, then we might be looking at all kinds of painful and mortifying extras—extras that might even be a reason for us not to carry the cross that we find in our everyday tasks and duties.

A Christian life in our world is in itself something of a cross. And if we bear it well it is at the same time utter joy: his joy.

Saturday of the Sixth Week

MARK 9:2-13

Transfigured

"...his clothes became brilliantly white, whiter than any bleacher could make them."

When Peter, James, and John looked at Jesus when he stood on Mount Tabor, transfigured, brighter than the brightest star, pure light before them, they not only saw him transfigured, they saw more than his future and risen life. Looking at him, they were looking at themselves. He showed them who he was. He showed them also who we are going to become. He showed them our future human glory and destiny, the glory and destiny of every human being.

Coming down from the mountain after this, the three started to discuss what "rising from the dead" could mean. They had just seen something like it; they had seen him as if he was risen already. Their discussion was a logical consequence of what they had seen.

This discussion has never ended as far as we humans are concerned. It is a discussion that has a wider dimension in our day. Reading the story, we hear that it is not only his body that begins to shine with the glory of the risen life; his clothes, too, become dazzlingly white, radiating light.

One of the reasons that we must respect our fellow human beings is the glory that is each one's personal destiny. We have to be respectful, too, for the rest of nature. The whole of creation will be taken up in glory.

We have many reasons to discuss further what rising from the dead could mean for us. We should also consider what it means for the whole of the environment we are so closely connected to, and even composed of. The resurrection of the body implies much more than we ever thought!

Monday of the Seventh Week

MARK 9:14-29

The Cause of Failure

"This is the kind that can only be driven out by prayer."

The disciples were astonished that they had not been able to drive out the evil spirit Jesus chased away. They might have thought it not completely fair. Hadn't he sent them out with the explicit assignment to cast out devils? Hadn't he given them the power and gift to do so? Had he been deceiving them? Had he been the reason they had lost face in the presence of a crowd of people?

They challenged him. Why hadn't they been able to help the possessed boy? His answer was simple: the cure demanded prayer. In other words, he told them that they were not close enough to God. Or to say it using a contemporary metaphor, they were not "online" with God.

God may have given us some gift, any gift, but unless we stay "online," that gift may wither and die. Many extra-ordinary people know that. There are doctors who pray with their assistants before an operation. Would you like your doctor to do that if you were the patient?

Two things happen when we pray like that. We keep in vital contact with the giver of the gift, and we do not lose the truth about ourselves—the truth that without God we are nothing.

The disciples had been equipped with power by Jesus himself. The power must have gone to their heads. They thought they would have been able to do it. They could not; they had lost the contact needed. This is quite a warning to all of us.

Tuesday of the Seventh Week

MARK 9:30-37

Social Program

"He then took a little child whom he set among them...."

Jesus is at home. The disciples are sitting around him. On their way home they had been arguing about who was the most important. (They were doing that while Jesus was explaining that he was willing to "deliver himself into the hands of men.")

He asks them, "What were you discussing on the way home?" They all fall silent. Nobody knows what to say. They must suddenly have seen the incongruity of the situation.

In their silence they hear some children playing outside. Jesus goes to the open door and calls a child, a street child.

These are the kind of children no one took seriously, the lowest level of the human hierarchy. Even in our world they often don't count. Just think of the little money available to help neglected children in our own society. So many things seem to be so much more important.

Jesus brings the child into their midst. The child stands there in their circle, a bit frightened, perhaps with a runny nose. Jesus embraces the child. Then he says: "Whoever welcomes a child such as this for my sake welcomes me. And whoever welcomes me welcomes not me but him who sent me."

It is not the only time that Jesus takes children as the model for his social program (see Mark 9:42; 10:13–16). It must have been quite a shock to his disciples. What Jesus is saying is that children are as important to God and to the Son of Man as the divine persons' self. Jesus is turning their whole world and its hierarchy completely upside down. Have a look at the children around you today; look at them with the eyes of God and Jesus Christ. A child should be present at all our decision makings! The more important the decision, the more important the presence of that child, for that child is God present with us.

Wednesday of the Seventh Week

MARK 9:38-40

Arrogance

"Master, we saw someone who is not one of us driving out devils in your name, and because he was not one of us we tried to stop him."

During a workshop for missionaries and evangelists, the participants were discussing their work and experiences. There was one thing they all agreed on: they had found many "Christian" values in people who had never heard of Jesus.

It was John who came to Jesus with a different, yet similar, experience: "Teacher, we saw a man who is not one of us driving out devils in your name, and because he was not one of us we tried to stop him."

It is the kind of surprise you hear often in a less obvious way. Pious persons can often say something like, "That person is so good, and not even Catholic!" When we say something like this, we restrict God's grace, we restrict God's presence, and we put ourselves on a special pedestal, as if we and those of our company are going to be the saviors of the world! We had better pay attention to Jesus' reaction.

He starts by saying to John: "Don't try to stop him!" He gives three reasons for this. The first is a practical one: anyone who works miracles in the name of Jesus is on Jesus' side. He then generalizes that reason: "Anyone who is not against us is with us." His third reason is the most important. Doesn't John understand that he himself will need some help now and then, if only in the form of a cup of water? And who is going to give him that help if he himself is the only one who can help? That is why Jesus adds: "Anyone who gives you a cup of water because you belong to Christ will not, I assure you, go without his reward" (Mark 9:41).

Thursday of the Seventh Week

MARK 9:41–50

Wisdom

"For everyone will be salted with fire."

On February 28, 1958, Thomas Merton, an American Trappist (1915-1968), had a dream. In his dream he was sitting next to a young Jewish girl who—to his surprise—embraced him tenderly. He asked her name. She answered: "Proverb." He, well versed in Holy Scripture, thought: "Proverb, the Book of Proverbs, Sophia, Wisdom, Spirit," and said: "What a beautiful name." She answered that she didn't like it, as she was often overlooked and sometimes even mocked.

On March 18 Merton had to see someone in Louisville—a rare occasion, as he was a cloistered monk. While he walked through its very busy shopping center he had a vision. He saw how the girl Proverb was present in everyone in the street. Young and old, rich and poor, black and white, male and female, they all were "salted" with God's Spirit.

The dream and vision changed his life. Before them he had been a rather aloof and otherworldly monk. After them he got interested in the people around him, all carriers of God's Spirit. He became aware of his interconnectedness with them and of their interconnectedness with each other.

He got interested in peace and justice issues, though it brought him into difficulty with his religious and secular authorities. Have salt in yourselves and be at peace with one another.

Friday of the Seventh Week

MARK 10:1–12

Marriage

"God made them male and female."

Jesus honors marriage. All through the tradition of his own people marriage has been considered a symbol of the final relation between God and humankind.

Mary didn't forget that theme, either. When she sees her son coming to the wedding in Cana, she goes up to him to say: "They have no wine!" Did she invite Jesus to begin the final wedding between God and humankind then and there? Jesus answers: "The hour has not yet come!" But as a kind of prelude to it, he changes water into wine.

Once Jesus was asked whether a husband is allowed to send his wife away. The question is not exactly about divorce, but about male domination. Jesus answers that such a male-biased approach to marriage is out of the question. Man and woman are created equal.

He quotes Scripture, saying that when marrying, a man leaves his own family, that his marrying doesn't mean the continuation of his family roots. The two are equal; they are one. Marriage is a relationship where love and friendship should be the norm and ideal.

That is the love and friendship we pray for when we attend a wedding. This is the bond married persons should be cultivating. This doesn't mean that there won't be difficulties. Any relationship experiences difficulties. The bond of married love, however, lies deeper than any of those problems.

Let us pray that that bond may exist between those who decide to marry, and let each couple cultivate it in equality and friendship. For the ashes of a burned-out marriage are bitter, indeed.

Saturday of the Seventh Week

MARK 10:13–16

Children and Reign

"Let the little children come to me."

These days many adults talk about the little child in them. Many would like that little child to be born in them. Considering what Jesus said about little children this might be a useful development. He invites us all to be like little children in their openness to the reign of God.

Parents can tell you stories about that candor. A mother told me how she was with her two children during a eucharistic celebration when the parish priest asked whether anyone would be willing to take a child, a refugee from Africa, into their home for a month or two. He quoted Jesus saying that anyone who receives a child is receiving him. Her children looked up at her but said nothing. A week later the pastor repeated his appeal. Her daughters looked up at her again.

After Mass the first thing these children asked their mother was, "Can't we take that child?" Their mother replied that she didn't think it a good idea, and that seemed to end the conversation. But that night when she was putting her children to bed, her eldest daughter asked, "Don't you think that Jesus would have done it?" At first the mother didn't even know what her daughter was talking about. But then she understood. She said, "I think he would."

That evening she discussed what had happened with her husband. They decided to contact their pastor and arrange things. The excitement at the breakfast table next morning was enormous!

Sarafina lived with them for about half a year. Her presence was a joy to the whole family. It was one of those cracks through which the reign of God broke through in our world.

Monday of the Eighth Week

MARK 10:17-27

Riches

"...he went away sad, for he was a rich man."

Lists are interesting things, as authors and publishers know. Sometimes they publish books that contain only lists, lists of all kinds of items.

You find many lists in the Bible. The ten commandments, the eight beatitudes, lists of virtues and vices. Jesus loves to use those lists. But sometimes he changes them. If he had used only the traditional lists, he wouldn't have contributed anything new. This is a good reason to listen carefully when Jesus gives his lists.

One day a young man falls on his knees in front of Jesus and asks: "Good master, what must I do to share in everlasting life?" Jesus answers with a list: "You shall not kill; you shall not commit adultery; you shall not steal; you shall not bear false witness; you shall not defraud; honor your father and your mother."

An old list with a variant! Do you recognize in this list the odd item, the one that is unusual and new? It is the term "defraud."

In classical Greek, the word Jesus uses means "refusing to return goods that have been given in deposit or loan." In biblical Greek it means "refusing to pay the wage of a hired laborer."

The man looks at Jesus and says: "Master, I have kept all these commandments from my earliest days." Jesus looks at him, with love and says: "There is one thing you lack. Go and sell everything you have and give the money to the poor, and you will have treasure in heaven; then come, follow me!"

Only at the end of the story do we hear that the young man was rich. In that time and region that can only have meant that he was a landowner or a businessman employing and hiring other people. Was that the reason Jesus added the admonition about defrauding?

ORDINARY TIME

Tuesday of the Eighth Week

MARK 10:28-31

The Bottom-line Question

"Look, we have left everything and followed you!"

Once when I was sitting on a train, a telephone buzzed in the pocket of the man next to me. Some passengers around us looked up. The man started a conversation about a business deal. At a certain moment we heard him ask: "What is in it for me? What am I getting out of it?" People looked for a moment at each other. They all must have recognized the bottom-line questions.

It was Peter's question: "We have left everything, what are we getting out of it?" Jesus' answer—that those who leave their houses, brothers, sisters, mothers, children, and land for the sake of the gospel will receive a hundred times as much—referred to the reign of God he came to introduce, the reign of justice and peace where we all will be brothers and sisters.

This new family is not just hanging somewhere as pie in the sky. No, it is being born among us from day to day. You can be sure that the Irish Sisters from Dublin working in the slums of Nairobi would love to have their own children and grandchildren. They gave them up for the gospel, and now are literally surrounded by hundreds, nay, thousands of children and grandchildren. That number has its own difficulties; so has their ministry. Didn't Jesus add that they will get all that plus persecutions? Giving birth to his new world is accompanied by pain, but a pain that will end in joy.

Wednesday of the Eighth Week

MARK 10:32-45

Ransom

"Can you drink the cup that I shall drink...?"

A woman was explaining to a group of children why Jesus died on the cross. She said that he did it to pay a ransom for our sins. He paid the price of his blood to his Father in heaven to save us. One child in class sighed audibly, "What a goofy father!"

Children aren't the only ones to have this reaction when they hear this type of theology. How could God ever ask such a thing? Yet, it seems to be the gospel story. In the gospel of Mark, Jesus explains that he is going "to give his life as a ransom for many."

The difficulty is not the concept of sacrifice. We all know of people who sacrificed their lives for others. The difficulty is in thinking that God would have had to wait for this ransom to be paid.

Luke narrates Jesus' death without any reference to this kind of need. In his gospel, one of the robbers crucified with Jesus explains to the other one why Jesus dies: "We die because we deserve to die, because we did evil, but this man dies because he is good!" He was right.

Jesus was willing to give his life to prove to us that the newness he brought is more than a possibility. It is the only answer to our problems caused by evil and sin. In his book, *The Spiritual Life of Children*, Robert Coles tells the story of another child, a nine-year-old girl, who explains it beautifully: "Jesus felt sorry for us. He knew we were in trouble, so he came here to save us.... He was 'too good for this world,' the nun says, and we should remember.... But he didn't mind dying. He was sad, but he knew he'd live forever, and 'because he died, so will we live forever,' the nun says. That's what our church says. It's what Jesus did for us."

Thursday of the Eighth Week

MARK 10:46-52

Called

"And at once his sight returned and he followed him along the road."

The last miracle Jesus works in the gospel of Mark is the one with Bartimaeus. The ideal miracle, it sums up all Mark wants to tell us about how Jesus relates to us and we to him. The story is simple. Bartimaeus is blind, sitting with cloak and stick on a street corner, begging. He hears that Jesus is coming, and he calls out, "Son of David, have pity on me!" Those persons anxious that they are losing Jesus' attention tell Bartimaeus to be silent, but he keeps calling. Jesus stops in the street and calls for the blind man. "Call him here!"

Mark stresses this last point by repeating twice more in the text that Jesus is calling him: "So they called the blind man. 'Courage,' they said; 'get up, he is calling you.'" Once healed, he starts following Jesus.

Bartimaeus' story is the story of the ideal follower of Jesus. It combines being healed by Jesus and following Jesus. This is the miracle that should happen to all of us. It is the meeting of two energies: the one in us that reaches out to God, world, and self; and the one coming from God through Jesus Christ reaching out to us.

Robert Coles's book on the spirituality of children contains this quote by Junior, a boy of twelve: "You know, I guess the Lord and us, we're all in this together. Us hoping to be saved, and him wanting to save us." That is what this miracle with Bartimaeus is all about.

Friday of the Eighth Week

MARK 11:11–26

For All People

"My house will be called a house of prayer for all people."

Jesus went that morning to the temple service. He had been there the evening before to survey things. As soon as he arrived he began driving out the tradesmen, upsetting the tables of the money changers and of the sellers of doves. We all know the scene.

But then there is a small sentence that escapes us sometimes. It reads: "Nor would he allow anyone to carry anything through the Temple." It meant that he practically stopped the temple service. People were carrying their offerings from the entrance over the temple square to the place where priests would receive their gifts. Stopping that continuous procession meant stopping the temple service!

To many in the temple this must have appeared as very disrupting, if not blasphemous, behavior. No wonder that the priests got so upset that they wanted to find out what was happening. They were informed that he had not only compared their temple to a "bandit's den," but also "a house of prayer for all peoples." That meant the end to any religious exclusivity.

They came together to discuss how to react to all this, and how to do away with him. He was too much for them.

Saturday of the Eighth Week

MARK 11:27-33

People's Authority

"They had the people to fear."

The issue is authority. The religious leaders came to ask Jesus, "Who gave you the authority to act as you do, to preach and even to upset our temple service?" They considered Jesus to be a layperson with no theological education, and no official approbation or mandate.

Church leaders today would have said that he had no "faculties." By speaking like that they were at the same time implying their own authority. It was the priestly caste and their education that gave them the authority to authorize others.

Jesus doesn't answer their question. He forced them to think about a third type of authority, an authority invested in the people of God. He said to them: "I will ask you a question, just one; answer me and I will tell you my authority for acting like this. John's baptism, what was its origin, heavenly or human? Answer me that."

They didn't. They couldn't. If they answered: "Heavenly," he would ask them, why didn't you believe in him? If they answered "Human," they had to fear the people, for "everyone held that John had been a real prophet."

So they gave no answer because they had to take into account—at least for that time—the authority of the people. And those people were right! John was a prophet. The people's authority was authenticated by the presence of God's Spirit in them. It still is!

Monday of the Ninth Week

MARK 12:1–12

Misappropriation

"They…sent him away empty-handed."

Immediately after the manifestation of God's presence in him at his baptism by John, Jesus was tempted in the way all of us are tempted once we discover our giftedness in the Spirit.

Those temptations are threefold, to use your charism, whatever it might be—as an economist, politician, scientist, teacher, lawyer, doctor, entrepreneur, industrial worker, worker in the service sector, artist, poet, musician, minister, theologian, entertainer, professional sports figure—to (1) make money, (2) get famous, or (3) exercise power.

The story today tells about tenants entrusted with a well-organized vineyard. When the time comes to account for the produce they made, they kill first the auditors and then even the owner's son, in the hope of acquiring the property for themselves.

The story is an allegory about those who give in to the first of the temptations the gospel mentioned, using your gift only for yourself. It is a tale about a misappropriation. The gifts given by God—hands and feet, heads and hearts, inborn talents and acquired skills—are not used to fulfill the intentions of the one who gave them, but only for one's own gain.

And the story ends by adding that Jesus, who did overcome that temptation, became the cornerstone to God's reign among us. The cornerstone to which we, God's actual tenants in this world, should be added.

Tuesday of the Ninth Week

MARK 12:13-17

Church and Flag

"Pay Caesar what belongs to Caesar, and God what belongs to God."

Some years ago Dan Grippo wrote an article on the custom of displaying a national flag in church (*U.S. Catholic*, March 1993). In his article he suggested that flag and church do not mix.

He wrote, "As a political symbol, the flag has no place among the religious symbols displayed in a church. It's fine to display the flag in the halls of government as a symbol of citizenship, but it is not necessary to put it up in the church to prove that Christians are good citizens. It would be better to demonstrate our civic virtue by following our Lord's instructions to feed the hungry, visit the sick, and shelter the homeless. Such works of mercy would make us model citizens in any country. If the church is to work for the justice and peace that characterize the reign of God, it must transcend national boundaries. Such artificial divisions must surely be irrelevant to the Creator of the one human family. If the church displays any flag, it should be that of the United Nations—or better yet an Earth flag."

In a survey done by the journal 47% of its subscribers agreed with the writer, but 41% said they liked seeing the national flag displayed in church; 12% had no opinion.

The scribes in Mark's reading today confront Jesus with a related kind of question: how do government and temple, Caesar and God, relate? Jesus answers by saying "Pay Caesar what belongs to Caesar—and what belongs to God to God." He indicates the principle; the rest we have to work out for ourselves in good conscience.

Wednesday of the Ninth Week

MARK 12:18–27

Living and Dead

"I am the God of Abraham, the God of Isaac, and the God of Jacob."

James Joyce wrote a story called "The Dead." In the story Gretta and her husband, Gabriel, return to their hotel after a New Year's party. They begin to undress. He approaches her. She hesitates. He asks her what she is thinking of. She answers that she is thinking of a song, "The Lass of Aughrim." She disengages herself, sits down on the bed, and begins to weep. She then tells him that she is thinking of Michael Furey, a boy who sang that song, a boy she loved and who died. He was sick when she was sent to a boarding school in Dublin. The evening before her departure she heard some gravel thrown against her window. She ran outside and found him there in the back of the garden, standing in the cold rain, deadly sick. "I implored him to go home at once and told him he would get his death in the rain. But he said he did not want to live.... He was standing at the end of the wall where there was a tree."

A week later she heard in the convent that he had died and was buried in Oughterard, where his people came from. The man who died for her sake remained a part of her life!

The dead and the living belong together, Paul wrote. Jesus had said it before, when he explained that we all belong together as the leaves and branches of the one tree of which he is the trunk.

In the end of Joyce's story it is snowing, "snow falling faintly through the universe and faintly falling, like the descent of their last end, upon all the living and the dead."

Thursday of the Ninth Week

MARK 12:28-34

Interdependency

"You must love your neighbor as yourself."

He was a very old African warrior, a Maasai. In his youth he had killed a lion with his bare hands to show his bravery in order to be accepted as an adult. He had also defended his family and homestead in fierce and bloody battles against others whom he considered hardly human.

Then an American missionary, Father Vincent Donovan, came into his village. All he ever did was tell the stories of the gospel. Everyone loves stories, the missionary reasoned, and his listeners were quite capable of drawing their own conclusions. He was right.

When he told the story of the Good Samaritan one evening, the Maasai elder spoke up. "If I understand you well, you want to tell us that God made the other people, too?" While he said this, he pointed to some faraway hills, behind which those "others" were living. "It is you who say so," the missionary answered. "If they are God's people, we respect them," the warrior said, "Loving God means loving God's offspring."

Didn't Paul write that we should love each other because we are all members of the same body, members of the same divine family? Doesn't the introduction to the gospel of John say that we are all created in the Son, God's offspring?

That we belong together is no longer only a spiritual feeling, but almost a physical reality. "When I call England, when I get my fax messages from Japan, I really feel part of the world in a way that I certainly didn't ten or twenty years ago," a student in the United States noted recently in *The Washington Post*.

Our interdependence is becoming global. We know about the most distant places; we suffer with everyone who suffers. We are becoming more and more the one people of the world. No wonder Jesus stressed that we should love our neighbor as ourselves.

Friday of the Ninth Week

MARK 12:35–37

Delight

"The great crowd listened to him with delight."

Why would they have listened to Jesus with delight? To find that out we might check our own experience. Do you remember a time that someone came up to you and told you: "You are great!" and, because you felt that the speaker really meant it, you heard it with delight?

Do you remember a time when you told someone the same thing, and suddenly their face lit up with sheer delight?

Did you ever witness one of those meetings in which speakers ask audiences to repeat after them: "I am someone, I am great, I am unique!"?

Have you ever seen crowds of people who were freed from one or another tyranny, a dictatorship or a foreign occupation, and how they danced in the streets because they suddenly did count again as human beings?

The crowds came to Jesus because of his liberating message. They considered him to be great because he made them feel their greatness. He didn't talk down to them. He didn't rub their noses in their sinfulness and speak about God's annoyance. He explained that God loved them unconditionally. He laughed with them at those who thought differently, and they loved it. It taught them how to relate to one another.

Saturday of the Ninth Week

MARK 12:38-44

Widow's Mite

"...but she in her poverty has put in everything she pos-
sesses, all she had to live on."

Jon Sobrino is a Central American theologian. Several years ago he wrote *The Hidden Motives of Pastoral Action*. In that book he explains that gospel stories are often not correctly interpreted and preached. In other words, the preachers manipulate the stories in view of other interests, very often their own.

One of the stories that is often used in a way that contradicts its original meaning is the one about the poor widow who offers all she has. She is so often referred to as the example of what we should do. She gave everything she had, and Jesus praised her for it.

True, Jesus praised her for her generosity, but he also did something else. Just before the incident about the widow is told, he is preaching against people who devour the property of widows. That done, he sits down in the temple opposite the offering box. He is studying—that is the meaning of the Greek word used—what is happening. That is how he comes to notice the widow with two of the smallest coins available. He sees her putting the two coins in the box. He calls his disciples together, praises her, and adds: "She put in all she had to live on. All the others contributed from their wealth." Her two pennies were worth more than all the other donations.

He praises her, that is true, but it sounds at the same time like a very bitter complaint. A complaint against a temple and a priesthood that doesn't protect a poor widow against something like this. How can they tolerate a poor widow giving all she has to live on?

In the gospel of Mark Jesus never goes to the temple again!

Monday of the Tenth Week

MATTHEW 5 : 1 — 1 2

Beatitudes

"How blessed are the poor in spirit...."

The eight beatitudes in the gospel of Matthew begin with "Blessed are the poor in spirit for theirs is the reign of heaven," and they end with "Blessed are those who are persecuted because of righteousness, for theirs is the reign of heaven." Those two beatitudes differ from the other six. The first and the last one promise the reign of heaven in the present. The six others promise things in the future:

"Blessed are those who mourn, for they will be comforted. Blessed are the meek, for they will inherit the earth. Blessed are those who hunger and thirst for righteousness, for they will be filled. Blessed are the merciful, for they will be shown mercy. Blessed are the pure in heart, for they will see God. Blessed are the peacemakers, for they will be called sons and daughters of God."

The poor in spirit belong to the reign of heaven now, and so do the ones who are persecuted because of righteousness. Why should that be?

The poor in spirit are those who know that, notwithstanding all our achievements, successes, and advances, the reign of God is not yet realized in this world. They sense that, though we might be quite happy about the way we have organized our society, there are too many left out who suffer, who starve, and who are abused. The poor in spirit are the ones who are intent on changing things as they are, in view of a greater justice for all. That is why they are the ones so often persecuted, vilified, ridiculed, and sometimes murdered because of their thirst for righteousness. The poor in spirit belong to the reign of God because they are living in this tension. They want to change the world so that the six other beatitudes may be fulfilled, so this world will be freed from weeping, arrogance, homelessness, injustice, darkness, and war.

Tuesday of the Tenth Week

MATTHEW 5:13-16

Light for the World

"You are the light for the world...your light must shine in people's sight."

Jesus tells us: "You are the light for the world." It sounds pretentious when we say it of ourselves. According to many contemporaries, it even sounds pretentious when it comes from Jesus' lips, calling himself the light of the world. They forget that he called *them* the light of the world, too.

That doesn't seem to be the only misunderstanding involved when using that analogy of light to describe his and our role. Light is enormous, light is a great help. Without light we would be in the dark. Yet, we shouldn't exaggerate. Light does much, but it doesn't bring anything. When I switch on the light in a dark room full of people and furniture, that light doesn't cause or create those people and those tables and chairs. Light only shows what is there already.

In a similar way, Jesus is a light in our world. It is in the light of his life that we see who we are and what we are capable of being. This is a role others play, too. It is what a lover, a friend, or an artist does. They reveal in us physical, psychological, and spiritual dimensions we would never have known if they hadn't helped to light them up inside us.

None of them, however, does it the way Jesus did. Nobody showed better what human love is capable of. Nobody showed better how to relate to the source of our being, or to each other. It is in his light that we discover our own depth, width, length, and worth. Who would we be without him?

Wednesday of the Tenth Week

MATTHEW 5:17–19

Law's Purpose

"...not one dot, not one little stroke, is to disappear from the law until all its purpose is achieved."

Jesus speaks about a purpose to the law. Popes Paul VI and John Paul II spoke about that purpose as well. They wrote in their encyclicals and said in their talks that God's laws followed by Jesus' beatitudes have as their purpose the establishment of "a civilization of love."

"Civilization of love" is a term that you don't find as such in Holy Scripture. Jesus uses another term. He speaks about the realization of the reign of God among us. He asked us to pray for it when he gave us his prayer of the "Our Father." He asked us to work at it when he gave us a share in his mission in this world. He asked us to celebrate it sacramentally in the Eucharist.

You could go one step further in analyzing the purpose of the law and beatitudes. The final outcome of the establishment of the reign of God among us is described as that time that "God will be all in all" (1 Cor 15:28).

So the purpose of the law has to do with God's presence in us! It has to do with the urge in you to be living in the presence of God—an urge you show by your readiness to read or to listen to this reflection. Even that term "God's presence in us" has to be well understood. It is not a presence of a mere in-dwelling. It is a being taken up in God's life-self, in God's trinitarian life. The old mystics described that life of the Trinity as a dance. The purpose of God's law and Jesus' beatitudes is to teach us how to get into step with that dance, with that life! They are the music to which our lives should be set.

Thursday of the Tenth Week

MATTHEW 5:20–26

Nothing to Eat

"Your brother has something against you...."

When I visited the religious community of a friend of mine, I was surprised by their behavior. They all were very kind and hospitable to me, but I noticed that some of them didn't talk to each other. I was the center of the conversation in a strange way.

It happened every time I ate with them. I mentioned it to my friend. He told me that some of his community members never ever talked to each other. Something had happened in the past that had made them decide to boycott each other forever. He added that he was sure that sometimes they didn't even remember what had caused the breach.

Sometimes we reason that it is better not to relate to someone anymore, sometimes for quite serious reasons. We keep a safe distance.

Jesus once said that anything done to anyone was done to him. On the cross he was hanging next to a murderer. So, according to Jesus' saying, Jesus himself was the victim of that murderer. Did Jesus turn his face away? Oh no! He told the man, "Today you will be with me in paradise."

God gives everyone the chance to "convert." We are asked to follow God's example. Trying to fight the difficulties that unavoidably arise between us with "a safe distance" and a deadening "silence" is no help. It hardens our hearts.

Friday of the Tenth Week

MATTHEW 5:27-32

Re-speaking Gender

"But I say this to you...."

In the Sermon on the Mount, of which this reading is part, Jesus sets the new standards of God's reign among us. The Sermon on the Mount could be read as its constitution. In the reading today we hear about the new place of women. The text speaks about adultery, fornication, divorce, and lust, but the background of it all is to redefine the place of women in a patriarchal world in which women played a secondary role.

In Matthew's gospel women seem to play a rather insignificant background role, but a closer study shows that Matthew is at the same time portraying the movement of women away from being victims and mere objects in a male dominated world.

Jesus came to reorder the entire world, including the households and the relationship of men and women, back to the original world intended by God in which male and female are equals.

They weren't equals in the world in which Jesus lived. A man could divorce his wife for any reason whatsoever—in one interpretation of the time even when her husband was attracted by another woman. A wife couldn't divorce her husband at all. If she did bring a valid charge against him in court, the court could only decide to force him to divorce her.

Revoking the right of a man to marry more than one woman, Jesus delivered one more blow against the patriarchal structures around him, structures due to their male "hardness of heart" (Mt 19:8).

Jesus raised the status of women, forbidding men to use their power to abuse them. He envisioned a new type of family relationship in which all would be treated in the same way. He began a movement, the end of which we have not yet seen in a world—unfortunately—still dominated by the old in so many ways.

Saturday of the Tenth Week

MATTHEW 5:33-37

Politically Correct

"All you need say is 'Yes' if you mean yes, 'No,' if you mean no."

Jesus tells us that in the new world to be born, the world of God's peace and justice, there is going to be no need anymore for oath taking—neither to God, nor to heaven, nor to earth, God's footstool. Some Christians already stick to this to the letter. The Quakers will not take an oath. They might add the word "verily" to their "yes," but that is as far as they are willing to go.

Other Christians, who do allow themselves to take oaths, justify their behavior by reasoning that the world is still far from perfect, far from the reign of God. We are only on our way. The new is only being born among us. The fact that oaths are still necessary is a proof of the evil that is not yet overcome in this world—something Jesus implied when he said that the need we feel to add to our "Yes" and "No" comes "from the Evil One."

What we can start doing is to avoid all unnecessary oaths, not only the real ones, but also the "minced" ones. "Oh golly," "By golly," or "Gosh," are, according to the dictionary, all substitutes for "God."

Another commonly used interjection is "Gee." The same dictionary defines it as "A form of Jesus, used in minced oaths." We might even have to rethink the use of expressions like "Good heavens" and "Good gracious"!

Does this seem exaggerated? Maybe it is. Jesus simplified the issue by just saying let your "Yes" be "Yes" and your "No" be "No"!

Monday of the Eleventh Week

MATTHEW 5:38-42

Equanimity

"Offer no resistance to the wicked."

She had been invited by her friend. She was happy to be invited, for it had been years since they had seen each other. It was only when her friend welcomed and hugged her at the airport that she suddenly thought, "I should have brought her something!" When they arrived at the friend's home, she told her so: "I should have brought you something." Her friend looked up and said: "You brought yourself. You are the present I was hoping for."

The way you are is the best offering you would be able to give to anyone in your life. By living a life of love, tolerance, and patience you are a wonderful sign of the love, tolerance, and patience of your Creator in heaven.

You would be a gift not only to the people and the world around you, but also to God's self. The practice of your life would sing God's praise much more than only your prayer.

Not only others would delight in you. To live like that will assure you, yourself, God's blessing, a tranquil and balanced life, happiness, and greater health. It will steep you gently deeper and deeper in the life of God's presence in you.

It will help you to accept any hardship you might face on your spiritual path, even loving and taking in your stride the wicked one who resists you.

Tuesday of the Eleventh Week

MATTHEW 5:43–48

Pacifism

"...love your enemies and pray for those who persecute you...."

The discussion on pacifism has been endless even in circles devoted to Jesus. Would Jesus have used violence if he had been in situations where many of us would have no hesitation to do so? This is a difficult question. It arises not only in the context of international or civil conflicts, but at any level where we harbor violent, defensive, or vengeful feelings against others in our own family, business, or other affairs.

Evangelii Nuntiandi ("The Gospels to Be Announced") states: "The church cannot accept violence—especially the force of arms which is uncontrollable once it is let loose—and indiscriminate death as the path of liberation, because she knows that violence always provokes violence and irresistibly engenders new forms of oppression and enslavement" (#37).

You can respond to evil with evil, and before you know it you are taken up in a cycle of ever-increasing violence. You see it around you: one child hits another, the other hits back, and so on until they both end up frustrated and crying.

Jesus presents us with the only way out of the issue. Respond to evil with love. Love your enemies, and pray for those who persecute you. A hard lesson and a difficult one, but it is the only way to break through the circle and cycle of violence. It is a lesson opposed to the way we usually arm ourselves against the other, verbally and physically, internationally and nationally, and personally.

Peace can only be made by peace.

Wednesday of the Eleventh Week

MATTHEW 6 : 1 - 6 , 16 - 18

Delegate

"Come after me...."

Many people don't delegate their power until they have to. There are many reasons to explain this difficulty. The main reasons are that we like to remain in power, that we do not like to be dependent on others, and that we don't trust the people around us. Many a saying confirms this attitude. For example, "You can only be sure something is done when you do it yourself!"

Jesus didn't have that difficulty at all. As soon as he begins the evangelization, or the "Good-News-ing" of his world he calls in others. He surrounds himself to have company. He doesn't want to be a "lone ranger." And he asks them to join his mission: "Come after me, and I will make you fishers of people." It is his way of demonstrating his trust in the ability of others, and to stimulate their commitment to him and his task. It also means that he made them share in his responsibility and authority.

He didn't only show that trust in the twelve he chose, or the seventy-two he would send out at a later occasion. Before he left this world he addressed all those who joined him. He addressed all of us. We all share in his responsibility and authority. It is one of the ways he wants us to be with him. It is one of the ways he wants us to be "on his wavelength."

Thursday of the Eleventh Week

MATTHEW 6 : 7 – 15

Babbling

"In your prayers do not babble as the Gentiles do."

If you believe all they say about this world on radio and television, you can become very upset. Everything seems to be going wrong and falling apart. Talk shows speak endlessly about what goes wrong and what to do about it. Convention centers fill up every day of the week with people coming together with their laptop computers, their papers and books, studies and research results. We ourselves can attend meetings, write and read papers, and talk until our mouths get dry, but what can we do?

On a smaller scale, in the family or at work, we often face that same need to come together, to talk things over again and again, until everyone is bored and some almost sick.

Jesus said: "Don't just talk, thinking that many words will help you out. They won't. Pray like this: your reign come!"

In a way, Jesus couldn't do very much about the world, either. Some people around him were healed and fed, but so many more remained sick and hungry. Yet God's reign broke through among us in him, because he practiced it in his everyday outreach to others, and in his prayer to God in heaven. He was capable of doing what he did because he always had that prayer on his lips. Praying for God's reign is not a question of words, or, as Jesus would say, of "babbling"; it is a question of being and doing.

If you pray "your reign come" with a sincere or open heart, you will begin to answer that prayer by your behavior. With the help of God, you will hear your own prayer and act in God's name and on behalf of God's reign. If you pray it with that same open heart together in a community or family, the same will happen to them. The reign of God is not simply a promise of the future that God will overcome sin and evil; it is a reign that has already begun.

Friday of the Eleventh Week

MATTHEW 6:19–23

Discovering Light

"If then, the light inside you is darkened, what darkness that will be."

Jesus tells us that we should be aware of the light inside ourselves. We should not only be aware of that for ourselves, but we should help each other, and especially children and adolescents, to be aware of it. They might be able to find light outside of themselves in their books and on the Internet. Without the discovery of the light within themselves, however, they, and we ourselves, remain in the dark.

A student in Holy Scripture complained to the rabbi of Rizhyn: "During the hours when I devote myself to my studies I feel life and light, but the moment I stop studying it is all gone. What shall I do?"

The rabbi of Rizhyn replied: "This is just as when someone walks through the woods on a dark night and for a time another joins him, lantern in hand, but at the crossroads they part and the first one must grope along alone. But if people carry their own light with them they need not be afraid of any darkness."

Practice the discovery of your own light with your friends and with your offspring. Help them to discern the Spirit that is guiding all of us if we are aware of her presence.

Saturday of the Eleventh Week

MATTHEW 6:24–34

Ownership

"You cannot be the slave both of God and of money."

"You cannot serve both God and money," Jesus says, leaving us with quite a problem. How then should we have money and possessions?

The same way Jesus did. We should own them at the service of everyone. That is what his "poverty" is about. It doesn't mean that he didn't need his food and drink, his rest and sleep, his clothing and sandals, his partygoing and picnics, but in the final instance these were in the service of all.

He never owned anything the way the rich man in Luke's gospel did (Luke 12:6–22). When God gives that landowner the bountiful gift of a rich harvest, he builds barns to store that harvest all for himself, saying, "You have plenty of good things laid by, enough for many years to come: take life easy; eat, drink, and enjoy yourself."

This is not only true of money or ownership. It is true also of our friendships, information, skills, talents, technical know-how, spiritual power, charisms, and gifts.

Jesus suggests that we should be like nature around us, the plants and the flowers. We should be as that beautiful flower, gifted with color and fragrance. It gives all it has to the world around, enriching our lives, pleasing our senses. We should be and live like a flower in the sun, like the sun itself!

Any property we own is God's gift, just like we ourselves are God's present. Nothing is really ours alone. Pope John Paul II says it very simply in his encyclical *On Social Concern*: "The goods of the world are meant for all."

Of course, the right to private property is valid. We obviously need to own things. But, writes the pope, this private property is under a social mortgage. It has to be referred to the "whole" of the human and creational "body."

Monday of the Twelfth Week

MATTHEW 7:1-5

Splinters and Logs

"Why do you observe the splinter in your brother's eye and never the log in your own?"

I once read a very simple story that brought home to me the issue about that splinter and log. The story was about a California woman who became extremely irritated by the hacking cough of her pet parrot. When this distressing symptom persisted, she took the bird to a veterinarian who checked the bird and found it to be in perfect health.

Then, listening to the woman who brought the bird, the veterinarian discovered that instead of having some exotic disease, the parrot had merely learned to imitate the raspy "barking" of its cigarette-smoking owner.

When the lady was informed of this, she was greatly surprised; but the insight she gained into her own problem caused her to go home and kick the habit.

So often we are highly critical of others without realizing that what we dislike in them is really a reflection of our own sins. We hate in others what we have discovered and dislike in ourselves. Jesus says the same thing in another way when he calls us hypocrites.

He advises us to apply the standard we use to judge others to ourselves, before others—and he himself—begin doing that.

Tuesday of the Twelfth Week

MATTHEW 7: 6, 12-14

The Golden Rule

"Treat others as you would like them to treat you."

We don't know where the golden rule, "Treat others as you would like them to treat you," originates. We do know that in all major religions this rule is expressed in practically the same words. In a way, Jesus mentioned that commonness when he said that it is the meaning of all laws and prophets.

All kinds of believers and unbelievers hold to it. That is why we know how it originated. It comes from the divine breath blown into all of us from our very beginning. It is a rule that betrays our origin, our Maker.

Our common belief in this rule is the reason we are surrounded by so much goodness. People stick to the golden rule in their lives. Have you never been struck by the human kindness that surrounds you? And this is, in a sense, even more true in our contemporary urban setting than before. Almost every aspect of our lives—health, education, power, food, and shelter—is dependent on others. A one-day strike by whatever group would grind any city to a halt.

This might sound overly cheerful. That doesn't mean, however, that it isn't true. All of us are so convinced that we should live according to the golden rule that sinning against it upsets all of us. That is why the media and we ourselves seem to be almost obsessed about injustice and crime. Those offenses are against the rule. It means that the rule remains the golden rule. And that is what Jesus meant, affirming in that way something we all know in the deepest part of us, there where our hearts are in touch with the one who created us.

Wednesday of the Twelfth Week

MATTHEW 7:15-20

Prophecy and Profits

"Beware of false prophets."

When you surf through your television channels or scan through the wavelengths of your radio, you are unavoidably confronted with people who call themselves prophets.

How do you distinguish the false ones from the true ones? The oldest known Christian manual, entitled *Didachè*, written about A.D. 100, gives this rule of thumb: "If they ask for money for themselves they are false prophets." Using this norm to discern the real prophets in the media instantly disqualifies most of them. Prophets and profit do not go together.

In his book *Prophets*, Rabbi Abraham Joshua Heschel notes that real prophecy is born from the pathos or grief of God. Heschel writes that many of us read the Bible for a sense of order, but when you read the prophetic part of it you get "Orations about widows and orphans, about corrupt judges and affairs of the market place. Instead of showing us a way through the elegant mansions of the mind, the prophets take us to the slums. The world is a proud place full of beauty, but the prophets are scandalized, and rave as if the whole world were a slum."

He then concludes by saying: "The things that horrify the prophets are even now daily occurrences all over the world." The real prophets among us are those who are sharing God's grief about the world in our days. They help us to listen to the cries of the poor, the neglected, the addicted, the abandoned, the hungry, and the thirsty. Real prophets are never out for personal benefits.

Thursday of the Twelfth Week

MATTHEW 7:21-29

Priorities

"...the one who does the will of my Father...."

In the final instance, all the exhortations in the Sermon on the Mount come down to one thing: doing the will of the Father. That is the foundation of it all.

What is your priority—doing the will of the Father, or something else? If our priority is doing the will of the Father, then another question arises: can we do that will of the Father on our own? Doesn't it ask for company?

Once he started his public life, one of the first things Jesus did was to look around for company. We need that company too.

It would be wonderful if we could find that company in our family or in our community. We might have to find it elsewhere, but wherever we find it, we need others to look again and again for God's will in the light and deeds of Jesus Christ. We need others not only to find that will, but also to realize it in our days and in the world in which we live.

It is the house we have to build together on the rock of God's will—a house that cannot be "mine," but a house that must be "ours."

Friday of the Twelfth Week

MATTHEW 8:1–4

Thy Will

"If you are willing you can cleanse me."

The man with a virulent skin disease who approached Jesus, bowed low in front of him, and said, "Lord, if you are willing, you can cleanse me," should not be misunderstood. The way he formulated his prayer didn't mean that he doubted Jesus' goodness or healing power. It meant that he recognized his need to be taken up in a world that was greater than his own personal world.

His prayer resembled the prayer of the good murderer in Luke's gospel who asked the dying Jesus to be remembered in his reign. Jesus told him in his last words: "Today you will be with me in paradise!" (Luke 23:42–43).

The man's "If it be your will" prayer was a decisive and daring approach to Jesus, asking straightforwardly for the healing he obtained. He was not exactly a non-assertive person; on the contrary! In his confidence the man took some risks. He wasn't supposed to accost anyone at all, and Jesus wasn't allowed to touch him according to the law.

When he qualified his request for healing by adding, "If it be your will," he meant to say, "I understand that you know better than I how I fit in your world."

It is the way we should pray, full of confidence that what will happen to us is going to be for the best, because God loves us and we are God's children. God's delight in us eliminates any need to worry.

Saturday of the Twelfth Week

MATTHEW 8:5-17

Reaching Out to Jesus

"And to the centurion Jesus said, 'Go back, then; let this be done for you, as your faith demands.'"

It was a hot evening at a college in Kenya. The Theological Association was meeting at Alliance High School, and they had invited other colleges from the area. There were over 600 students in the hall. They were obviously interested in the topic: "Healing and Miracles in Our Time." They also had a hidden agenda. The real question they wanted to explore was, "Why did miracles and healing take place in the early days of the church, but not in today's Christian communities?" A good question!

Do you remember the story of the Roman officer who comes to ask Jesus to heal his servant who is sick at home? Jesus is touched by the loving care of the officer and decides to go with him to his house. The officer says that this is not necessary: "Just give the word and my servant will be cured." Jesus, amazed by the man's faith, gives the word, and when the officer returns home and checks the time of the healing, he realizes that his servant was healed at the moment Jesus spoke.

The Roman officer doesn't do the healing. He asks Jesus to do that. Yet, if he hadn't asked Jesus, and if he hadn't believed in Jesus, his servant wouldn't have been healed. So in a way we might conclude that the officer, too, healed his servant.

How did he do it? By reaching out to Jesus. The lack of healing and miracles in our communities and in our lives is due to a lack of reaching out to Jesus! When you reach out, when you get on his wavelength, when you have faith, all becomes possible!

Monday of the Thirteenth Week

MATTHEW 18:18-22

Without Delay

"Lord, let me go and bury my father first."

All of us know them, those missed moments of grace. Again and again we hear the story of those moments, of people who knew that they should change something in their lives, but didn't follow up immediately, and nothing happened afterwards. They should have followed the impulse to change their life, but they procrastinated. The moment didn't come back.

We knew that we should have said a word of sympathy, of warning, but the word was never spoken. The moment passed. It is the tragedy of the unseized moment.

It might have been the story of the disciple who came to Jesus to tell him, "Let me first bury my father, and then I will follow you." We don't know exactly what he meant. Was it that his father had actually died and that he asked to go to his burial first? That would not have been too much of a delay. That is why some commentators think that his father was still alive, and that he meant to say, "I am coming to follow you once I have fulfilled all my family affairs after my father's death." And that could have taken quite some years.

We don't know what happened to him, whether he followed Jesus or not. We do know, however, what Jesus told him: "It is now or never, make up your mind. Don't let this moment of grace pass you by."

Tuesday of the Thirteenth Week

MATTHEW 8:23-27

Calming the Storm

"He stood up…and there was great calm."

"When the fearful breakers roar, then, while leaning on Thy breast, May I hear Thee say to me, 'Fear not—I will pilot thee!'" This prayer express a reaction to what happened in that boat our text speaks about. It isn't the only possible response, and maybe not even the one Jesus himself would prefer to hear.

It is nice to see ourselves in his company while he is calming the storm for us. But would that be all he expected from us when he said: "Follow me"? Modeling ourselves on him, shouldn't we be the ones who calm the storms that rage in the world around us?

While apartheid was creating havoc in his country, South Africa, Father Albert Nolan wrote: "To believe in [Jesus] is to believe there is a power that can resist the system and prevent it from destroying us. There is a motive that can replace, and can be stronger than the profit motive. There is an incentive that can mobilize the world, enable the 'haves' to lower their standard of living and make us only too willing to redistribute the world's wealth and population…. It has generally been called faith, hope and love; whatever you choose to call it, you must understand it as the unleashing of the divine but thoroughly 'natural' power of truth, goodness and beauty."

Father Nolan didn't only rest on the breast of Jesus when that storm raged in his country, but he stood up, and was a pilot like Jesus was, commanding the wind and the water.

Wednesday of the Thirteenth Week

MATTHEW 8:28–34

Possessed

"Two demoniacs came up to him."

While writing this reflection, and wondering what to write about it, I came upon a book with a small piece of paper sticking out of it. At first I thought it was just a piece of paper used as a bookmark, but then I saw that it contained a text. And as happens so often, it was just the insight I needed to continue.

The quote began: "How easy it is to hate oneself. True grace is to forget." Hating yourself is like being possessed by some evil. It might be something you did, or didn't do in the past. It might be that you accuse yourself of the way you are disposed or oriented. It might be that you interiorized what others have been saying about you. It might be that you allowed yourself to be defined by them.

True grace is to forget. There was a third sentence on that small piece of paper. It gave the reason why it is so difficult to forget. "Yet if pride could die in us, the supreme grace would be to love oneself in all simplicity—as one would love any of those who themselves have suffered and loved in Christ."

When those two possessed men came out of their tombs (!), Jesus just said to the evil spirits in them, "Go!" They did. The old was gone and forgotten; the two were healed!

To forgive others is easy in comparison with the difficulty of forgiving ourselves. In the presence of Jesus' love it can be done. Thanks be to God.

Thursday of the Thirteenth Week

MATTHEW 9:1–8

Human Beings

"They praised God for having given such authority to human beings."

The crowd saw Jesus heal the lame man, and thus prove that he was able to forgive sins. Matthew notes how a feeling of awe came over the crowd and how they began to praise God for having given such an authority to "human beings."

Jesus linked his ability to heal body and soul (through the forgiveness of sins) to his authority (in Greek, *exousia*). He told them: "But to prove to you that the Son of man has authority on earth to forgive sins—then he said to the paralytic—'Get up, pick up your bed and go off home.' The man got up and went home."

According to Matthew, however, the crowd didn't understand this authority as being limited to Jesus alone: "They praised God for having given such authority to human beings." In the light of Jesus' action they understood their own "authority" and power.

We find this same "sharing" expressed in Matthew's gospel just before Jesus leaves his disciples at the ascension. Jesus then says: "All authority (*exousia*) is given to me, and therefore you go…" (Mt 28:18). We, who understand and accept ourselves in the light of Jesus' presence among us, share in Jesus' power and authority.

As one commentator explains: "He [Matthew] sees the function of the earthly life of Jesus as bestowing the transcendent authority of Jesus Immanuel [God-with-us] to the believing community" (J. Reese, *Biblical Theology Bulletin*, 7, 1977).

Sharing this "power," we should use it in our lives. We should forgive and be willing to be forgiven! Forgiving and accepting forgiveness is the only way to make up for the past.

Friday of the Thirteenth Week

MATTHEW 9:9-13

Sitting at Table

"Now while he was at table in the house...."

A Latin American theologian once wrote: "Anyone who needs more than half an hour to explain what the Good News is about, is disfiguring it." And a primary schoolteacher told me once before I entered a classroom for a religious instruction: "Keep it simple, because that's what it's about."

They are right. Just look at Jesus as he is described in today's reading. He is sitting at table with his friends. If there was a door, it was definitely open. All kinds of people are walking in and out, tax collectors and sinners.

The Son of God is sitting in the midst of them, and in the midst of us, with their—and our—worries, sicknesses, human relations, jobs, unemployment, beds, breakfasts, affairs, businesses, sports, children, grannies, all saints and sinners.

The drinks go round, the bread is broken, the sun is shining, the birds twittering, children are running around, mothers shouting, and a cat is rolling on its back in the shade. It is all so simple, it is all so human, it is all so rich.

Some of the local Reverends were saying, "this cannot be done! It is a shame. How can someone like Jesus allow something like this?" He knows what they think, he hears what they say, and leaning back on his seat he says: "Mercy is what pleases me, not sacrifice!"

Saturday of the Thirteenth Week

MATTHEW 9:14–17

Enjoy!

"Surely, the bridegroom attendants cannot mourn...."

John's disciples spoke about fasting. Jesus spoke about feasting, comparing himself to a bridegroom. In one story about him he plays the role of a bridegroom. It was at the wedding feast at Cana, when a bridegroom couldn't live up to his task of providing wine for his guests. Jesus, mercifully, took over the poor groom's responsibility and produced wine such as they had never drunk before.

He compares himself to a bridegroom who is calling for celebration. We should listen and celebrate. We in the West have wormed our way through so much soul-searching, and often mind-boggling theological interpretations and re-interpretations, that we forget that the best way to honor God is to celebrate the life we've got.

It was at the beginning of the summer holiday season. The pastor suggested in his homily that Christians should enjoy those days. He got some anonymous letters to reprimand him for his lack of earnestness. The letter writers thought him to be frivolous. The pastor told me the story with great joy. He added that it was one of the rare times in his life that he was reproached as Jesus had been before him.

We all know from our own experience how nice it is when a gift we give is enjoyed by the receiver. The more they use it, the more they enjoy it, the greater our own delight. And as we are made in God's image, so it must be with God!

So let's enjoy our life, our body, our spirit. Let's work and be serious in the services we render, in the justice we help to establish. But let's not forget to celebrate, dancing and singing, eating and drinking, loving and making merry. The bridegroom is with us! Enjoy!

Monday of the Fourteenth Week

MATTHEW 9:18-26

Courage, My Daughter!

"Jesus turned around, saw her, and he said to her: 'Courage!'"

It is sometimes obvious in life that you don't count as a person. For example, you are buying something and the salesperson who is supposed to be helping you keeps talking to someone else and doesn't even look at you. Some people reason that this kind of anonymous behavior is the price we pay for the kind of world we live in. A remark like that isn't much of a help; in fact it makes things even worse!

In today's reading a woman in the crowd around Jesus touches the fringe of his cloak. She isn't supposed to do that. She wasn't even allowed to be in a crowd, because, according to the Law, her sickness made her impure. According to that Law everything she touched became unclean as well. But she took the risk, thinking "even if I only touch his cloak I shall be saved."

At the moment of that touch everything else around Jesus seems to fall away. It doesn't count anymore. What counts is that woman and no one else. Jesus turns around, looks at her, and says to her, "Courage, my daughter, your faith has saved you!"

She was for that instant the only one who counted for him. He gave his whole self to her. In a moment of great mystical insight W.B. Yeats once wrote: "The love of God is infinite for every human soul, because every human soul is unique; no other can satisfy the same need in God."

It is that unique love of God for each of us that should make us halt in the crowd we live in and look at one another and at ourselves with greater care.

Tuesday of the Fourteenth Week

MATTHEW 9:32–38

Unclean Spirits

"The harvest is rich, but the laborers are few."

On the street I saw a small girl, cold and shivering in a thin dress, with little hope of a decent meal. You must have met her now and then, too. I became angry and said to God; "Why do you permit this? Why don't you do something about it?" For a while God said nothing, but that night God replied, quite suddenly: "I certainly did do something about it. I made *you!* Now why don't *you* do something about it?"

We often don't accept our own authoritative power over misery, sickness, and evil. Matthew says explicitly that Jesus summoned his followers and gave them authority over unclean spirits with power to drive them out (Mt 10:1).

We could do all kinds of things, but we don't. It isn't unwillingness on our part. It is often not even our lack of imagination that hinders us. What hinders us most often is the poor idea we have of our own influence, of our own weight and authority. Yet, we are charged with God's Spirit, and with the mission Jesus left us to bring God's reign to life among us.

As Pope John Paul II has said, "At stake is the dignity of the human person, whose defense and promotion have been entrusted to us by the Creator, and to whom the men and women at every moment of history are strictly and responsibly in debt.... Every individual is called upon to play his or her part in this peaceful campaign" (*On Social Concern*, #47).

We are put in this world as participants and executors in God's creative and salvific project. We have to execute this project in the place and situation where we are engaged as parents, educators, doctors, postal workers, priests, or retired senior citizens. And next to that we should also take into account that there is always a great demand for volunteer workers chasing the evil from our world.

Wednesday of the Fourteenth Week

MATTHEW 10:1–7

The Repair of the World

"Jesus summoned his twelve disciples."

Jesus summoned his disciples, made them share in his authority, and told them to go out to clean and repair the world. They became his partners in the universal restoration work he himself had come to do (Acts 3:21). Their honeymoon was over, the work had begun.

Many people feel this vocation to do something about the world. It lies at the root of innumerable religious congregations and societies, but it also explains contemporary associations like Catholic Relief Services, Bread for the World, Amnesty International, and Greenpeace, to mention only a few.

The repair of the world is an old theme with roots that lead down to the Creation story itself. Jewish wisdom calls it *tikkun olam*, the restoration of the world.

Jesus, who came to fulfill this mission, rallied his first partners to start that work. They had to chase the evil spirits away, to cure all sickness, and to announce the actualization of God's reign.

He added that they should start at home. The temptation is always to blame the evil in the world on others, scapegoating them. Later, just before Jesus leaves them at the end of Matthew's gospel, they will be sent by him to all the nations of the world commissioning us too, to contribute our share in his repair of the world.

Thursday of the Fourteenth Week

MATTHEW 10:7–15

Hospitality

"Provide yourselves with no gold or silver, not even with coppers for your purses."

The way Jesus sent his disciples out—with not a cent in their pockets, no food, and no spare clothing—made them totally dependent on the hospitality of others. The first thing they had to do after arriving in a village was, as he suggested, to look for a house where they could stay, "to seek out someone worthy."

The seminarians of the All India Seminary in Goa, India, are sent out as evangelizers in that way for their pastoral practice. They are sent in pairs to villages that often have never heard of the Good News before. Their travel is taken care of, but for the rest they, too, depend on the hospitality of the places where they are. When I asked some of them whether they were welcomed when they come like that, they told me that they hardly ever had any difficulty finding a place. They explained to the villagers that they had come to pray with them and to speak about God, and the doors, most times those of the poor, always opened.

"God is never absent from any place in the world. Hospitality to us is the first sign of God's presence," one of them added.

When Jesus sent them out the way he did, he wasn't only sure that God's Spirit would be with the twelve he commissioned. He also was sure that the same Spirit would take care that they would be received. He foresaw that some would refuse to receive them, but they always would be able to find someone who would. He, too, reckoned that God would never be completely absent from any place, and that hospitality would be the first sign of God's presence. It is!

Friday of the Fourteenth Week

MATTHEW 10:16-23

Persecution

"You will be universally hated on account of my name."

Jesus didn't only assure his disciples that they always would find the hospitality they needed to begin their mission. He added that they unavoidably would meet persecution when announcing and practicing the reign of God.

Justice is at the heart of that message. Jesus sent them out to promote justice. Identifying with the cause of justice in an unjust world means trouble.

According to church statistician David Barrett, some forty million Christians have been martyred since the time of Christ. Barrett's total is not based solely on stories headlined in newspapers, but on numerous kinds of accounts, some of which surfaced years after the incidents.

His definition of martyrs is believers in Jesus Christ who lose their lives while witnessing to their belief as a result of human hostility. Martyrs are not necessarily people who would be considered unusually heroic or pious, Barrett said. The church knows the names of only 15,000 such heroic martyrs.

Bishop Oscar Romero is a contemporary heroic one. Alexander Muge, bishop of an Anglican diocese in Kenya, is another one. He was killed on August 14, 1990, when his car collided head-on with a truck. The accident occurred only hours after a Kenyan cabinet minister had publicly issued a death threat to intimidate two Anglican bishops who were outspoken in condemning official corruption.

They died persecuted "in the cause of uprightness, and God's reign is theirs" (Mt 5:10). I wouldn't be surprised if all of us know some persons who would qualify as martyrs according to Barrett's definition, whose names are hardly known, or not known at all by others.

Saturday of the Fourteenth Week

MATTHEW 10:24-33

Trust

"So do not be afraid...."

Etty Hillesum was a young Jewish woman arrested and killed in one of the Nazi extermination camps. Years after her death her diaries were published under the title *An Interrupted Life.*

Etty discovered what Jesus assured us of when he said, "Do not be afraid of those who kill the body, but who cannot kill the soul." She had not only read these words. She understood them.

On New Year's Eve, 1941, she discovered the possibility of listening in to her inner self. She learned "a greater awareness and hence easier access to my inner sources." Soon she understood that she was "listening in" on God in her innermost being.

She discovered in the deepest center of her soul, her still point, the presence of God: "Somewhere there is something inside me that will never desert me again."

She found that God had a dwelling place in her. Having located this "home" in herself, she is at home everywhere. "I have no nostalgia left. I feel at home. I have learned so much about it here. We are at home. Under the sky, in every place on earth, if only we carry everything with us. I often felt, and I still feel, like a ship with a precious cargo—the moorings have been slipped and now the ship is free to take its load to any place on earth. We must be our own country."

Realizing this, she knows nothing can happen to her. There is, indeed, no need to be afraid of those who cannot steal your soul! Nothing can happen to us that can undo the divine presence. We are always in God's hands.

September 7, 1943, she sat in the freight train that brought her to her death. She threw a postcard out of that train. It was found by a farmer. She wrote: "Opening my Bible at random, I read 'the Lord is my dwelling place.'" She had opened Scripture at the place that explained her trust in God: "Do not be afraid!"

Monday of the Fifteenth Week

MATTHEW 10:34 – 11:1

Peacemaking

"It is not peace I have come to bring."

Of course, Jesus came to bring peace. It is what the prophets foretold he would do. It was what the angels sang about at his birth. But we all know how difficult it is to bring peace. Think about the official peacemakers in our world sent out by the United Nations or other international organizations.

Peacemaking isn't an easy and peaceful activity. It isn't about smiles. If there are smiles they often hide a deep anguish. Peacemaking hurts and is often humiliating. It never gives up, it demands endless travel, it is never at rest, it is always looking ahead, and more often than not it is very risky and dangerous. Our contemporary history is full of tales about those risks. Cars are blown up and shots are fired.

The members of *Pax Christi*, an international Catholic peace movement, can tell you horror stories about how they have been manhandled and arrested, beaten up and humiliated in practically all the countries where they are active, including the United States. All peacemakers in our world have the same kind of tale to tell.

Even at the home level peacemaking and peace keeping are often an ongoing burden. Trying to harmonize the different ages, granting enough freedom and self-assertion but not too much; controlling without disturbing initiative; stimulating enthusiasm, creativity, generosity, and self-determination; and wishing sometimes that you had never let things go as far as you did.

Peace is not an easy thing. It is the gathering into one of what is scattered. According to the Good News of John it is the reason they killed Jesus on the cross (John 11:52).

Tuesday of the Fifteenth Week

MATTHEW 11:20-24

Alas for you!

"Alas for you, Chorazin! Alas for you, Bethsaida!"

She is speaking to her daughter, the apple of her eye. He is speaking to his son, of whom he is so proud. Both son and daughter got involved with what any parent would call bad company, the drug scene and all that comes with it.

The scenario is as old as the hills. She is not threatening her daughter; he is not menacing his son. What they say might sound like it, but it isn't like that. They aren't angry either; they aren't even warning. They are just sad, full of sorrow. What that mother and that father say comes from their broken hearts: "Alas, for you, my daughter." "Alas, for you, my son."

It is the way Jesus speaks about those two towns, Chorazin and Bethsaida, who refuse to get reorganized in the light of his Good News. He worked miracle after miracle there—that is what the text says—but they refused to turn round.

What he says sounds like a menace and a warning. In a number of translations the "Alas" of our version is translated "Woe." But what we hear him express is sorrow. Sorrow that they didn't accept the most valuable thing in their world.

Alas for you who continue the old ways; alas for you who don't want to change. It isn't an angry man who speaks, but one with a broken heart.

Wednesday of the Fifteenth Week

MATTHEW 11:25–27

Letter and Spirit

"I bless you, Father, Lord of heaven and earth, for hiding these things from the learned and the clever and revealing them to little children."

It is as if Jesus is here on a kind of anti-intellectual tour, something Paul seems to do, too, when he makes almost the same remarks about the foolishness of those wise in the eyes of the world, and the wisdom of those wise in the eyes of God.

Does this mean that all scientific studies of the Bible are useless? No one who ever seriously tries to engage in a Bible group will ever think so. Scientific research and exegesis are a great help, and they are needed. It is definitely helpful for any Bible group or Bible reader to consult a good commentary on a text one intends to use. It would be good to go—even as a group—to a Bible study session or update.

The main goal of a Bible reader or Bible group, however, shouldn't be an intellectual insight into the letter of the text; the real goal is the Spirit. The study of the letter of the Bible text and its life stories should lead us to experience the Spirit of God alive in our own lives.

There is a written Bible, and there is the Bible of our lives. There are the Acts of the Apostles that continue in the acts of our own communities and lives. God's Spirit is hiding in, through, under, above, and beside all we do, and in all that happens around us, inspiring, cajoling, taunting, warning, and sometimes just opposing. Tracing all those reactions in ourselves should be the intention of our Bible reading and study, digging out the "hidden" things in our own lives.

Thursday of the Fifteenth Week

MATTHEW 11:28-30

Solidarity

"Come to me, all you who labor and are overburdened, and I will give you rest."

You can listen to sayings of Jesus in different ways. You *should* listen to them in different ways. In today's text Jesus invites us to come to him with our burdens and sorrows. So we should go to him and, indeed, we will find our rest.

There is also another way of understanding this saying. We are like he is. Haven't we received his spirit in us? We should be to others as he is to us. We should be the ones to say to others: "Come to me, all you who labor and are overburdened, and I will give you rest."

Jesus doesn't mean this in just a vague way. He means what he says. People did come to him and left him refreshed, having found new meaning in life and new ways of living. He restored their human dignity, helped them to overcome crippling obstacles, healed, and forgave them.

Pope John Paul II put it in a different way: "'Solidarity' then is not a feeling of vague compassion or shallow distress at the misfortunes of so many people, both near and far. On the contrary, it is a firm and persevering determination to commit oneself to the common good; that is to say, to the good of all and of each individual, because we are all really responsible for all...a commitment to the good of one's neighbor with the readiness, in the Gospel sense, to 'lose oneself' for the sake of the others instead of exploiting them, and to 'serve them' instead of oppressing them for one's own advantage" (*On Social Concern*, #38).

If anyone starts to tell you of her or his worries, don't shrug them off. Take your time, offer a cup of tea or coffee, and listen. Show them your solidarity. Be an oasis in the desert of their lives, just as Jesus is in yours.

Friday of the Fifteenth Week

MATTHEW 12:1-8

Sabbath Rest

"The Son of Man is master of the Sabbath."

Jurgen Möltmann is a great theologian who took the lead on many theological issues. He wrote one of the first books on the theology of creation that speaks of the spirituality of care for the earth in contemporary terms.

His approach is simple. He believes that what we have to do is consider the old life laws as found in the first book of the Bible.

One law he would like to see restored is the Sabbath law, not only to guarantee every human being, every animal, and every plant a seventh day of rest, but also to guarantee such a rest to the land every seventh year.

We desperately need that kind of respect for ourselves, for others, for all that is alive and gives life, to begin to offset the ecological disasters we have allowed. A seventh day of rest, a simpler life, another order of priorities.

Another theologian who stressed this point not so long ago is Pope John Paul II in his encyclical *Centesimus Annus*. He writes that every worker has a right to that rest, not only to obtain the leisure it provides, but also because it gives us the time to reflect on who we are, on how we relate to the world and to God, the source of it all. John Paul wonders whether that human right is sufficiently respected in our industrialized societies.

Maybe it is through our ever-growing respect for animals and plants, the water and the sky, that we might rediscover a greater respect for ourselves, for our own human environment.

Wasn't it said and written that we should learn from creation around us?

Saturday of the Fifteenth Week

MATTHEW 12:14-21

Serenity

"He will not brawl or cry out, his voice is not heard…he will not break…or snuff [out]…."

To "brawl" means to argue or to quarrel, and the Greek verb that in our text is translated with "cry out" is the word that is used for the barking of a dog, the croaking of a raven, the screaming of a drunken man, and the uproar of an angry crowd. Jesus is not going to do anything like that.

We often do make those noises in our polarized Christian communities. We are divided over liberals and conservatives, liberation theologians and creational ones, left and right, and so on.

The great Australian cartoonist Leunig reflected on this polarization in his Christmas cartoon of 1997 in the daily *The Age.* A Christmas angel is dialoguing with a Christmas shepherd. The angel says: "I am the angel of good tidings." The shepherd asks: "Are you a left-winger or a right-winger?" The angels answers: "I am equally right-winged and left-winged. If I was only left-winged I would be condemned to fly in clockwise circles like a creature chasing its tail. And if I was only right-winged I would end up flying in equally meaningless anti-clockwise circles. But I have meaning! I have two good wings of equal strength. I fly where I like and say what I want." The shepherd asks then, "And what do you want to say?" The angel answers: "I want to say that hope is alive, and that life can still be good!"

Isaiah prophesied about Jesus that he would not brawl or cry out, that his voice would not be heard in the streets, that he would not break the crushed reed or snuff the faltering wick, and that all nations would experience him as their hope.

Monday of the Sixteenth Week

MATTHEW 12:38-42

Overlooked Signs

"Master," they said: "we should like to see a sign from you."

Their question was silly. Calling them "an evil and unfaithful generation" showed Jesus' exasperation. How could they ask him for a sign while they were surrounded by the signs he gave them? Wasn't he God's sign to them?

Since the Second Vatican Council we have been accustomed to the expression "signs of the times." It was mentioned four times, once in the *Constitution of the Church in the Modern World*, #4, once in the *Declaration on Religious Freedom*, #15, once in the *Decree on Ecumenism*, #4, and once in the *Decree on the Ministry and Life of Priests*, #9.

It proved to be a term that spoke to the mind of many a theologian. Pope John Paul II has mentioned it in many of his documents and most emphatically in his encyclical *On Social Concern*, #7.

In that document he complains that one of those signs is the situation of poverty and of underdevelopment in which millions of human beings live. He calls them the "griefs and anxieties of today," and he adds: "Before this vast panorama of pain and suffering, the Council wished to suggest horizons of joy and hope."

All of us should make that grief and anxiety our own, because it is Jesus who identifies with the hungry and naked around us. He gives us that sign. Are we, too, asking for another sign from him?

Tuesday of the Sixteenth Week

MATTHEW 12:46–50

The New Family: Church

"Stretching out his hands towards his disciples, he said:
...'Here are my mother and my brothers.'"

Jesus' mother, brothers, and sisters, in other words his blood family, are waiting outside. When Jesus is told about them, he asks the crowd in front of him: "Who is my mother and who are my brothers?" He then stretches out his hands toward his disciples and says, "Here are my mother and my brothers! For whoever does the will of my Father in heaven is my brother, and sister, and mother."

At that moment he distinguishes between his blood family "outside" and his new family "inside," those who later will be called his "church." In Matthew's gospel he makes this distinction in a different way than Mark does in his gospel. In Mark Jesus pointed at all those in front of him, here in Matthew only to his disciples.

His earthly family, who had come to bring him back home, and who must have been forcing his mother Mary to come with them, was left cooling their heels outside, cut off from his new family—the church—inside. What Jesus had asked of his disciples before, to change their ties to their blood family in view of the reign of God (4:22; 8:21–22), is here explained further.

It is a transition from one household to another one. Those disciples who are doing God's will form together with him in their new community, his new family. This reality is often lost in the Western context, where we are addressed as "brothers and sisters" but have difficulty calling each other like that, in contrast to the non-Western church communities in our midst and in the wide world around us. In the Synod for Africa in Rome some years ago the African church decided to make this sense of the new family their central plan of action.

Wednesday of the Sixteenth Week

MATTHEW 13:1-9

Family

"Jesus left the house and sat by the lakeside...."

It sounds perfectly normal. It is something all of us like to do now and then—just leave everything behind, go into nature, and sit quietly at a lakeside. There is, however, more to this text than just a hike to the lake.

We know from the gospels that Jesus had difficulties at home. His family and the villagers of Nazareth were afraid that he was out of his mind. They had tried to get him home. His disciples didn't understand him very well either. When he left the house, he got away from them as well. He didn't like to be fenced in.

While he is sitting there a crowd of people gathers around him. The crowd is so large that he can't address them. So he gets into a boat and addresses them from a bit offshore.

He found a new family, a larger circle, the family of God. Matthew uses that theme of "leaving his house" six times. But Matthew not only notes when Jesus *leaves* his house, but also when he goes home again.

"Then, leaving the crowds, he went to the house" (Mt 13:36). He returns in a different way than he left. He left his family alone, and he returns to them in the company of a crowd.

Jesus is someone who constantly leaves a home to start a larger household. He refuses to be restricted to a group, however charismatic it might be. He leaves the closeness of Nazareth and settles in Capernaum. He leaves Capernaum to move on. Every house seems too small for him, all limits too restrictive. He will not rest until all of us are relating to one another in a reign of God that is like one great kin-dom. He remained faithful to his roots, but he grew out into a tree in which all of us will find a home.

Thursday of the Sixteenth Week

MATTHEW 13:10–17

Seeing

"Blessed are your eyes because they see!"

It was at a meeting of religion teachers. The theme of the in-service day was "Signs of Hope in a Culture of Death." The introduction sounded rather abstract and out-of-this-world, and some of the participants proved to be irritated about this at question time. "How do you make your students experience the presence of God in their world?" they asked. "Where does God's light and presence break through this darkness of our world?" "How can you see God in our world?" One teacher quoted Jesus' saying that "Blessed are they who see," but added, "I am sorry, but I don't."

The whole session got deadlocked. The facilitator, trying to overcome the impasse, suggested a half hour of quiet time to consult one another in small groups or to think the matter over on their own. The proposal was accepted, and people dispersed.

When they came back together, they had an exchange on the results of their quiet time. The most striking report came from a small group that had asked one another to mention something they were really grateful for.

In all cases it had been something "extra," a friendly word or gesture, something that betrayed another world from the dark one, "the culture of death."

They all mentioned something they hadn't paid for, something showing a dynamic with roots deeper in human beings than what is often called the bottom line: money, fame, and power. They hit on a realm of goodness and—so they thought—godliness. Indeed, happy the eyes that see and take into account what they see!

Friday of the Sixteenth Week

MATTHEW 13:18–23

Yielding Fruits

But what was sown in good soil was the one who hears the message and takes it in.

Archbishop and Nobel Prize laureate Desmond Tutu once told how the believers in the reign of heaven see and organize themselves in two ways.

There are those who see themselves as people dressed in white with palm branches in their hands, singing solemn "Alleluias," marching with serious faces towards a light in the sky. Others see themselves as laughing, singing, dancing, playing cards, and affirming life in all its ways.

It is the second group, he said, that is yielding the fruits we are supposed to yield. They understand what the message of the reign of God is about.

God's reign is about life and the celebration of it. Jesus always gloriously affirmed life around him, healing it when it was sick, seeing the good in those who were overlooked by all, clearing away evil that was obstructive, and sitting down with them to have a good meal.

It is that affirmation of life, of the reign of God that made Archbishop Tutu do the things he did. Affirming that life and reign made him a valiant champion for justice and peace, opposing the injustice of apartheid, and fostering the reconciliation needed to assure peace.

The seed of the "word of the reign" yielded a harvest in him and in his country that surpassed humanity's wildest dreams.

Saturday of the Sixteenth Week

MATTHEW 13:24-30

Gentle Powers

"But he said: 'No...let them both grow till harvest.'"

We have the awful tendency to wage war—and not only to protect ourselves against political enemies. We declare war on crime, drunken drivers, cancer, abortion, and drugs. In many cases this isn't only a figure of speech. It is a reality. In Washington, D.C., about 2000 people were killed in drug wars from 1989 to 1991. People shot each other, or were shot by the police.

War has something to do with old apocalyptic ideas: heaven should open and destroy everything that hinders us.

Jesus' companions thought in those terms. When a town in Samaria didn't wish to receive them, James and John asked Jesus, "Lord, do you want to call down fire from heaven to destroy them?" Jesus rebukes them. That isn't his approach. He doesn't believe in that type of force. He prefers another power, the fantastic power of a seed, the penetrating power of yeast. He prefers energies that change things from within.

We often think that change can come from outside, that you can force it upon people as you can force it upon things. Jesus asks us to trust the soft powers in ourselves, in others, and in the world.

The reign of God begins with an inner potential that is given to everybody, something that will grow. If stimulated correctly and gently it will overgrow the weeds and all evil.

Jesus is a friend of all of us. You can notice that even in the examples he uses. He is inclusive. He speaks about a man who goes out to sow, and about a woman who is kneading the yeast through the dough.

Jesus has the bold gentleness attributed to God in the Book of Wisdom—a gentle confidence in our inborn goodness and possibilities. Let us trust those gentle powers in ourselves and in others. Let us stir them up in ourselves and others, before we burn.

Monday of the Seventeenth Week

MATTHEW 13:31–35

What Has Been Hidden

"I will speak to you in parables, unfold what has been hidden...."

The parables Jesus tells lead us into a world that often remains hidden to us in the world in which we live. According to him the world has a kind of double bottom.

Saint Paul, too, works with that "doubleness" when he writes in his first letter to the Corinthians that "those who are involved with the world [should live] as though they were people not engrossed in it" (1 Cor 7:31).

The reason he gives is that the world as we know it and live it is not the real world. It is the "factual" world, but not the real one. How could the world in which we live—in which, according to some statistics, 45,000 people die of starvation each day, in which about 25% of its population consumes 80% of its goods, in which millions of refugees are fleeing from each other—be the real world? The actual world, yes; the real one, no.

It is the reason Jesus speaks in parables—stories that tell about another world, a world where people have awakened from the nightmare in which they had been living.

"He would never speak to them except in parables." It is only in that way that he could introduce us to the counter-world that broke into this world by his presence.

At first hearing, his world, the world of the beatitudes, doesn't make sense in our world. Yet, it is as our world should be. It is the world as willed by God since its foundation.

Tuesday of the Seventeenth Week

MATTHEW 13:35-43

Dawn

"Then the upright will shine like the sun in the reign of the Father."

I know a woman, a very nice person, who now and then will suddenly comment: "I don't understand how God can tolerate this world." It is what people so often say when they are confronted with the evil around them.

Once a secretary told me all that was going on in her family, and she made that very same statement as she wiped the tears from her eyes. How can God tolerate all that is going on? Why doesn't God let the divine light shine? Why doesn't God show God's power?

But the question backfires. The same question should be asked about us: how can we tolerate this world? We want God to do something about it, but shouldn't we do something about it?

Listen to the prophet Isaiah: "This is what pleases me—it is the Lord who speaks—to break unjust fetters, to undo the straps of the yoke, to let the oppressed go free, and break every yoke, to share your bread with the hungry, and to shelter the homeless poor, to clothe the one you see naked, and not run from your own kin. Then will your light shine like the dawn, and your wound will be quickly healed over" (Is 58:6-7).

We are asked to be a people after God's own heart, acting as God's love and justice in this world. It is our light that should start shining like the dawn over a dark world that badly needs light. As Teresa of Avila once wrote: "Christ has no body on earth, no hands, no feet, but yours...."

Wednesday of the Seventeenth Week

MATTHEW 13:44-46

The Games God Plays

"The reign of God is hidden...[and] found."

It is as if the world around us is nothing but an invitation to look for hidden things. Think of all the discoveries made—gold, diamonds, silver, but also water and oil, and all kinds of minerals. What about the terrific powers hidden in the smallest atoms around us? What about all those waves around us that carry mobile phone calls, radio stations, and television programs? And at the moment only God knows what is still hidden in them.

Remember the secrets of plants, their hidden dyes and spicy tastes, and their medical properties: moss and molds that heal sores, an insect-eating plant that, when refined, is a cure to whooping cough; the quickening power of coffee, tea, and cocoa; and the calming power of chamomile and valerian.

Recall the genius hidden in poets, painters, and musicians, writing, painting, and composing pieces of art you wouldn't have thought possible before they were created.

Remember your own wonder about the first drawings you and your children and grandchildren made. And how Michelangelo, looking at a large piece of marble, saw that beautiful statue of David in it.

God is playing games with us, a kind of endless and infinite hide and seek. And now Jesus explains that in the field of this world God has hidden a treasure that is greater than all those things we summed up. He calls it the reign of heaven, a human/divine work of art, in which all the gifts God has hidden in us will be shared by all, and we will never come to the end of telling the story.

Thursday of the Seventeenth Week

MATTHEW 13:47-53

Storytelling

"The reign of heaven is like a householder...."

"Those who tell the stories rule the world," wrote a Navajo author as an introduction to a collection of old American stories. You know that from your own family. You know how some stories can be told, and how others are banned. Just listen to the stories we tell each other at home, at work. Listen to the stories children tell their parents, and parents tell their children. Listen to the preachers and their sermons.

Isn't it true to say that the world around us doesn't change more than it does because we are listening only to certain types of stories? Who is listening to the stories of the poor and the neglected, of the abused and wretched? And even when those stories are told in a documentary about the hunger in Africa or war in the Middle East, aren't we inclined to switch off our television or radio because we don't like to hear those tales of endless woe, those stories that come from the underside of our society?

Jesus was an accomplished storyteller. He told marvelous parables about the reign of God. The reign is like a fish hiding in the deep water that must be fished out. It is like a pearl, like a treasure, hidden in the earth. They have to be found. It is like a householder who brings forth the new and the old.

Hiding in the old, the newness of the reign has to be brought out. You can't bring it forth when you are repeating the same old things. You fail to discover it when you are listening only to the traditional melody.

The greatest challenge to the world and the church of today are the new stories that come to us from Africa and Latin America, from Asia and Australia, from our own inner cities, from minority groups and the marginalized people among us. Are you willing to listen to them? Are you willing to be like that householder who brings out from the storeroom things both new and old?

Friday of the Seventeenth Week

MATTHEW 13:54–58

Their Low Self-Esteem

"This is the carpenter's son, surely?… Where did the man get it all?"

His own hometown and his own family wouldn't believe in him. They wanted to cut him down to their size. This is a story all of us know. We probably know about it in two ways: we have been cut down to size by those related to us, and we ourselves have cut down to size those nearest to us.

"A prophet is despised only in his own country and in his own house," Jesus says. You can hear how disappointed he is by the little word "only," which he adds to his words: "A prophet is despised only in his own house." That wee word is at the same time an understatement and an exaggeration. He is not only despised in Nazareth. But the word expresses his disappointment. He was disappointed, too, because it meant that he couldn't help them, as he would have liked to.

Their judgment on him was also a judgment on themselves. How could someone like them do the things Jesus did? It is the kind of fatal self-fulfilling prophecy that is no help to anyone. Because of their low self-esteem they would never be able to lift themselves out of their apathy.

Lifting others out of their apathy, showing them their greatness was exactly what Jesus had come to do. In his company people felt better and greater than they had ever thought possible before. It was the reason that those crowds of people surrounded him. At home it didn't seem to work.

Saturday of the Seventeenth Week

MATTHEW 14:1-12

The Great Why

"[John's] head was brought in on a dish."

A dancing girl, a wicked mother, a petty king, a set of loose guests, and on a dish the head of the man Jesus had called the greatest ever born to a woman. Why did God allow a gruesome thing like this? Why? It is the great question all of us carry under the surface of our skins in the dark depths of our hearts. Why? It is a question answered in so many different ways, that it seems as if no answer has ever been given.

In his book *The Conversations at Curlow Creek*, award-winning Australian author David Malouf relates the answer as given by an old Irishman, Eamon Fitzgibbon:

> God may exist—I do not deny that, though as you know I am no great friend of the Church—and be responsible for all this. It is our business to make good his mistakes, to achieve as far as we are able, that just world of perfect reason and order that He, for whatever reason, has failed to provide for us. Perhaps because the greater glory is to stand by and let His creatures do it through the gifts he has given us.

Is that the answer? Maybe it is. If God would have done all for us, we would have nothing to do. We would be glorified dummies and nothing more.

Something is surely happening all around us in the world and definitely also within us. God and we are partners in what is happening. Is it so that in the end we will be able to say, that —with God's help—we were able to do it?

Monday of the Eighteenth Week

MATTHEW 14:13-21

Equality

"… to say nothing of women and children."

The last words of this reading—"to say nothing of women and children"—have caused some critical commentaries in our days. It is as if women and children are mentioned as a kind of after-thought, as if they really didn't matter. Why should one speak about them at all? It is those 5000 men that counted.

Matthew makes that remark "to say nothing of women and children" twice, both times after a miracle in which Jesus provides food to the crowds (Mt 13:21 and 15:38).

The words he uses in both cases for "men," "women," and "children" are words that indicate family relations. The word he uses for men (my apologies for these technicalities but they are needed to make the point) is a word that is only used in the context of a man's relation to his wife. It is a word that—for that reason—was rarely used. The word used for woman has the same kind of connotation; it indicates her relation to a man. And the word used for children is also a term that describes little children in relation to the rest of the family.

Matthew describes those enormous, wonderful picnics as a family affair, a family affair where men (fathers), women (mothers), and children are fed in a way different from what normally happened in a patriarchal family, where this equality didn't exist when taking meals. Jesus made those who never ate together eat together. He created a new family pattern and model.

When the American missionary Vincent Donovan, a Holy Ghost Father, celebrated the Eucharist for the first time with Maasai Christians in the Great Rift Valley in East Africa, men and women ate together for the first time in their lives. The young unmarried girls came to thank him for that equality in Christ.

Tuesday of the Eighteenth Week

MATTHEW 14:22-36

Fear

"Courage! Do not be afraid!"

We all know the story of the storm on the lake. Jesus had left the disciples to be by himself. The disciples were trying to get to the other side of the lake, but were hit by a head wind that became stronger and stronger, finally turning into a storm. They were afraid, but when they suddenly saw someone walking toward them over the water, they were terrified.

Fear is a killer. Fear is a murderer, not only because fear can lead us to murder others, but also because fear can kill *us*. It can make us deadly sick.

Those disciples were not only afraid of the wind and the water; they were terrified to see *him*. It wasn't the first time they were scared of him. They often must have had mixed feelings about that man, Jesus, who was changing their lives so radically.

Are you always happy to be one of his disciples? Did you ever have the feeling that you would like to be left alone? That he is asking too much of you? That the cross you are supposed to bear is too heavy?

Jesus finally had left the disciples alone. They were trying to go home, but then, suddenly, he reappears on the lake walking over the water.

"It is a ghost," they said, and cried out in fear. Jesus called out to them: "Courage! It is I! Don't be afraid." Peter wanted to cut his fears and doubts once and for all and shouted, "Tell me to come to you, and I will come!" Peter got out of the boat but he didn't make it. He started to sink, yelling: "Lord, save me!"

That is what Jesus did, adding: "Man of little faith, why did you doubt?" suggesting that Peter had it in him to believe. And Peter did, when he said with the others and all of us: "Truly, you are the Son of God!"

Why should we, why should you, be afraid of him?

Wednesday of the Eighteenth Week

MATTHEW 15:21-28

Mission

"Woman, you have great faith!"

Part of the requirements of their course on "The Practice of Interreligious Dialogue" had been to participate in a non-Christian religious service or event, and to give an oral report on the experience in class. They reported on a great variety of contacts and experiences, Muslim, Sikh, Buddhist, Hindu, Bahai, and several others. Practically everyone expressed the kind of appreciation Jesus had for the Canaanite woman, when he said of her: "Woman, you have great faith!"

The beginning of her dialogue with Jesus had been difficult. He was hardly ever so harsh in his words as when meeting her. She made a nuisance of herself too, up to the point that the disciples got really upset about her. But then, once contact was made, things eased, and in the end he expressed his admiration for her, and she must have admired him when she found her daughter free of whatever had possessed her.

No wonder that most commentators think that the story is a text remembered and used by the early church to justify their mission among the non-Jews after Jesus' death and resurrection. It is a story shot through with an early Christian mission theology: "First to the Jews and then to the Gentiles."

The story about Jesus' reaction, however, wasn't only told to help the early Christians two thousand years ago. The intent of the story remains valid for our days. Many of the recent statements from Rome insist on the need of every Christian community, and in fact of every Christian, to be in interreligious contact and dialogue with those who are not Christians.

Thursday of the Eighteenth Week

MATTHEW 16:13-23

Peter's Faith

"It was not flesh and blood that revealed this to you..."

When Jesus asks his disciples: "Who do people say the Son of Man is?" he is not asking them a rhetorical question. It is a real question. He wants an answer.

At first they all try to dodge the issue. Jesus repeats his question. It is Simon who finally gives the answer: "You are the Christ, the Son of the living God!"

Jesus replies: "Simon, the son of Jonah, you are a happy man, because it was not flesh and blood that revealed this to you, but my Father in heaven." And he gives him a new name: "I now say to you, you are Peter and on this rock I will build my church."

Peter not only discovered the real identity of Jesus that day. Jesus helped Peter to discover his own identity, too. Simon the fisherman discovers that he has something in him that makes him Peter. That something is the reality of God in him.

Peter isn't the only one who carries God's presence, but he is the first one who discovers it through Jesus. Millions of others would follow him in that discovery. Yet, he is the first one to understand and to feel what all this will lead to. He remains a first among equals.

The others in the early Christian community never let him forget that. They respected him as the leader, but they were also the ones who sent him on his mission (Acts 8:14). They called him to give account of himself and of his way of handling issues, when they thought that necessary (Acts 11:1-4).

Peter's conviction is shared by others, and by you and me. It is that faith that taps into the same divine presence in all of us.

All of us sharing that belief are built on the persuasion that made Jesus call Simon "Rock." "Everyone who hears these words of mine and puts them into practice is like a wise man, who built his house on the rock" (Mt 7:24-25).

Friday of the Eighteenth Week

MATTHEW 16:24-28

Giving up One's Life

"Anyone who loses his life for my sake will find it."

Hearing this text, many think about martyrs, like Father Miguel Pro in Mexico, who stood against a wall to be shot, and whose last cry was in praise of Jesus. Or someone like Father Maximilian Kolbe, who gave his life to save that of the parent of a large family.

Those who think so are right. Yet, there is more to Jesus' saying than just that supreme martyrdom. All those who undergo a real conversion, a total transformation of their life, for the sake of Jesus and the reign fall under this category: the alcoholic man or woman who deliberately joins an Alcoholics Anonymous group; the addicted gambler who is willing to pay the cost and spend the time to overcome his or her obsession; the lukewarm Christians who take the risk of making a thirty-day retreat hoping to convert and lose the lives they had been living; a bishop like Dom Helder Camara in Brazil who in 1965 decided to leave his episcopal palace to live in a simple three-room apartment. People who make decisions like that lose their life to find it again.

It isn't easy to do that. It isn't without reason that Jesus speaks about "renouncing yourself" and "taking up your cross." We have to overcome not only our fear, but also our pride to take his words seriously. We have to admit the sad condition our lives might be in, to find our real selves.

Saturday of the Eighteenth Week

MATTHEW 17:14–20

Moving Mountains

"If your faith is the size of a mustard seed…nothing will be impossible to you."

The Sunday School class had been listening to the story about the mustard seed and the moving of mountains when one small boy put up his hand. Not waiting for an acknowledgment of his hand he shouted: "My father can do that." "Your father can do what?" "Move mountains. He told us that he can do that. He has a bulldozer. That's what he said." The boy was right. We can move mountains from here to there, even long before the invention of bulldozers. It has been done many a time.

Jesus was speaking in metaphors. There are more mountains in life than the physical ones, mountains that have to be moved to make human life feasible and the reign of God realizable. They can be moved, too.

Just take the Berlin wall that divided Europe and even the world in East and West, the hurdle apartheid was in South Africa, and the many obstacles that keep the human family—and very often our own families and communities—divided and apart.

In the apocryphal Gospel of Thomas we find an echo of Jesus' saying in our text today: "Jesus said, 'If two make peace with one another within a single house, they will say to a mountain, "Go elsewhere," and it will go elsewhere.'"

If we believe in the truth, the goodness, and the beauty—or in one word in the Spirit that is given to all of us—and connect with it, we will be able to do great things.

Jesus said that we would even be able to do greater things than he was able to do (John 14:12). We will be able to move mountains and obstacles that need to be moved. We did, and we will do it again.

Monday of the Nineteenth Week

MATTHEW 17:22-27

Freedom and Scandal

"So that we shall not be the downfall of others...."

When Jesus and his disciples arrived home some collectors of the temple tax approached Peter and asked him, "Doesn't your master pay the temple tax?" Peter answered impetuously while entering the door, "Yes, he does." Even before he could say anything else Jesus challenged his answer, telling him that he was wrong.

He being the Son of God is not obliged to pay any temple tax. Children don't pay tax to their father. Peter and the other disciples, doing the will of the Father, become Jesus' brothers and sisters (Mt 12:49–50) and consequently, God's children. Together with Jesus they form the new family of God and as a result don't have to pay any temple tax either. They are free.

This freedom, however, doesn't exclude responsibilities toward others. And it is here that an important lesson is given to all of us.

Our freedom shouldn't cause scandal. It shouldn't offend others, hindering them to see who Jesus is. And that is why, though not obliged, Jesus is willing to pay the tax for himself and for Peter voluntarily. To show, however, that he is not obliged to do so, he doesn't pay from the common purse they have or with the help of a rich supporter; he does it from the mouth of a fish.

Peter has to go fishing, cast a hook in the lake, catch a fish, open its mouth, and find a shekel, just enough to pay the tax for two, for Jesus and for Peter. This is one of the many comic situations in the gospels: they paid their tax, but, in a way, they didn't pay it themselves; a fish paid to avoid "scandal!" A fish provided by their Father in heaven.

Tuesday of the Nineteenth Week

MATTHEW 18:1–5, 10, 12–14

Solidarity

"Suppose a man has a hundred sheep and one of them strays; will he not...go in search of the stray?"

Jesus asks the disciples about the good shepherd who lost a sheep: "Will he not leave the ninety-nine?" We are so accustomed to the answer Jesus gave to this question that it doesn't strike us that in real life the answer might be "No."

Doesn't the shepherd going in search of the stray put the ninety-nine at risk? Wouldn't it be more logical for him to take care of *them*? Should he leave all those others behind because one got lost? Isn't leaving those ninety-nine not only absurd, but even irresponsible?

It is Saint Augustine who recommends that we should have a closer look at numbers when we read the Bible. Numbers have a deep meaning. Sometimes their significance escapes us because the biblical numerology is too foreign to us. Yet, in this case that meaning is not too difficult to grasp. Even for us 100 is a special number. It indicates completeness. It is a rounded-off number.

The number 100 has the same kind of importance in the Bible. It is a serious matter when such a whole number is broken. It only takes one to break it. So, in a way, it doesn't even matter whether one is missing, or sixteen, or thirty-four. Losing even one means losing completeness.

Humanity, God's flock, belongs together like the number 100. If even one is lost or marginalized, we are no longer complete. That is why Jesus came to find the lost and marginalized one. We human beings belong together, and we should reform our attitudes and lives accordingly. Jesus came to find us, to bring us together, and to lead us all home.

Wednesday of the Nineteenth Week

MATTHEW 18:15–20

Two or Three

"For where two or three meet in my name, I shall be there with them."

It happened regularly, and yet I was surprised every time. I was accustomed to prayer. I prayed a lot with my family at home. In those days we went to church every day of the week. I prayed by myself, and later on with the community of missionaries I belong to. We would sit in the chapel for hours and hours a day, meditating, examining our consciences, celebrating the Eucharist, and even preparing for death!

Yet, I was surprised by it once I got to Africa. Practically every time I was invited to a family, celebrated one or another occasion together, visited a sick person, or was invited for a cup of tea, my hosts would ask me to pray together with them. I often forgot. I would already be at the door, shaking hands and saying "God bless you," when my friends would say: "Aren't we going to pray together?" And that is what we did, sometimes with only two or three, sometimes in a family.

I once read a report written by a student evaluating his pastoral experience in one of the West Indian Islands. He mentioned the same kind of experience. Once he had been awakened in the middle of the night by someone who was obviously disturbed. After a terrible nightmare she had gone to the rectory to knock on the door for help. He didn't know what to do. Should he give her something to eat, to drink? She saw his consternation, and she said: "I don't need anything. I only came to pray together with you for a moment. I am alone at home."

He did, and while the two were praying her anxiety disappeared. In Jesus' presence her anxiety cleared. Jesus promised: "When two or three are meeting in my name, I will be there with them."

Thursday of the Nineteenth Week

MATTHEW 18:21 – 19:1

Reconciliation

"Were you not bound, then, to have pity?"

Sometimes we speak about nature as if it is a person. We have that kind of instinctive feeling deep in ourselves that, if we force nature too much, it will take revenge. You hear that feeling expressed when a dam breaks, when a bridge collapses, when a new sickness breaks out, when an over-busy person suffers a heart attack, or when all the trees in an area suddenly start to die.

The older religions are full of rites to appease nature, to be reconciled with her. That is what the old shaman did, putting people back in the rhythm of nature with which they had lost contact.

It is a reconciliation we urgently need. It is a need that up to now was hardly ever mentioned in any of the church's documents on reconciliation and penance.

Only one bishop spoke about it at the Special Synod on Penance in 1983. He came from Japan, the country with a very bitter atomic experience. Bishop Stephen Fumio Hamao said: "Work for peace will be effective if all become aware of their deep connection with nature, especially with all living beings. We must not only dominate nature, but also seek harmony with it, and admire in it the beauty, the wisdom, and the love of its Creator. Thus men and women will be freed from their frenzy for possessions and domination and will become partisans of peace."

The Lord, our God, created this world as a beautiful garden for us, just as a lover gives flowers to a loved one. The whole of creation is God's gift to be enjoyed by all of us. On several occasions Jesus said: "Look at the flowers, the birds, the sky, the trees, the water, and the sunset!" Appreciate God's gifts from your heart, and make up for the damage done to it. Reconcile yourself with Sister Water.

Friday of the Nineteenth Week

MATTHEW 19:3-12

Marriage

"...and the two become one flesh."

The Pharisees who came to ask him a question on divorce didn't come because they were interested in marriage. They came for another reason. They wanted to catch him. They hoped to force him to choose sides in an ongoing discussion between two rabbinical schools of thought. They wanted to involve Jesus in the controversy between the strict view of Shammai and the lax view of Hillel. Hillel allowed practically anything as a pretext for divorce, from bad cooking to aging. Shammai interpreted the law more strictly, giving proven adultery as practically the only reason for a divorce.

Jesus saw through their intention to trap him in a controversial position, and he didn't answer their question. He did, however, speak about marriage and divorce. One of terms he used was "and the two become one flesh," giving as the example the relation between Adam and Eve.

Everyone of good will who ever attends a marriage hopes that this will be true of the bride and the groom marrying. No one of good will ever marries with anything else in mind. Yet, it doesn't always happen. The two don't always become as one.

Human nature being what it is, things might go wrong. The two might have been mistaken about each other, or their relations prove to be no help to either of them at all.

It is in those unhoped for and in fact tragic circumstances that our church community sanctions separation. This is a development that is always tragic and deplorable. Both parties will suffer in the bitter ashes of the fire that did not last. Children will be a further pain to cope with, and they will be hurt too.

Let us pray that in all marriages the two may become one flesh!

Saturday of the Nineteenth Week

MATTHEW 19:13–15

Children

"Let the little children alone, do not stop them coming to me."

One of the things I remember from my time in kindergarten, run by the Sisters of Mercy, is a large painting in soft colors of a sitting Jesus with little children all over him. In the background you could see some grumbling older men, his disciples.

Like many of the paintings of that time (though they still remain popular in many places these days) the whole set-up was rather sweet, not only because of the nice pastel colors, but also because of the figures of the children, all with curly hair and not a single one with a snotty nose or a soiled and smelly diaper.

There is another reason why such a painting doesn't tell us what this meeting with children was about. The disciples had been scolding those children. Those children should have known their place; they didn't really count. They should be seen, but definitely not heard.

Matthew uses this event to show the new kind of house-order Jesus came to introduce. All community members, young and old, count as equals not only in the eyes of God, but in the practice of Jesus' community itself. Quite a lesson in our days!

Monday of the Twentieth Week

MATTHEW 19:16-22

He Left

"And now a man came to him and asked: 'Master, what good deed must I do...?'"

Pope John Paul II uses the story of the man in question as his main theme in *The Splendor of Truth*. He says we can recognize in this man (whom Matthew's gospel doesn't name) every person who approaches Jesus Christ questioning him not so much about rules to be followed, but about the full meaning of life.

This youth expresses the aspiration at the heart of every human being. Who am I, what should I do? What is the meaning of my existence? It is the echo of God's call in us, the only one to satisfy the desire of the human heart. Those questions come from the depths of the heart. These questions are essential and unavoidable.

Jesus' answer, "Keep the commandments," doesn't satisfy the man, who asks a further question: "I have kept all these; what do I still lack?"

Conscious of the young man's yearning for something greater, which would transcend a legalistic interpretation of the commandments, the Good Teacher invites him to enter upon the path of perfection: "If you wish to be perfect, go, sell your possessions and give the money to the poor, and you will have treasure in heaven; then come, follow me."

When the young man heard these words he went away sad. He was as yet not ready to follow the perfect road. It is interesting to note that halfway through the story we hear that the man is young. A lot could still happen to him. It is as if a hint is given that not everything is lost. It might be an indication that Jesus' conversation with the rich young man continued, just like it does—as Pope John Paul II mentions—"in every period of history, including our own."

Tuesday of the Twentieth Week

MATTHEW 19:23-30

Last Equals First

"Thus the last will be first, and the first, last."

We have thousands of ways of dividing ourselves against each other into first ones and last ones. The one who is driving an eight-cylinder car expects the one in a two- or four-cylinder car to give way to him. The one with more money is sure to be treated first in an emergency. The first-class passengers leave the plane first, just like they were the first ones to leave the sinking Titanic. The non-smoker feels superior to the smoker, and, until recently, right-handed people felt superior to left-handed ones. The able-bodied people look down on the so-called disabled people; those who went through therapy look down on those who did not, and the other way around.

There is no end to the categories we have for letting the "first" ones look down on the "last" ones: money, beauty, muscles, race, skin, age, smell, gender, abode, origin, street, piety, religion, health, name, ordination, and so on. The list is endless and the difficulties that these prejudices cause are enormous.

When Jesus tells us that the last ones will be the first ones and the first ones the last, he doesn't want to reverse people's positions. He doesn't want to put those who are presently standing in front of the row in the back. That would only perpetuate the differences. Jesus wants to *abolish* those differences. The first ones and the last ones are equal—regardless of age, race, gender, religion, or all the rest. In his vision we are equal as sisters and brothers, who are friends.

Wednesday of the Twentieth Week

MATTHEW 20:1-16

Work and Wages

"They...grumbled at the landowner."

The behavior of the landowner who paid the same wage to his workers, whether they had worked the whole day or only for an hour or so, remains today as confounding as it was to the workers in the story who had been working the whole day. You can notice this when the story is read in a community service. It simply doesn't seem to be fair.

We don't think it fair because we connect wage and work. If you don't work you don't earn. And if what you do isn't considered to be work by those in power—like the work of a mother at home—you aren't paid either.

Jesus touches here upon the economy around him. In Matthew's gospel he frequently uses economic themes to talk about God's reign: planting and sowing, wealth and poverty, buying and selling, hiring and firing, the just and unjust, and in this case the payment of wages. In his book *House of Disciples*, Michael H. Crosby shows how in Matthew the very proclamation of the gospel, then as now, could never be divorced from economic and religious considerations. Jesus wanted to introduce a new social order.

And isn't our own actual economic situation as confounding—if not even more so—than the one in the parable about those laborers in the vineyard? What about our salary imbalances? What about the CEO salaries in comparison with their factory workers who are often in the poorer regions of the world; or the salaries of our entertainers and sports stars? And shouldn't mothers be paid for all the work they do? Doesn't their unpaid work make all paid work possible?

Thursday of the Twentieth Week

MATTHEW 22:1–14

Refusal

"'Come to my wedding.' But they were not interested."

The banquet is prepared. Everything is in order. The roast is sliced, the salad bar ready, the vegetables steaming, but the guests don't come. The guests have other things to do.

Those hesitations have a special significance in this case. It is God who did the inviting! Accepting such an invitation is a serious issue. To be invited by God and Jesus Christ? You never know how that will end. Or maybe you do guess, and you don't want it.

Many of us live on that kind of edge. We are attracted by God, we know we are invited by Jesus' love, and yet we don't dare accept. We hesitate. We refuse. And yet we can't deny that that invitation has come to us. We can almost hear the music in the hall and smell the roast on the fire. The American Quaker Thomas Kelly described this intuition in a striking way: "And we are unhappy, uneasy, strained, oppressed, and fearful we shall be shallow. For over the margins of life comes a whisper, a faint call, a premonition of richer living which we know we are passing by. Strained by the very mad pace of our daily outer burdens, we are further strained by an inward uneasiness, because we have hints that there is a way of life vastly richer and deeper than all this hurried existence, a life of unhurried serenity and peace and power. If only we could slip over into that Center. If only we could find the Silence which is the source of sound" (*A Testament of Devotion*).

All of us are more religious and more mystical than we appear to be. We have seen more than we want to admit even to ourselves: bits of light, rays of goodness, fragment of songs, patches of heaven. Most times we act as if we never heard or saw a thing.

Friday of the Twentieth Week

MATTHEW 22:34-40

As Yourself

"You must love your neighbor as yourself."

They asked him, "What is the most important commandment?" He answered, "You must love the Lord your God with all your heart, with all your soul, and with all your mind. This is the greatest and first commandment. The second is like it: You must love your neighbor as yourself."

Love your neighbor as yourself! Did you ever ask yourself why we should do that? We often ask ourselves how we *should* do it, but do we ask why?

It is because we are all together in this creation. In your essence you are the dwelling place of God. So is your neighbor. You might not feel God's presence, but that doesn't mean that God is absent. Your neighbor might not feel God's presence, but again that doesn't mean that she or he is not carried by God's love. We belong together, God, you, and I.

When we are one like this, we can see God and Christ in everyone. You might even go further and say that we ourselves are in the heart of everyone. What we do for another is done to ourselves. When another is hurt, we are hurt. We can repeat in our lives the words of Jesus: "Anything done to any of my sisters and brothers is done to me!" Our heart is not as large as the one in our chest; it is as large as Jesus' heart, as God's heart!

Sociologists, psychologists, and philosophers have been expressing worries about the ever-growing self-consciousness and consequent individualization of the younger generation. If you stick to Jesus' words, that growing self-awareness can only be a blessing, not only for those persons who are so highly conscious of themselves, but also for all humanity. The more you love yourself, the more you see who you are, the more Jesus' directive "Love the other as you love yourself" will be a blessing for all humanity!

Saturday of the Twentieth Week

MATTHEW 23:1–12

On Being Humble

"…those who humble themselves will be exalted."

People either attract each other, or their "vibrations" do not meet. It has to do with physical appearance, body language, the way people are dressed, and all kinds of other indeterminable factors. Most times it also has something to do with personality characteristics and deficiencies.

A modest and simple person, a mild and good one attracts. An arrogant and haughty person antagonizes everyone. Nobody is more difficult than the person who doesn't know his or her place, who looks and talks down to others, who condescends and uses others for his or her own advancement.

We ought to know our place. Psalm 8 might help us to do so:

> I look at your heavens made by your fingers,
> At the moon and the stars you set in place—
> Ah, what are men and women
> that you should spare a thought for them
> and that you should care for them? (8:3–4)

Those who know their place will be mild in their relation to others. They will have a sense of humor, and they will see the relativity of things. They will not get haughty. They will be neither fanatic nor intolerant. They will be exalted and carried on hands!

Monday of the Twenty-First Week

MATTHEW 23:13–22

Shutting up the Reign

"You shut up the reign of heaven in people's faces...."

Ten days before his retirement in December, 1997 the seventy-five-year-old Austrian Bishop Reinhold Stecher made a statement on the pastoral situation of the church. He said that "It shows no concern for the health of the community." Speaking about the lack of priests and the church's refusal to engage non-ordained laity, he wrote: "For some time now we have been offering people tacitly but in reality, a non-sacramental way of salvation. Those familiar with scholastic theology can only shake their heads in disbelief. For that theology strongly emphasizes the necessity for salvation of the Eucharist, penance and anointing the sick.

"Millions upon millions are unable to receive the sacraments of salvation...," he said. "Literally hundreds of millions of Catholics are unable to come to sacraments of forgiveness, which are morally necessary for salvation—and because they now cannot come, in a generation they will not want to come. In a day in which health care is directing greater attention to the whole person there is a wonderful opportunity for the anointing of the sick. Millions are unable to encounter Christ the good physician in this sacrament, however, because we insist that it can be administered only by a celibate priest."

Bishop Stecher notes that he is not opposed to celibacy and doesn't question its value for the sake of the reign. He does oppose, however, the tendency to make Jesus' teaching subject to administrative practices and the exercise of human authority. It is, he suggests, what the Pharisees did whom Jesus condemned for "shutting up the reign of heaven in people's faces."

He ends his letter by expressing his undiminished hope in the future of Jesus' gospel, but he warns that all of us need to be more sensitive to its real demands.

Tuesday of the Twenty-First Week

MATTHEW 23:23-26

The Inside

"Clean the inside…so that it and the outside are both clean."

Some call it our "still point." Thomas Merton wrote that he couldn't find an English or American word for it, so he called it by a French term "Point Vierge," our "Virginal Point." All agree that it is the point in us where we meet God's breath blown in us from the beginning, keeping us alive.

An old Hasidic story speaks about it as our "Innermost Point." It also tells that Satan can wrest that Innermost Point away from a person, leaving everything else just at it was. The wheel keeps on turning at the outside, but the Innermost Point is missing. The story ends with the raised voice of a rabbi praying: "But, so help us God, we must not let this happen!"

The story exaggerates. The Innermost Point in us cannot be lost. You cannot lose the inside without losing the outside. You cannot have the inside of a cup or hat, or anything without having the outside at the same time.

Your Innermost Point can be ignored, fogged over, sullied, and hidden under layers of waste and dirt, but it can only get lost like you lose something in your room—you can't find it, but you know it is there.

Those who have found their Inner Point all assure us that life only begins when inside and outside are one, or one again. They even add that it shows on your face!

Wednesday of the Twenty-First Week

MATTHEW 23:27–32

Tombs

"Your own evidence tells against you!"

The late papal theologian Cardinal Hans Urs von Balthasar, a specialist in Christian Esthetics, once wrote that he was always suspicious about over-decorated tabernacles. He didn't like the gold, diamond-studded ones that open with difficulty and the noise of a deep sigh, closing with a solemn bang. They reminded him of tombs in which we carefully bury Jesus out of sight, safely away from our lives. The more diamonds, the thicker the door, the more expensive the security system, the safer Jesus is away from us!

Jesus, though in another context, accuses the people around him of burying their prophets and decorating their tombs. The text suggests that the same kind of psychology is at work. Out of sight is out of life. Voices that still should be heard were buried once and for all. The tombstone assured that they would remain where they are. Their decorations are the hypocritical facade. Jesus added: "They are your own evidence telling against you!"

In our veneration and adoration of the Blessed Sacrament we have to be sincere—a sincerity that makes Jesus' presence a reality not only in the tabernacle in a church or chapel, but in the reality of our lived life. The Sacred Presence in that tabernacle is there to be broken open and to be eaten by us!

Thursday of the Twenty-First Week

MATTHEW 24:42–51

Awake

"Blessed that servant if the master's arrival finds him...
awake!"

She comes from an island with a saint's name, Santa Lucia. For some days in the week she takes care of the people in a presbytery. She takes care not only of the people, but also of the house, the plants, the cat, and those who ring the doorbell. Part of her time she cooks in a Franciscan community. When you see her she will always ask whether you would like a cup of coffee. She attends many of the liturgical services. She often acts as the sacristan, and when there is no Mass server she will do that too. She is a member of the Legion of Mary, a very active member who not only comes to the weekly meetings and visits people in the neighborhood, but also saves money to go on apostolic tours during her holidays. She went to Copenhagen and to Moscow. She didn't go as a tourist, but for apostolic reasons. Sitting in a park or at a station she will ask passersby whether they speak English, and when they do, she asks them whether they have ever heard the story of Jesus. I asked her if people listen to her when she does that. "Oh, yes," she said, "They do!"

The priest in the presbytery where she works told me, "She is always doing something for God." And she is! She is the kind of person Jesus would call "blessed!" Not because of something that is going to happen to her afterward in the life to come. She is blessed here and now. You can see it in the smile of her face and the way she asks you whether you are sure that you don't want that cup of coffee. I never saw a person more awake, and that is how her Master will find her, I'm sure.

Friday of the Twenty-First Week

MATTHEW 25:1–13

End of Time

"Stay awake…you do not know either the day or the hour."

As I write this, we are approaching the year 2000. That number 2000 is a very full, very complete number. We will not only end a century, we will end a period of a thousand years.

It is a number that makes people afraid. They fear that it might mean the end of this world. We seem to live in a dangerous and thrilling time. Prophets and pseudo-prophets are rereading the Hebrew Scriptures, especially prophetic books like Daniel, or the Book of Revelation in the Christian Scriptures.

It isn't the first time that this has happened. We have a report of the Mass that Pope Sylvester II celebrated in the old Saint Peter's Basilica in Rome at midnight December 31 of the year 999. The basilica was full. Some people had given everything they had to the poor just before Mass began. They were sitting in sackcloth and ashes in the church. Some of them didn't even dare to look up at the moment of consecration. They were lying flat on the earth with their arms outstretched as on a cross. At the moment that the bells started to ring at midnight, some of those present died of pure fear. But when the tolling of the bells was over, and the earth didn't open, and no fire came down from heaven, it was as if everyone woke up from a nightmare. Weeping and laughing, the crowd started to embrace each other, man and woman, friend and foe, master and servant, and the bells of all the churches in Rome started ringing.

Jesus asks us to be prepared. We should be as ready as the five sensible bridesmaids at the moment of the bridegroom's arrival.

We have to do some long-range planning for the coming of Jesus at the end of our own days, and even for his return at the apocalyptic end of human history. It is just as important to do some short-range planning for the coming of Jesus in the "now" and "here" of our daily life.

Saturday of the Twenty-First Week

MATTHEW 25:14-30

Gain

"The person who had received five talents promptly went and traded with them and made five more."

Several times Jesus expresses his amazement about what people do to enrich themselves. He calls them children of the darkness, because they misjudge what their lives are about, but he admires their dedication.

He does *not* admire what they do. He makes it clear that it is very difficult, if not impossible, to combine a mere interest in money with an interest in the reign of God.

We don't need Jesus to know this. Human history itself witnesses to that difficulty. Hundreds of years ago Bartolomé de las Casas wrote what became a classic about the greed of the Spanish conquerors of Latin America. In it he says: "I am not saying that they are out to murder, but I do say that they want to get rich. They want to swim in gold by the labor of and the sweat of the wretched natives, which they use as if they were tools, with the unavoidable result that they all die in exhaustion and misery."

The people de Las Casas wrote about were not bad. They were not necessarily aggressive. Maybe they didn't even want to kill, but they did want to get rich. Their greed blinded them to any reign-of-God value.

This kind of attitude is at work all around us. Shops are kept open even at the most impossible hours. Appointment books are overbooked. The deadliest deals are made. Wars are waged. Health, honor, integrity, and leisure are sacrificed to make more money. Jesus must be again amazed.

Jesus says: "If only the children of the light would be as eager to establish the reign of God as the children of the darkness are eager to get rich."

Monday of the Twenty-Second Week

LUKE 4:16-30

Faithful

"And he won the approval of all and they were astonished by the gracious words that came from his lips."

Jesus taught with a new authority, his amazed listeners told each other. Many explanations of that newness have been given. You can find some of them in other reflections in this book.

One of the explanations is that Jesus interpreted the Scriptures from his own viewpoint and that of his listeners. He didn't leave it in the hands of the Pharisees and the scribes. He applied it to himself and to his listeners from the moment he talked to them.

Think of the scene at Nazareth when he reads them some verses from the prophet Isaiah and then applies them without further ado to himself and his own life: "This text is being fulfilled today even while you are listening."

His main interest is not to interpret the Scriptures, but to interpret his own life with their help. He is faithful to the meaning he discovers in the text as it applies to his own life and that of his listeners.

So you have to be faithful to two things: the Bible text, and your own life and struggle. You should meditate not only on what Mary might have felt at the moment she sang her Magnificat, you should also meditate on what her song means in your life.

You can do that alone. It is better, however, to do it in a group, a group that is neither too large, nor too small. That means that a third faithfulness comes in. You have to be faithful to the others and their experience.

Carlos Mesters writes that those three faithfulnesses—(1) to the Bible text, (2) to its application to your own life, and (3) to community—belong together like coffee, milk, and sugar in the same cup. Each influences the taste of the other.

Tuesday of the Twenty-Second Week

LUKE 4:31-37

Evil Spirits

"Jesus [said], "Be quiet! Come out of him!"

Let me tell you how a fourteen-year-old boy in Kenya once made me suddenly see what being possessed by an evil spirit might mean. There are, of course, many more cases to be taken into account and many more explanations to be given. But listen to this one.

The boy was very poor, in fact he was a street boy. In one way or another he had obtained a bike. It was an old, rusty one, and both wheels needed some alignment. He aligned them himself, more or less. Then he decided that he was going to enhance his treasure—because that was what the bike meant to him—with gears. The bicycle shop was willing to do the job supposing that a boy with a bike would be able to pay for the job. When he went to fetch his bike, the bill for the gears was so high that he couldn't pay it. He was told that if he didn't find the money within a fortnight his bike would confiscated.

That's when he decided to steal a radio from the school's office. Nobody knew who had stolen the radio, but he was found out. He hadn't yet been able to sell the radio, and he produced it from its hiding place. When he handed it over to me, he told me: "Father, don't think that I stole that radio!" I asked him, "If you didn't, who did?" He answered, "The bike." He was right. The bike had become an obsession, like an evil spirit mastering him.

And Jesus said to the man possessed by an evil spirit: "Be quiet," and it went out without hurting him at all. How often I wish I had heard those words in time!

Wednesday of the Twenty-Second Week

LUKE 4:38–44

Pray and Move On

"I have to proclaim the reign of God to the other towns too."

When you read the lives of mystics you find the same kind of dynamics as you do in the life of Jesus. To be correct, you should say it the other way round: the dynamics you find in the life of Jesus are also found in the life of those mystics.

Early in the morning Jesus leaves the house to be alone. He wants to be alone to pray. He wants to be in God's presence. He often absents himself for that reason, sitting at the lakeside, going into the mountains or, as in today's reading, somewhere in the back of the garden. Every time he does this he returns to move on in his activity among the people around him.

Teresa of Avila describes in detail how you can enter your inner castle in seven stages. She also points out that every time she "touched" God, she was sent back prompted to do something.

Her contemporary and friend John of the Cross, who described the path to God as a mountaineering journey in seven stages, reports the same thing. It is as if in swinging up to God you are swung back into the world.

This is Jesus' experience in today's gospel reading. He disappears to be with the Father, and consequently tells the disciples that he has to move on.

We should allow ourselves to pray taking that risk in our lives. Do you dare? He is challenging you, too!

Thursday of the Twenty-Second Week

L U K E   5 : 1 – 1 1

Ichthus, Fish

"...he said to Simon: 'Put out into deep water and pay out your nets for a catch.'"

Why did Jesus choose fishermen as his first disciples? Many explanations have been given. John A. Sanford, an Episcopalian priest/psychologist, says that a fish is the symbol of what is swimming around in our inner depth: possibilities, riches, expectations, potentialities, combinations, creativities hidden from our eyes because they are swimming in the dark—silent, mysterious, and unfortunately unseen. The disciples are called fishers because, once confronted with Jesus, they fished those possibilities up from within themselves and helped others to that realization.

Jesus feeds the crowd around him with fish; he fries fish for the disciples at the breakfast he eats with them after his resurrection, and he eats some to prove that he isn't a ghost.

In the earliest African communities Jesus was symbolized as a fish, the symbol for the totality of our inner possibilities brought to light by Jesus. Julius Africanus wrote: "God's well produces a continuous flood of water, a stream in which there is one fish, caught on a divine hook, feeding the whole of humanity." It is in the presence of Jesus—the *Ichthus* or "fish"—that all of us can discover who we are.

No wonder that fish play such an important role not only in the life of Jesus, but also in the life of so many Christians, who eat fish instead of meat on the days of abstinence during the forty days of Lent.

Mysterious, indeed. Symbolism is the matter our dreams are made of. In that matter the "fish" plays an important role.

Friday of the Twenty-Second Week

LUKE 5 : 33 – 39

Dancing in his Presence

"…while the bridegroom is still with them."

He, a Catholic in good standing, participated in a church conference in Africa. He happened to be the only Catholic present. That is probably why everyone at the conference supposed that he also was a non-Catholic Christian.

During one of the informal conversations someone asked the question, "If you can't find a church of your own denomination in a foreign place, where would you join?" As he listened to the answers he noticed that no one would go to a Catholic community.

This intrigued him greatly, so he asked them: "Would you ever think of going to a Catholic worship service?" They all looked at him with amazement, and asked: "Did you ever go there? They don't know how to celebrate." One of them even added: "The Spirit is not there!" The Catholic was shocked, and rightly so, because what they said was hard to take, and only true up to a point.

Hearing him tell the story I was reminded of the many Catholic eucharistic celebrations I had been attending, during which priests and the choir conductors had had the greatest difficulties in getting the faithful to participate. Many in the assembly didn't even take the trouble to open their hymnals, let alone their mouths. Many left even before the "celebration" was over.

They never realized that they had been invited to a "celebration" as a "bride" by one who calls himself our "bridegroom."

Saturday of the Twenty-Second Week

LUKE 6 : 1 – 5

Time Control

"The Son of Man is master of the Sabbath."

Are you really master of your Sabbath? It would be good to ask yourself that question. It would mean that you live "your time" in such a way that you control your use of it. It would mean that every seventh day is free from work, allowing you to rest and to have time for those dimensions in your life that are "deeper" in you and "nearer" to you than your work: your family, your personal growth, and your relation to the divine presence within you and all around you.

Keeping the Sabbath is a discipline that helps us escape from being away from ourselves, engrossed in the pressure of endless labor. Sabbath means that we come to a stop, that the body gives a rest to the heart.

It is a liberation or, as Walter Brueggemann wrote in *The Book of Exodus*, "[It is] a disciplined and regular withdrawal from the systems of productivity whereby the world uses people up to exhaustion. Sabbath is a daring recognition that with the change in sovereigns from Pharaoh to Yahweh, unrewarded and unrewarding expenditure of labor is no longer required."

It is a liberation, a control, and a discipline that have slipped away from the life of many. According to research done in 1991, the time the typical American worker today spends on the job is one whole month more per year than in 1969.

We should once again become stewards of our time, taking into account the four elements to be realized—work, play, love, and worship. We should learn to say "No," not only to others but also to ourselves! We should be masters of the Sabbath!

Monday of the Twenty-Third Week

LUKE 6:6-11

Common Sense

"'Is it permitted on the Sabbath to do good…to save life?"

Jesus asked them a question: "Is it permitted to save life on a Sabbath day?" They were experts in the law. They knew that their law interpretation stated: "Whenever there is doubt whether life is in danger, the doubt overrides the Sabbath." Here was a man with a withered hand. There was no life in danger.

One of the apocryphal gospels—a writing as old as the gospels but that never gained admission into the New Testament—tells us that the man in question had asked Jesus' help saying, "I am a stonemason earning my living with my hand. I ask you, Jesus, give me back my health that I have not to beg my bread with shame." The man only asked for the healing of a hand.

When Jesus asked his question he simply appealed to the common sense of the people around him. He could do it, he could help the man, what was the problem? He said: "Stand up. Come out! Stretch out your hand!"

One of Luke's major commentators, Joseph Fitzmyer, adds that this incident brings out "the freedom Jesus' followers will have in the face of such regulations, when there is the opportunity to do good for people or save a life." Our hands should be stretching and helping.

Tuesday of the Twenty-Third Week

LUKE 6:12-19

Praying

"...he went onto the mountain to pray, and he spent the whole night in prayer to God."

Luke is interested in prayer. He is especially interested in the kind of prayer in which you contact the Holy Spirit. That Spirit is the first thing he mentions when writing Acts. "You are going to be baptized with the Holy Spirit...you will receive the power of the Holy Spirit which will come on you" (Acts 1:5, 8). Luke mentions the role of the Holy Spirit eighteen times in his writings. According to Luke praying is making and keeping contact with the Holy Spirit in you.

That is what Jesus does, from his baptism to his death on the cross. In four of the parables Luke recounts, Jesus speaks about prayer. He tells us that we should pray constantly, that we should pray for the coming of the reign of God, that we should pray against temptations that might make us forget that reign, and that we should pray constantly for the Holy Spirit.

Those intentions relate to one another. The realization of the reign of God among us is the reason that we should remain in contact with the Holy Spirit, and it is the Holy Spirit who pushes us towards that fulfillment. That is not all, however.

There is another aspect to the presence of the Holy Spirit in us. That other aspect is the Holy Spirit's presence itself. Wherever we are, whatever happens to us, we are always "at home" with that Spirit.

This is a terrific reality, one that we don't take sufficiently into account. Its realization would change our whole life. Once a guest master apologized to Charles de Foucauld, the founder of the Little Brothers and Sisters of Charity, for leaving him alone in a parlor. Charles laughed and said that he was never alone. You aren't either!

Wednesday of the Twenty-Third Week

LUKE 6:20-26

Beatitudes

"How blessed are you who are poor, the reign of God is yours."

Luke's version of the beatitudes sounds like an echo of Mary's Magnificat when she meets Elizabeth. They both express a hope to be realized in the future. But that isn't the only thing they do.

Not everything in Jesus' message about the coming reign of God can be explained simply in terms of the future. It is in the present time, in our "now," in the present, that he asks us to address God as our Father, and to pray for the realization of God's reign. It is in the "here and now" that we have to forgive those who sin against us. It is in the here and now that those we have sinned against should forgive us.

It is in these, our days, that we sit with Jesus at the table, where he breaks his bread with us and shares his wine as a sign and pledge of sharing, with him and each other, the final banquet in heaven.

It is here and now that the poor, the hungry, and those who weep are happy, not only because they have Jesus' sure promise of the reversal of their lot in God's reign, but because his disciples are reorganizing their own lives and the world in which they live to bring them into line with that reign to come.

The reign of God is in some sense already with us in word and deed, not only because of Jesus' presence among us, but also because of the presence of those who follow in his footsteps.

Thursday of the Twenty-Third Week

L U K E   6 : 2 7 - 3 8

Proverbs as Verbs

"I say this to you who are listening...."

Any language has its proverbs, pithy truths in one short sentence. They state a lot without too many words. They are a treasure based on age-old wisdom and experience. They can turn, however, into slogans, clichés, and stereotypes that mean almost nothing at all.

Jesus' language has its proverbs too. They often become slogans, too easy and handy to use. They become passwords we use opportunely and importunately, until they lose all meaning.

Our reading contains a whole set of them. "Bless those who curse you...," "treat others as you would like them to treat you..." and so on. You can find them hanging nicely embroidered and framed on the walls of our homes at the edge of our lives, beyond our reach and far away.

Jesus would like us to take those proverbs off our walls and put them in the center of our living rooms, kitchens, offices, and working places, at the core of our lives. He would like us, who are listening to him, to use them as "bookmarks" in our daily lives.

Jesus didn't give us these sayings to have them decorate our spiritual lives. Those "proverbs" are meant to turn into "verbs," becoming all we decide to do and not do.

Friday of the Twenty-Third Week

LUKE 6:39-42

Discipleship

"The disciple is not superior to the teacher, but the well trained disciple will be like the teacher."

Once an Indian disciple asked her master: "Maharajah, Sacred Scripture says that a guru, a teacher, is needed to make progress. Is that true?" The Swami answered, "It is necessary in the beginning; after that it is the teacher in yourself who can play the role of guru."

Jesus intended something like that when he told us that he was going to the Father, and that after his departure we would discover ourselves to be with his Spirit.

There is a divine spark in us. It is due to the Pentecost event. The little tongues of flame that would have appeared above our heads if we had been there, disappeared inside us to be with us forever and ever.

That doesn't mean that all will go well with us from here on. We all know stories about disciples who became as powerful as their master, but who didn't use that power in the way their master did. One of the stories in Acts concerns Simon the witch doctor, who wanted to buy the power of the apostles to earn money and get rich, and not to build up a Christian community.

Perhaps this is the reason that Jesus at times dramatizes the relation between master and disciple so powerfully. Take the instance when he washed their feet at the last supper. Having done that he says: "You call me Lord and Master and rightly so, I am. If I, then, the Lord and Master, have washed your feet, you must wash each other's feet. I have given you an example, so that you may copy what I have done to you" (John 13:14–15). Or as Jesus says in our Scripture for today: "The disciple is not superior to the teacher, but the fully trained disciple will be like the teacher."

Saturday of the Twenty-Third Week

LUKE 6 : 43 – 49

Goodness

"...the store of goodness in their hearts."

We often overlook the ordinary things in the life of Jesus and those who accompanied him. They were hungry and thirsty, just as we are hungry and thirsty. They depended on ordinary, everyday human goodness and kindness, just as we do. They had to go to bed and get up in the morning. That ordinariness can be found even at the most important moment of Jesus' life.

Take what happened on Easter morning. Some women, Mary of Magdala, Mary the mother of James and Joses, Salome, and some others came to the tomb to bury him properly. They had brought some oils, herbs, and spices. They went to the tomb to wash and clean him, to anoint him. Simple acts of friendly kindness.

It was all they could do. They knew that he had been buried in a hurry. He had been taken down from the cross late in the afternoon, and there had been no time to do anything but put him in the tomb. He had to be taken care of. They couldn't just leave him like that.

It was simple human kindness and friendship that made them take this initiative. It was the kindness and friendship they had learned from him. Even before they knew about the resurrection, his life had begun in them, a life that manifested itself not only in all kinds of extraordinary things, but in the way their ordinary lives had changed.

Their fears had passed. In him they found new meaning and an immense joy.

Monday of the Twenty-Fourth Week

LUKE 7 : 1 – 10

Jesus' Amazement

"I tell you, not even in Israel have I found faith as great as this."

In 1988 the International Association of Mission Studies met in Rome. The discussion in one of the working groups began with the missionaries exchanging personal experiences. They had much in common. One of the participants said: "When I left my seminary I had not been told that I would meet God working with the Hindus. From my theological training I expected the contrary. It was a great surprise for me to discover that they, too, walked with God."

He and the others had discovered that God is wider than the Christian circle.

Jesus seems to experience something like that himself when he expresses his amazement about the faith of the Roman officer. In fact, Jesus doesn't meet that officer himself, because when he approaches his house to heal the officer's favorite servant, the man sends him the message: "I am not worthy to have you under my roof, and that is why I did not presume to come to you myself. Let my boy be cured by your giving the command. For I am under authority myself, and have soldiers under me; and I say to one man, 'Go,' and he goes; to another 'Come here,' and he comes; to my servant 'Do this,' and he does it."

When Jesus expresses his amazement about the officer's faith, Luke uses the same word he used for Mary's faith at the beginning of his gospel, a faith not restricted to the Jewish circle, just as our faith in God is not restricted to the Christian circle.

God is not just with *us*, God is with all of humanity, in many different ways.

Tuesday of the Twenty-Fourth Week

LUKE 7:11–17

Death and Hope

"And the dead man sat up and began to talk, and Jesus gave him back to his mother."

One gospel text that is often read at funeral services, especially for young people, is this story of the widow at Naim who was burying her only son. In those days, her son was probably also her only hope and livelihood. Jesus was struck by her grief, stopped the funeral procession, and returned the dead son alive to his mother.

At first hearing, the text seems an almost cruel choice for grieving parents. Parents should not be burying their children. When they do, it is because of something tragic—cancer interrupting a young life, an accident tearing someone away from their loved ones.

What consolation does such a text offer? Jesus is not present now, and the miracle is not going to be repeated. We human beings can do a lot, but we can't bring the dead back to life.

It is exactly at this point that the story about the young man at Naim makes sense. We can't do anything about death, but God can. At Naim God breaks through the hopelessness of this world. God opens new possibilities. The road is open to new life, life assured!

The story is about that hope, a hope that counts not only at the physical death of a child, but of all death: the death of a marriage, when a couple gets divorced, the death of a job when it is lost, the sad death of your plans for life.

The hope revealed in this story about Naim does count at those moments when we are confronted with the apparent deadliness of death.

Wednesday of the Twenty-Fourth Week

LUKE 7:31-35

Joining In

"...you wouldn't dance...you wouldn't be mourners."

The bishops of the United States have been taking on many issues. There have been many letters on peace and disarmament, on the economy, on poverty, and on mission. All kinds of deeds have been added to those words.

The emergence of the Catholic peace organization *Pax Christi*, RENEW programs, RCIA programs, hundreds of national networks, and all sorts of action groups and activities on a local level are signs of a change. More and more Christians see their professional skills as talents to be used on behalf of God's reign. The percentage of those who join these groups, however, still remains relatively low.

Too many don't dance with the Lord when the reign makes some progress, and many more don't mourn with God when the reign in this world is betrayed and people suffer.

As Jesus said: "We played the pipes for you and you wouldn't dance; we sang dirges and you wouldn't be mourners" (Mt 11:17).

Wouldn't it be wonderful if we did dance and did mourn, harnessing all the faith and all the energy there is? This is what the American bishops and the pope are hoping for: "There is no justification for despair or inertia. Though it be with sorrow, it must be said that just as one may sin through selfishness and the desire of excessive profit and power, one may also be found wanting with regard to the urgent need of the multitudes of human beings submerged in conditions of underdevelopment through fear, indecision, and, basically, through cowardice. We are called, indeed obliged, to face the tremendous challenge…, because the present dangers threaten everyone" (*On Social Concern*, #47).

Thursday of the Twenty-Fourth Week

LUKE 7:36-50

Forgiven and Accepted

"It is someone who is forgiven little who shows little love."

During the party a rich Pharisee gave in honor of Jesus, a woman came in. Those present recognized her; she had a bad name in town. She went to Jesus and waited on him; she wept, and at a certain point she knelt at his feet and anointed them with the oils she had brought. Even before Simon, his host, could make any remark Jesus addressed him: "I tell you her sins, many as they are, have been forgiven her." It is strange that he tells this to Simon, even before he says anything to the woman anointing his feet.

That woman already knew. She is not forgiven because she is anointing Jesus' feet, showing her love. She anoints Jesus' feet because she is forgiven! "It is someone who is forgiven little who shows little love."

From our own human experience, it is not difficult to grasp what happened here. It is the case of someone who is despicable in her own eyes. Everyone despises her. She is a nobody to others. She is not anointing his feet to be forgiven. In that case forgiveness would have depended on her initiative. She understood and felt that Jesus forgave her, that Jesus—unlike all the others—accepted her.

She knew that he was willing to recognize her as a person, notwithstanding all that had happened to her. She remained valid in his eyes. That is why she came in with her perfumes and oils.

She anointed him because she loved him, and she loved him because she knew that he loved her.

Friday of the Twenty-Fourth Week

LUKE 8:1–3

Women Disciples

"...with him went the twelve as well as certain women...."

The apostles were not the only ones accompanying Jesus. Many women followed him as his disciples. Their role is always minimized, though in this text Luke mentions them here together with the Twelve in one and the same sentence.

And just as he did with those men, he calls some of them by name: Mary, surnamed the Magdalene, Joanna, Susanna, and many others. Luke adds that Jesus lived from their resources. They paid for him and his male disciples. It would be an interesting, and to many persons probably a disturbing, question to ask whether they also paid for his last supper with them.

Yet, the role of those women in Jesus' ministry is often minimized in the church. When David Bosch wrote his recent brilliant study *Transforming Mission*, one of the complaints was that he had overlooked almost totally the role of women in the apostolic outreach of the churches through the centuries.

In his writings Luke is clearly aware of the independent role of women during the life of Jesus and in the early communities. He names no fewer than twenty-six women participants in the story of the church, together with several groups of women. Luke saw a fairness, a dignity, and an opportunity accorded to women in the early church that contrasted sharply with the ways and morals of their time.

In Christ a new era had dawned for women, offering liberation, equal value in God's sight, and wide social vocation. Luke would have us know it.

It is good to remember all this, especially in a time when the church is again—and rightly so—reconsidering the position of her female members.

Saturday of the Twenty-Fourth Week

LUKE 8:4–15

Abundance

"A sower went out to sow his seed."

In her book *The Color Purple*, Alice Walker tells a story about God going out in the world sowing seeds, planting plants. Lavender was one of the seeds God threw with divine abundance all over a countryside, anticipating the joy their purple color and their smell would give to humankind.

The seeds sprouted, the plants grew up, buds developed and opened their candles of purple flowers. The field lit up in a brilliance of purple that beat the nicest sunset.

People passed those fields. They hurried through them. Even those who walked were in such a hurry and so intent on their work, that no one looked up to notice the color purple, or to inhale the glorious lavender smell.

Walker then uses a rather indecorous term telling what God thought about this lack of reaction. God really felt "pissed off." When she asks, "What do you think God did after that?" the answer was, "Oh, God just will try something else."

Jesus' gospel story seems to suggest that the sower went out only once to sow his seed. In human affairs it is often like that. In God's affairs, in the reign business, it is not like that. The seed is in abundance, and God is endlessly patient. As long as we live here on this earth God will come out to us again and again hoping that one day the seed will be caught and sprout. God will not give up on us, nor will he give up on others around us; and being created in God's image, neither should we.

Monday of the Twenty-Fifth Week

LUKE 8:16–18

Let It Shine

"..so that people may see the light..."

Some animals started a school. The school had classes in things animals do, swimming, flying, and running. The duck, a good swimmer, was asked to run, and soon became an average swimmer. The rabbit, good at running, broke his leg while trying to fly. The eagle, the top one in the flying class, was disabled for life when she tried to swim. By the end of the school term none of the animals were very good at anything.

A silly story, but that silliness is the point. God gave every one of us a unique set of strengths and weaknesses. The gospel often calls them talents. As Saint Paul remarks in his first letter to the Corinthians, they all come from "the Spirit, who distributes them at will to each individual."

Those talents are not God's gifts to *us*, they are God's gifts to the *world*. Not all of us are equally gifted, but we all have the capability to shine the light God's love entrusted to us.

We might be limited in our talents and in our sphere of influence. But if we are faithful to them, our words and deeds may be exactly what others need in order to find their talents and gifts in their own hearts.

It is the way friends and lovers, artists and cooks, academicians and surgeons, preachers and authors—the list of our talents is almost endless—enlighten and help one another in this world of ours.

Know your strengths, recognize your talents, engage your abilities, develop your capacity to love, to console, and to support. Don't put your light under a bowl or a basket. And in case you do hide your light, you will be found out in the end, so Jesus says!

Let your light shine, please, let it shine!

Tuesday of the Twenty-Fifth Week

LUKE 8 : 1 9 – 2 1

Practice

"My mother and my brothers are those who hear the word of God and put it into practice."

The Good News as told by Luke is full of high expectations. Mary sang that the starving would be filled with good things, Zechariah prophesied that we would be guided into the way of peace, and Jesus himself said the year of favor (or the year of the Jubilee, the remake of the world) started with his coming.

All this didn't remain a question of words only. Jesus did begin the newness in his own life, and after his death and resurrection the early community reorganized its life accordingly. What can the poor and mangled in this world expect from our actual Christian community?

You must have heard what happened at Toronto's Airport Vineyard Church, January 20, 1994. During a church service practically the whole community burst out in laughter. This "Toronto Blessing," as it has come to be known, has, over the years, touched more than 200,000 visitors and spread to Great Britain, where about 2,500 to 4,000 communities from all kinds of Christian denominations had the same experience, and thousands of newsletters, manuals, and guidelines have been published about it.

One commentator is very harsh in his interpretation of this strange phenomenon. Joseph McAuliffe, suggests that the Toronto Blessing is a concrete indictment of most of actual official Christianity. The church became something like a joke in the world, he noted, instead of being its salt and its light. Its presence became laughable because those who heard the word didn't put it into practice. His interpretation might not be right, but it is definitely something to think about.

Wednesday of the Twenty-Fifth Week

LUKE 9:1-6

Experience

"He sent them out to proclaim the reign of God."

A bishop appeared on television. He expressed his worry about the spiritual condition of the teenagers in his diocese. He blamed their poor spiritual condition on their lack of religious knowledge. A religious educator joined the bishop and was asked what to do about it. Bishop and teacher decided that the youth needed better and more straightforward textbooks and texts. They were going to provide those texts, so they said.

Of course, texts are needed. The Bible itself shows that. It is a book with many pages. Those texts should be analyzed, taught, disseminated, and explained to others. It is, however, good to note that the greater part of Sacred Scripture consists of stories.

When asked a question Jesus almost always answered by telling a story. Stories are always about human (and, in the case of Sacred Scripture, religious) experiences. It is that experience that counts in the first place. A text, even the very best one, will only begin to count when it is connected to experience.

Jesus spoke to his disciples; he taught them; he introduced them to a greater understanding of the stories they already knew; he told them lots of stories they had never heard before. Those stories told of the experience of others.

Sending the disciples out, like he did in our reading today, he helped them to experience for themselves that they were charged with his Spirit. It is crucial for teacher and pupil to have personal experience of the stories they tell and are told, the texts they teach and are taught.

Thursday of the Twenty-Fifth Week

LUKE 9:7-9

Bad Conscience

"And he was anxious to see him."

Herod had a bad conscience. He decapitated John the Baptizer. It made him anxious to see Jesus. "Who was he? What did he know? How did he react? Was he a prophet? Was he Elijah? Or, God forbid, was he maybe John the Baptizer, whose murder still haunted him?" Thinking about that last possibility, "Herod said, 'John? I beheaded him. So who is this I hear such reports about?'"

We don't know whether Herod ever got an answer to his question about who Jesus was. We do know that when later informers come to tell Jesus that Herod wants to kill him, Jesus calls Herod a fox (Luke 13:31).

In the end the two met when Pilate sent Jesus over at his trial. Herod didn't get any reply to his questions from Jesus. He didn't take any responsibility for Jesus' fate, either. He had been anxious to see him, now he was anxious to get him out of his sight.

There is an old saying: "Conscience does make cowards of us all." A bad conscience certainly does. We are hiding things not only from the others, but even from ourselves. We live in constant denial and at the same time in fear of being found out. Some psychologists even suggest that this is what makes us so interested in court cases. Will the defense be able to outdo the prosecution, so that the accused will be able to keep his crime hidden, sometimes against all evidence?

Herod can be our example in one way: his bad conscience makes him want to see Jesus. When we are in bad conscience it would be a good thing for us to have the same desire—not for the reason Herod had, but in view of an admission of sin, forgiveness, conversion, and also to get rid of the constant anxiety of that bad conscience.

Friday of the Twenty-Fifth Week

LUKE 9:18-22

Christit of God

"It was Peter who spoke up, 'The Christ of God,' he said."

People around Jesus were always asking, "Who is he?" It was a question asked from the very beginning of his life. He is obviously someone who touches everyone, someone who causes a strong reaction, either favorable or unfavorable. There are all kinds of rumors and ideas about him. Why does he do the things he does? Why does he always seem to be on the side of the sick, the poor, and the abused?

He himself asked that question: "Who do the crowds say I am?" There are two answers: the one from Peter, who says, "You are the Christ of God, which means you are the anointed of God," and his own, "The Son of Man."

Immediately afterwards he describes what those names entail. He uses four verbs doing that: to suffer, to be rejected, to be put to death, and to rise.

Why would that be? Why does it still happen day in and day out to those who follow him?

It has to do with the divine dynamic in our world, a dynamic described in the main event of Hebrew Sacred Scriptures: the Exodus.

The God of the Exodus is an "ethical" God, a God who takes the side of the oppressed poor. This option for the poor implies the willingness to do something about this world, to convert, change, restore, and heal it. It is an option that isn't well received by those who are profiting from the world as it is at the moment, and who are powerful in it.

Consequently, to opt for the healing of the world is dangerous. It means being gripped by God's dynamic in this world. It is what he asks his followers to do and be. It is the cross all of us have to carry. It is the task we face in the exercise of our daily work and skill.

Saturday of the Twenty-Fifth Week

L U K E   9 : 4 3 – 4 5

Pain and Suffering

"For your part, you must have these words constantly in mind...."

He was sitting in the waiting room of a clinic, preparing to undergo a painful operation. He started a conversation with the woman next to him. He learned that she had undergone the same operation he was in for. But he was afraid to ask her about it.

We often don't want to hear about things like that. When we ask someone, "How do you do?" we would be upset if the answer would be about suffering and pain. We don't want to hear that truth. No, thank you!

In the gospel reading of today Jesus and his disciples had just come back from his transfiguration on the mountain. The light still dazzled in their eyes. Coming down, they had been confronted with the pain of a father whose only child was suffering from seizures. When his disciples hadn't been able to help the child, Jesus had intervened. He cured the child and returned him to his father. "And everyone was awestruck by the greatness of God." Pain had been overcome. A new restored world sparkled in front of their eyes.

At that very moment of glory he warned them again about the price he would have to pay to overcome the evil in this world—how he would be delivered into the hands of evil, how it would murder him, but how he would prevail.

They understood the glorious part; they didn't understand the pain. They didn't want to, that's why they didn't even ask a question about the price that would have to be paid. Would we dare to ask that question in our own lives?

Monday of the Twenty-Sixth Week

LUKE 9:46-50

His Mirror

"...he took a little child...."

They had been discussing who was the greatest, the most powerful, and the record breaker. It is the kind of conversation that goes on all the time. The *Guinness Book of World Records*, the Emmy Awards, the Oscars, the Salesperson of the Month, and so on are all part of a system that has pervaded our whole life. In any home, school, parish, or community hall, you can find the swimming, fencing, running, soccer, and football trophies in special displays.

All those items are mirrors, ways to gauge yourself against others, to see who you are and who you are not; where you are and where you are not; what your status and rank are and what they are not.

In today's gospel, the disciples are ranking themselves and each other when Jesus interferes. He takes a little child, puts the child at his side and asks the disciples to mirror themselves "in" the child.

A child is as he or she is. A child has an eye and an ear for the small, almost insignificant, everyday things of life—things that in our lives are often overlooked and considered to be of little value. Jesus tells them, "The least among you is the greatest of all!"

John doesn't agree. He must have been telling the others that he was the best loved among them. He insists that there is a difference between those who are with Jesus and those who are not. Jesus doesn't agree with John. Those who are with Jesus have no monopoly on doing well and being good. Anyone who is doing good who is not against Jesus is on his side.

Tuesday of the Twenty-Sixth Week

LUKE 9:51–56

Making His Choice

"He resolutely turned his face towards Jerusalem."

All of us know in our lives of a decisive moment, a final choice to make, the point of no return. You find the story of it in practically any biography. It is often told in almost the same way.

Take the story of the best-selling British author Jack Higgins. He was terrified by the prospect of giving up his secure well-paying job to become a full-time writer. He tells: "On a rainy day in Cornwall I visited an old church where I got talking to a priest. I explained my dilemma, and he said: 'What you are telling me is that you afraid of going forward. If you don't decide one way or the other, the problem will make you neurotic. Take a sheet of paper, draw a line down the center and list on either side the reasons for and against resigning.' Whichever argument had the most points should be my answer, to be acted on resolutely. That evening I took the priest's advice. By a strong lead it showed me what to do. I typed my letter of resignation and posted it that same night."

In today's gospel, Jesus makes up his mind once and for all. He decides to turn his face toward Jerusalem. He had drawn a line through the center of his life, and he had weighed his reasons to the left and the right of it.

He opted for the Father's will, for the final test of the feasibility of God's reign in this world. He knew the test would mean going through his execution. He knew that he would be executed in the Roman way on a cross. He also knew the final outcome: he would be raised by the Father. His reason and motive should feature on our own list when deciding what to do!

Wednesday of the Twenty-Sixth Week

LUKE 9:57-62

No Procrastination

"Leave the dead to bury the dead..."

Any mother or father, teacher or speaker knows that repetition and using different examples help to make a point. When Jesus is telling his prospective disciples that they shouldn't delay or procrastinate, he makes the point twice. Don't delay burying the past, don't even go to bid it farewell. Follow me now, or never. He asks us to confront our hesitation and procrastination

If recent surveys can be trusted, out of every one hundred people, only sixty-seven have actually set goals for themselves, goals they can put into words anyway. Of those, only ten have actually made realistic plans to reach their goals. Out of those ten, only two will have the self-discipline to succeed in implementing their plans, that is 2% out of the one hundred! (Greg Harris, 1995).

When we procrastinate, it is almost always because we're afraid of something. We may fear we won't measure up, or that we will fail. We may even fear to succeed, which will mean a greater responsibility. Maybe we fear emotional closeness, or that we'll have to surrender some of our cherished autonomy.

The only solution to procrastination is to do what you know you should do. Delay is no help to anyone. Doing only the same old thing will never bring any change.

It is that change Jesus was looking for. That is why he adds that once the hand is laid on the plow you shouldn't even look back. If you procrastinate and only look back, you are not fit for the reign of God.

Thursday of the Twenty-Sixth Week

LUKE 10:1-12

The Whole World

"...the Lord appointed seventy-two others and sent them out ahead of him...."

Luke is the only evangelist who reports the mission Jesus gives to seventy-two disciples. There is another mission given to the twelve, but the report of the mission of the seventy-two is exclusive to Luke.

Bible scholars wonder what the number seventy-two referred to. They all agree on the twelve. Those twelve indicate that Jesus' mission extends to the twelve tribes of Israel.

There might be a hint given by the fact that Luke is a Gentile, the only non-Jewish evangelist. Another clue might be that he is writing for Gentiles.

Bringing these hints together and looking for a corresponding number in the Hebrew Scriptures, many scholars now agree that the number refers to the seventy-two grandsons of Noah, who left their grandfather's homestead, spread out all over the world, and thus became the origin of all the peoples that live on the earth.

The twelve refer to the whole of the Judaic nation, the seventy-two to the whole of the world. The Good News is that we together form one family, one father, one brother, and one Spirit. In the Book of Revelation, the last book of the Christian Scriptures, John describes how he sees all the nations coming together to the New City, the New Jerusalem, each one bringing its own treasure to it. It is the movement started by those seventy-two.

It is the movement that was symbolized from the moment of Jesus' birth, when the magi from the East came to bring their gifts to his cradle in Bethlehem. All of us are taken up in that swirling movement started around him, each one of us bringing in our gifts.

Friday of the Twenty-Sixth Week

LUKE 10:13-16

Online

"Anyone who listens to you, listens to me…[and] the one who sent me."

Most of us know the term "conference call." It means having a number of people talking together on the telephone. The people talking are online with each other. In this way you can have a meeting with people scattered all over the world. It is even possible to arrange those communications in such a way that you can see each other "online."

Jesus couldn't use the term "online" or "conference call" in his time as a metaphor. Yet, he was speaking about something like that. When you get into connection with him, you are online with the Father. When you connect to people who listen to Jesus, you are going to be put through to Jesus, and through Jesus to the Father.

It is the kind of networking we do in our communities when listening to the Good News he came to broadcast to the world. Jesus hopes that we all might get online, receiving his signals faster and faster, and living our lives better and better according to the data we receive.

Saturday of the Twenty-Sixth Week

LUKE 10:17-24

Childhood Memories

"I bless you, Father…for hiding these things from the learned and the clever and revealing them to little children."

This is an amazing statement: the Lord of heaven and earth revealed "these things" to "mere children." Jesus was speaking of you and me. Not about us as we are now, but as we were long ago. At one time we knew what the reign of God was all about.

Try to remember your first religious experience. Was it praying with your mother? Was it at your first Holy Communion? Revive it in your mind and heart. Was it when you saved your money to help the poor or a missionary in a far-off land? Revive it in your mind and heart. It will connect you to your own spiritual roots. It will help you to drink from your own spiritual well. Write it down to make it a lasting memory.

A Sister once told me how as a small child she walked through a brook on a sunny afternoon. When she saw how the sun was shining on her feet under the water, she suddenly realized that God is in heaven, that all is well, and that nothing would ever ultimately go wrong. As children, we knew—just as children around us today know when they trust adults without reservation, when they share their food, shout enthusiastically when they see a flower, a bird, a horse, a cat, or a dog, and communicate with all without any difficulty. Pope Paul VI once said never to trust a theologian who can't explain the Good News to children.

Jesus shows a fascination with little children, those who bear the full genius of the human personality, the ones who haven't yet forgotten the reign within, as Jean Houston wrote in one of her books. It is in ourselves that we can trace God's reign. We all carry within ourselves the little child that Jesus talks about. It is a matter of finding that child in us again and freeing it, of recapturing our original joy.

Monday of the Twenty-Seventh Week

LUKE 10:25-37

In Your Heart

"Jesus said to him, 'You have answered right, do this and life is yours.'"

A lawyer comes to test Jesus. He asks him, "What should I do?" Jesus doesn't give him the answer. In the gospel of Luke Jesus rarely gives answers. Instead, he returns the question. He asks his interrogator, "What do you think you should do?"

The lawyer gives the correct answer: you have to love God with all your heart and your neighbor as yourself. So why did he ask? The man asks another question to justify himself: "Who is my neighbor?"

Again Jesus doesn't give a direct answer. He tells the story of the Good Samaritan. When the story is told he repeats his examiner's question: "Who was the neighbor in that story?" Again the lawyer gives his answer.

Jesus often dodges questions. He doesn't want to answer. He leaves the answer to us. He's not going to take over. He respects us too much for that. He tells stories and parables, he gives examples and poses riddles, but it is up to us to make up our mind.

Jesus doesn't write encyclicals or pastoral letters. In the whole of the gospels he wrote only once, and then in the sand, so that in no time the wind had blown away whatever he wrote.

Jesus is faithful to the ancient text in Deuteronomy: "For this law which I am laying down for you today is neither obscure for you nor beyond your reach. It is not in heaven...it is not beyond the sea.... No, the word is very near to you, it is in your mouth and in your heart for you to put into practice" (Dt 30:11–14).

Tuesday of the Twenty-Seventh Week

LUKE 10:38–42

Martha and Mary

"Mary sat down at the Lord's feet."

At the end of his commentary on the Martha and Mary story Joseph A. Fitzmyer, the great commentator on Luke's gospel, notes that the Mary/Martha episode is addressed to the Christian who is expected to be *"contemplativus (a) in actione,"* "a contemplative in action."

We should not play out Martha against Mary, or Mary against Martha, neither when judging the lives of others nor our own life. The ideal is to combine the two attitudes Mary and Martha symbolize. *"Ora et Labora"* is the old saying you often see in monasteries and convents: "Pray and Work."

Yet, Jesus speaks about a "better" part, stressing the listening or contemplative side. Let's not forget, however, that afterward he only could sit at table to eat because Martha had continued fussing in the kitchen. He never asked her to come and sit down with Mary and himself. He knew, you might say—rather irreverently in a way—on what side his bread was buttered.

There should be a balance between word and deed, between talk and action, between prayer and work. Both are important. The two belong together; they are interwoven.

Wednesday of the Twenty-Seventh Week

LUKE 11:1–4

Not What but How

"Father, may your name be held holy, your reign come...!"

The famous theologian Karl Barth once wrote that praying is nothing but reminding God of God's promises and holiness. That is how Abraham prayed. When God tells him that Sodom and Gomorrah are going to be destroyed, Abraham reminds God of God's promise: "Is the judge of the whole world not to act justly?" (Gn 18:25).

This is what Jesus does when he teaches his disciples how to pray: "Father, may your name be held holy, your reign come!" It is on that foundation that you ask for a new start in your life and for everything you need for that life. You also have to ask God to forgive you for all you did wrong in the past, and don't hesitate to remind God that you are doing the same—that you are forgiving anyone who might have harmed you. And ask not to be misled, but to be guided in the correct way.

Jesus doesn't tell us what we should pray, but how. No nonsense, no long prayers—just straightforwardly tell what you expect from the one who put you in this life, and whom you trust in everything.

In Luke's gospel, after giving them the Lord's Prayer, Jesus tells the story about the man who asks his friend for three loaves in the middle of the night. He gets those loaves, not so much because of his friendship, but because of his persistence. The word Jesus uses is the Greek word *anadeia*, which really means "shamelessness."

To be too timid when praying to God is no sign of confidence. On the contrary, ask God to stick to the promises given!

Thursday of the Twenty-Seventh Week

LUKE 11:5-13

On Being Asked

"Ask and you shall receive...."

There are three persons in the story Jesus tells us today: there is (1) the guest who turned up unexpectedly at (2) his friend's house, and (3) the third friend who is asked for three loaves of bread in the middle of the night. Which of the three are we supposed to identify with?

We can exclude, I think, number one, the guest who arrived unexpectedly in the middle of the night at his friend's house. Of the two left over the likeliest one is number two, the one who knocks at his friend's door and asks persistently for help to be able to fulfill his duties as a host to his hungry guest.

The parable is then about the persistent—the word Luke uses really means shameless—friend. The story is then on how to pray to an unwilling God, cajoling and coaxing him to give a help that God is initially not willing to give at all.

But it is also possible that we are supposed to take number three as our model. It gives the story an interesting twist. In that case the story is about God who always hearkens to the cry of the needy and comes to their help.

Maybe we ourselves should identify with that third friend in the story. Aren't we created in the image of God? Aren't we the carriers of God's presence in this world?

When you take that third friend as the most important one, when you identify with the neighbor who was awakened and asked for help, the story is about you, yourself, helping out when asked for help by those in need.

Friday of the Twenty-Seventh Week

LUKE 11:15-26

Scattering

"Anyone who is not with me is against me; and anyone who does not gather in with me throws away."

We are living in a time when all seems to point at the fulfillment of the old prophecy that one day all human beings will come together. When you read the latest papal documents on mission and social teaching, you can't help but notice that he repeats that theme again and again.

We all know the slogan: "One world or no world." Yet, at the same time, we seem to be more divided than ever before. It is in this context that the words of Jesus take on a new meaning. We are accustomed to sayings like: "He who does not gather with me, scatters." Those words don't engage us. We gloss them over. They don't enter our spirituality or piety.

If they did, we would be busy at the process Jesus came to introduce in our world, a process that intends to bring the whole of humanity together as the one family of God. The process he illustrated by leaving us the breaking of his one bread as the symbol of his intention.

Perhaps his verdict is less a condemnation than the observation of a fact. If we are not busy gathering and bringing together, the opposite will take place.

At the same time, his words question each one of us. Are you a gatherer or a scatterer in the exercise of your profession, in the way you educate the ones dependent on you, in the urban legends you tell?

According to Jesus' words, there is no middle here. You are either gathering or you are scattering.

Saturday of the Twenty-Seventh Week

LUKE 11:27-28

Mary's Policy

"Among women you are the most blessed...."

Just imagine that we would be able to sit down with Mary at her kitchen table to ask her some questions about herself. One of those questions could be why she had been willing to bring Jesus into this world. It would be interesting to hear her answer. I wonder whether she would just answer, "I did it because I was asked to do so!"

We often think of Mary as a simple, young, and pious woman living in a small village, Nazareth. She wasn't as simple and naive as all that. She was full of dreams, hopes, and expectations. She wasn't just a "follower," she was full of ideas, intention, initiatives, and programs.

You can hear that when she sings her "Magnificat" when she meets Elizabeth. In that song Mary shows that she had been reflecting upon the world in which she lived. Nowadays we would say that she had made a kind of social and cultural analysis of her situation. She was like a "center of concern" in the world in which she lived.

Her song is the reaction of one who is keenly aware of what is going on around her—the political intrigues and the power plays. It is the hymn of someone who not only made that kind of social analysis of the world, but who was also keen on the role she had to play.

The world is full of rumors about her appearing again and again. Those apparitions show that her interest in this world did not wane! Neither should ours.

Monday of the Twenty-Eighth Week

LUKE 11:29-32

Crowds

"The crowds got even bigger."

The crowds around Jesus were growing all the time. He did something to those who surrounded him. They listened to him. They saw him. They touched him. Something in them started to vibrate when they did all this. They heard the melody he sang resound in their hearts. That is how they recognized him as someone special, and that is why so many accompanied him. It is the reason they "converted" to him and changed their lives. He awakened something in them. His dynamics became theirs. It didn't happen to all of them. Some came to trap him. They asked for more signs. But the growing crowds came because they felt empowered by him.

There are immense depths in us. There are fantastic possibilities, realities that remain hidden if we are not stimulated by someone else.

John once said of Jesus that he came to baptize us with the Holy Spirit and fire (Mt 3:11). Jesus himself said: "I have come to bring fire on earth, and how I wish it were already kindled" (Luke 12:49).

What was lighted in those who let themselves be affected? What was the change in their orientation? What was the difference Jesus made? What did they hear in themselves when they listened to him? What does it mean to be taken up in the process he launched in our world? When and how do we begin to live his energy and love?

Do we, too, need more signs?

Tuesday of the Twenty-Eight Week

LUKE 11:37–41

Outside and Inside

"He who made the outside made the inside too."

He asked her to go down to the basement to find him an empty pot. She went down and came back telling him that there were plenty of pots, but not a single empty one. He told her that he couldn't believe her and that there were plenty of empty pots.

She went down again and came back with the same announcement, "There is not a single empty pot." He then went down with her, and pointed at a whole row of empty pots. She looked at them, and said, "But not a single one of them is empty." He said, "What do you mean? There's nothing in them." She tilted one of the pots and pointed at its inside, "Look there's something inside." He finally understood what she meant.

She was right. The pots were all filled up with a substance he overlooked. A pot without any filled-up inside at all would collapse and crash.

We are better at recognizing the outside than the inside, not only in the world around us, but even in our own personal case.

From the very beginning we are told how God blew God's breath in our bodily frame, making at the same time our inside and outside. It is the divine breath in us that each one of us shares with all the others. Doesn't Paul say, that we hold "treasure in earthen vessels" (2 Cor 4:7)?

ORDINARY TIME

Wednesday of the Twenty-Eighth Week

LUKE 11:42-46

Lawyers and Mediation

...while neglecting justice and the love of God.

Jesus foresaw that we would meet many difficulties on our way to the reign of God. One of the ways in which people try to solve their difficulties is by going to court. Jesus warned us against that practice (Mt 5:25–26), and so did St. Paul (1 Cor 6:1–7).

It is a warning that is greatly overlooked by Jesus' followers. Consider these statistics from the National Center for State Courts. Between 1984 and 1991, civil caseloads in courts rose by 33%, yet the national population only rose by 7%. In 1990, "new cases filed in state courts exceeded 100 million—about one court case for every three persons in the United States." Things are no better in federal courts where the number of cases filed between 1981 and 1991 increased by nearly 60%. Unfortunately, many Christians rush to litigate whenever they have a grievance.

Jesus, himself called the Mediator between God and us, recommends a different approach, that of mediation (see Mt 18:15–20; Luke 12:57–59). It is a better way, and it is God's way. It is a system for handling disagreements that is seen throughout the pages of the Bible.

We are fortunate to have a legal system to turn to when all other recourse fails. We should, however, be able to find mercy and justice outside of the courtroom. Mediation is gaining popularity because it is generally quicker and cheaper than litigation. For Christians it also holds the potential to demonstrate that hallmark of our love for one another. In fact many church communities have begun to provide those mediation services. If your parish doesn't offer such services yet, why not begin, involving some lawyers from your community? Contact your diocesan offices, and if they aren't able to help you, contact The National Christian Legal Society, P.O. Box 1492, Merrifield, VA 22116-1492, (703) 642-1070.

Thursday of the Twenty-Eighth Week

LUKE 11: 47-54

Conscience

"You have not gone into yourselves."

Once I read the story of a child preparing for a biology test the next day. His name was Eric. The test was about insects and their reproduction. Eric had studied the matter carefully, but to be sure that he would be good at the test he put his textbook under his pillow before he fell asleep. Then Eric began to dream. In his dream he entered an illustration in his textbook, a meadow full of insects. He saw a beetle and told her, "Be careful with yourself. You are going to lay some eggs soon." The beetle blushed deeply. It was true! From that moment all kinds of insects came to ask Eric to check in his book whether it was time for them to lay their eggs, and where and how to do it. At first he answered, but then he began to understand that he was upsetting the insects. They were becoming afraid that the things they had been doing, normally guided "from within," were not according to the rules in Eric's book.

This story might illustrate—in a way—the point Jesus made. He told the lawyers that they—with their laws—didn't "go into themselves," and that their laws prevented others from doing so.

We need laws. Yet, it is from the voice of the Holy Spirit within us, speaking through a well-informed conscience, that we know how to act. To kill someone is against the law. It isn't wrong, however, because it is against a rule that comes from *outside* of us, but because it is against the voice of God present *within* us. It is against our conscience. If legislators don't make that connection, they risk receiving the same condemnation Jesus gave to the lawyers in his time.

The *Catechism* says: "Sin is an offense against reason, truth, and right conscience" (#1849). It also quotes Cardinal Newman on conscience: "Conscience is the aboriginal Vicar of Christ" (#1778). Christ is the one we meet when we go into ourselves!

Friday of the Twenty-Eighth Week

LUKE 12:1-7

Sparrows

"Not one [sparrow] is forgotten in God's sight."

People often try to convince me the world situation is getting worse and worse. And, indeed, things are often unbelievably rough for those who are poor and marginalized. And yet, I wonder whether the world isn't improving. What about the Universal Declaration of Human Rights in 1945 and its influence in the world? What about the sudden appearance of all kinds of provisions for the other-abled people in our society—like ramps for wheelchairs in the sidewalks, kneeling buses, and traffic lights for pedestrians that make a sound when green?

Another sign of this type of progress—and you might also call it this growth into God's reign—are those stickers on several body-care products: "Not animal tested." I still remember when I heard for the first time the term "animal rights." It wasn't so long ago, and I was very surprised. Remembering that Jesus said that not even a sparrow is forgotten in God's sight, I wondered why I hadn't heard about those rights before.

It is so obvious that they have rights. They, too, though in a different way are "knitted together" by God (Ps 139:13–16). If you help those sparrows Jesus speaks about through a freezing winter, you provide a service that in a way is divine!

Saturday of the Twenty-Eighth Week

LUKE 12:8–12

Witness

"If anyone openly declares herself for me...the Son of Man will declare himself for her."

It was during a terrible ethnic clash in Africa in 1994. She was the headmistress of a school. All the children had been evacuated, but some of them hadn't been able to leave. They would have been murdered because of the ethnic group they belonged to, so she was hiding them in the school. She was safe because she belonged to the group responsible for the ethnic cleansing. She was hiding the kids because she felt it her duty to do so as a Christian.

She must have been betrayed by one of the children who went home. One evening a band of excited and half drunk soldiers came to the door of the school. She opened it with her rosary in her hand. They asked her for the keys to the school so that they could search for the children she was hiding. She refused to give them the keys. She was overrun and killed. She was found in the doorway with that rosary of hers still in her hand.

This is only one of the thousands of similar testimonies from all over the world, where witness like this is given to the presence of the Holy Spirit in our world. A presence that will be honored by Jesus himself for all time to come.

For all of them—the well known and the hidden ones—it was their ultimate test. The trial we ask not to be led into, when we pray the Our Father.

Monday of the Twenty-Ninth Week

LUKE 12:13-21

Capital and God's Reign

"...for life does not consist in possessions...."

Eighteen times in his gospel Luke mentions wealth and its dangers. Mary sings about the difference between the poor and the rich even before Jesus' birth. Luke is the only one who mentions that the (poor) shepherds are the first ones to hear about Jesus' birth. He notes that Jesus belongs to the poorer class and that Mary and Joseph brought the sacrifice of the poor to Jesus' circumcision in the temple. He is the one to tell us that John the Baptizer asked those who had two shirts to give the second shirt to those who had none.

Yet, Jesus isn't against wealth as such in Luke's gospel. He definitely doesn't center his message directly on a redistribution of goods. The essential thing is to be with Jesus, to be Christlike. That is the real treasure, the genuine pearl.

To be with Jesus leads to a new style of life, a life that leads unavoidably to love and care, to justice and peace, and to the development of anything that would bring those qualities about. Our wealth, our gifts, and our talents should be used to build the reign of God. In certain situations, that can be done by giving alms. That, however, is neither the only nor probably the best way to tackle the problems of the world.

In Washington, D.C., a famous Christian community has many rich and influential members. They formed a "Ministry of Money" group. They meet regularly to discuss how to invest and use their money in view of God's reign. For instance, they might invest in the research on sicknesses of the poor that would otherwise be left unresearched and untreated, the sort of research that is usually not interesting for the shareholders of the pharmaceutical industry.

The medical doctor Luke would have had no problems with *that* use of wealth.

Tuesday of the Twenty-Ninth Week

LUKE 12:35-38

Waiting Upon

"Be like people waiting for their master to return."

"What exactly are we waiting for?" asked a young woman during one of the Year 2000 Jubilee preparations. The answer was that nobody really knew. They all knew that it had something to do with their hope that the Holy would be revealed to them, or descend upon them as never before. But if that were to happen, would they really be ready to deal with it? They hoped it would happen, and they hoped it *wouldn't*, all at the same time.

Søren Kierkegaard tells many stories to illustrate this ambiguity in us. They all go something like this: A church congregation somewhere in Denmark is singing enthusiastically "O come, O come Emmanuel," when the sacristan comes from the sacristy, runs up to the pastor, and whispers in his ear, "He did come, he's in the sacristy, he wants to see everyone personally." The pastor is the first one to enter the sacristy and, indeed, there he is, the Lord himself. He asks the pastor only one question: "Are you really serious about that hymn you were singing?" The pastor doesn't dare to give an answer; neither does anyone else from the congregation, when their turn comes. Yet, once back in the church, they continue singing "O come, O come!"

Annie Dillard once wrote about this "waiting for him" as so often expressed in our liturgy: "Ushers should issue life preservers and signal flares; they should lash us to our pews," for one day it will happen and he will come and draw us to a place of no return. "See that your belts are done up," Jesus says, fasten your seat belts and light the lights on your life jackets!

Wednesday of the Twenty-Ninth Week

LUKE 12:39-48

Holiday

"You too must stand ready, because the Son of Man is coming!"

He was an old missionary who had been in Uganda for over fifty years. He never intended to come back home, but doctors and nurses there convinced him that he should go home to heal from what they thought were stomach ulcers. Once back home and in the hospital, he was told that his sickness was much more serious than some stomach ulcers. He had those, too, and they could be healed. But something else was wrong, and he wouldn't be able to eat any food through his mouth anymore. They assured him, however, that they would be able to help him live for years to come. They brought him to a nursing home.

Some days later we brought him communion in the morning. It was the only substantial thing the doctors allowed him to eat. All the rest went through tubes and drips.

When he had finished his thanksgiving, he made some bank arrangements and things like that. Before we left, he told us that he looked forward to his death. He added: "It will be my final holiday!"

In the afternoon we got a phone call from the nursing home. They told us that he had died. The nurse said, "He must have given up, they sometimes do!" He hadn't given up, he had looked forward to his final—and in a sense even first—real holiday in the place where Jesus said that God, our Father, puts on an apron, sits us down at table, and asks us to tell our story (cf. Luke 12:37).

Thursday of the Twenty-Ninth Week

LUKE 12:49-53

Dove or Hawk

"Do you suppose that I am here to bring peace on earth?"

Pacifists, or the doves among us, are often deadly serious people. This is understandable; once you have chosen against violence, there is no place for compromise.

The same is true for the hawks among us, the ones who believe in the use and the efficiency of violence.

All that seriousness has a negative side. There is hardly any space left for some playfulness, for some humor. If you lose your sense of humor you will definitely have trouble with Jesus' words about peace.

Did Jesus come to bring peace? If he did, why then did he say, "Do you suppose that I am here to bring peace on earth? No, I tell you, but rather division." (But if you say that he did *not* come to bring peace, a whole new set of difficulties arises.)

The correct answer is, of course, yes, he did come to bring peace. That was his intention, that is why he came. But that wasn't how it had worked. His presence brought tension and tore families apart, as it still does. Some favor him, some are against him.

He didn't come to conquer the world with violence. He didn't come to force us.

He left us the word *shalom* as our greeting. It is the Hebrew word for peace, for wholeness. It is this kind of wholeness Jesus came to bring to the whole of humanity, a peace that asks for a choice. You are in favor of it, or you are against it—dove or hawk! It was a dove that descended on him at his baptism, not a hawk!

Friday of the Twenty-Ninth Week

LUKE 12:54-59

Reconciliation

"...make an effort to settle with him on the way...."

The violence people unleashed against one another during the twentieth century was extremely brutal. And the church's leadership didn't always stand on the side of the oppressed and the poor. It often has been on the side of the oppressor; even when it wasn't, it often didn't resist the oppression in the way it should have.

That is why the church cannot always assume the right to mediate between victims and oppressors, or even tell them to make an effort to settle the past without any further ado. The church often wasn't an outsider to what happened. Robert Schreiter notes in his book *Reconciliation* that the church may be in need of reconciliation itself.

In 1988 the United Church of Canada apologized for what they did to the native peoples of Canada. In 1990 the Catholic Church in Poland admitted its failings during the Holocaust years to the Jewish community in that country, and apologies like that have been offered more and more over the last years.

A good example of a church that had the right to help in a reconciliation between the suffering and the oppressed was the Catholic Church of Chile, by far the largest religious body there. Raul Cardinal Silva made his opposition to the Pinochet government clear from the beginning in 1973. When that regime came to an end, the church helped establish "houses of reconciliation" throughout the country where victims of the regime could come to tell their story "to settle" with their victimizers.

Another example of an even more reconciliatory approach is happening in South Africa under the guidance of the Anglican Archbishop Desmond Tutu. These are examples to be followed even in our family and community contexts.

Saturday of the Twenty-Ninth Week

LUKE 13:1-9

Healing and Growth

"'Sir,' the man replied, 'leave it one more year and give me time to dig round it and manure it: it may bear fruit next year....'"

Luke was a doctor. He made Jesus one as well. It is Luke who reports that Jesus says of himself: "No doubt you will quote me the saying, 'Physician, heal yourself.'"

According to Luke the world is sick, and so is the human family. Humanity should be healed in many ways. Luke describes Jesus' work among us as that of healing.

Yet, Luke is a good enough doctor to know that healing has to come from within the one who is sick. If any sick person asks a doctor, "Can you heal me?" the wise doctor will say, "No, I can't heal you. I can help you to create the conditions under which you might heal, but the real healing has to come from within you." It is what Jesus says after practically all of his healings: "Your faith has saved and healed you!"

It is like the parable Jesus tells about the fig tree without any fruit. Its owner will come, dig around it, manure it, and water it. That is all the owner can do. The rest is up to the tree. It is only from within the tree that the fruits will come. Without the cooperation of the tree nothing will ever happen.

Luke describes in his gospel what fruits we should deliver to be healed. We have to convert, to change. According to Luke, that change is the aim, the high point, and the summary of Jesus' presence among us—conversion, the forgiveness of the past, and a healed existence.

The questions of how and why we got into our present sad state are less important than that other question: how are we going to get it healed?

Monday of the Thirtieth Week

LUKE 13:10–17

Bent Double

"Woman, you are freed from your disability."

The woman in the text of today has no name. Some Bible commentators think that persons without a name, anonymous persons, stand for all of us.

If this is true this bent-over woman stands for all women. "She was bent over and quite unable to stand upright." Jesus would call her, and consequently all women, "a daughter of Abraham," that is to say a person in whom the powers and promises of God are mightily at work. This activity, however, was hindered in the society in which she lived. In her social context she was crippled, dysfunctional, and worthless. Besides, as Walter Brueggemann notes in his book *Texts Under Negotiation*, she had accepted that debilitating status as her place in life.

She is surrounded by men, the maintainers of the "order" in which she was "as" she was. Jesus called her over in front of them, and said, "Woman, you are freed from your disability," and he laid his hands on her. And at once she straightened up, and she glorified God.

Jesus refuses to accept the way the woman is, bent over and locked up in the mentality and judgment of her time. He frees her before her oppressors' very eyes, making her again the one she really is, a daughter of Abraham. The woman accepts the role immediately: "At once she straightened up and glorified God."

Jesus showed them the counter-world he came to introduce, the world of God's reign that in so many ways is still suffering violence among us.

Tuesday of the Thirtieth Week

LUKE 13:18-21

As Yeast in the Dough

"What does the reign of God resemble?"

The reign of God is like yeast, Jesus says, yeast that is leavened all through the dough. If you take that image literally then the reign of God is in everything, inside and outside, whether we see it or not.

Some people see it everywhere. It is everywhere.

•One day I left my wallet with my driving license, credit and telephone card, and a lot of cash in the supermarket. I noticed my loss when I was looking for my car key. I thought: "Oh...!" Turning round I saw the young woman who had been helping me to pack my shopping bag. She came running from the store waving her hand and holding my wallet: "Sir, you left this."

•A security officer in a dark and paramilitary uniform bent over to me when he handed me my bag that had just passed through the x-ray machine, and said: "Sir, you might zip your trousers."

•A child looked up at me in the bus, and offered me a piece of sticky candy.

All of us could go on and on telling each other stories like these. Many of us don't notice that constant presence of God's yeast all around them. We are too accustomed to it. We do see when it is missing. And that is bad news, indeed!

Saint Francis of Assisi saw God's presence in everything he ate and drank, smelled and tasted, heard and saw, touched and felt, and in everyone he met. That is why he left us his song, the "Canticle of the Sun."

Wednesday of the Thirtieth Week

LUKE 13:22-30

No Number of Saved Ones

"Sir, will there only be a few saved?"

Finding the right question is often more difficult than finding the answer. If you have all the answers but don't know the questions, you haven't learned very much. Saying that someone knows all the answers is no compliment.

Sometimes Luke groups together a set of answers that Jesus gave at different times. Luke does that by introducing a question. Luke uses this literary device when he introduces a voice from the crowd that asks: "Sir, will there be only a few saved?"

A whole set of answers follows. Jesus speaks about a narrow door; a householder who keeps his door closed; about people who come in from the East and the West; about how the last ones will be the first ones and vice versa, and so on.

But he doesn't directly answer the question of how many will be saved. What he is willing to tell is how to be saved. He doesn't want to play the numbers game, or give a body count. He is only willing to tell what kind of people enter. He tells us that Abraham, Isaac, Jacob, and all the prophets are there.

It is a pity that he doesn't mention any women, at least not by name. He mentions them indirectly by indicating the type of people you find in heaven, those who dedicated themselves to the reign of God here on earth.

If you are busy here only eating and drinking, producing to consume without any further perspective, you don't belong to the reign of God here on earth. You are saving neither yourself nor anyone else. The correct question to Jesus' answer is not: "Will there be many?" It is: "*Are* there many here who *are* saved?"

Thursday of the Thirtieth Week

LUKE 13:31–35

As a Hen

"I longed to gather your children together, as a hen gathers her brood under her wings...."

Many years ago some members of the "Women of the Grail" from Loveland, Ohio, told an international group of theology students how they invited children from the city to their farm to show them where milk and eggs come from. The children knew where to get their eggs and their milk, but they had no idea about hens and cows.

Much of the rural imagery the Bible uses was lost on them. They would have no idea what Jesus might have meant when he compared himself to a hen, when he wanted to express his frustrated and jilted love for his co-patriots in Jerusalem. Many adults today wouldn't understand it either.

Have you ever observed a mother hen looking after her young? If she sees a hawk circling overhead, she instinctively gives a warning sound, and immediately the baby chicks come running to hide beneath her wings. When menacing storm clouds fill the sky with rolling thunder and jagged lightning, she quickly makes a noise that beckons her brood to herself, where they find protection from the elements. As night approaches and the shadows lengthen, she gives a quiet call that gathers her young to rest.

Jesus did observe her behavior. He knew what he was talking about. He also knew that he had had no success. They hadn't listened. His love and care hadn't been accepted. He experienced the bitterest tragedy in human life—to give your heart only to have it refused and broken.

Friday of the Thirtieth Week

LUKE 14:1-6

A Child in a Pit

"Which of you, if his son falls in a well will not pull him out?"

Sometimes it's as if we are tested to see whether our human solidarity still works. It happens every six years or so. A child falls in an old, deep pit. The walls of it are fragile. The slightest touch makes them come down. The child, about five years old, is standing in water. Nobody knows what to do. First the child's parents and brothers and sisters, family and neighbors try to help. They don't dare to approach the opening of the well, afraid that it might collapse on the child.

The local fire brigade comes in. That evening the news is on the local radio and television. The next day the county emergency services appear on the scene. Ladders are put flat over the earth and some food is lowered to the child, who is too frightened to eat. That night the national television services arrive. A camp of tents, vans, and a free coffee shop surround the child in the pit, who is now on the international news. The president sends word, and so does the pope. When finally the child is back in the arms of his or her mother, the whole world gives a sigh of relief.

The solidarity Jesus spoke about did work again. It does in a case like this. So our answer to Jesus' question is, "Yes, we would get the child out, even on a Sabbath."

That is, however, not the full answer. To be truthful our answer should also be, "No, we wouldn't, not even on a weekday," because so many children in the streets and alleys of our world are even in greater difficulties, with no help at all.

Saturday of the Thirtieth Week

LUKE 14:1, 7–11

Option for the Poor

"When you have a party invite the poor, the crippled, the lame, the blind...."

Many theologians today use this gospel text to justify the church's "option for the poor," but few seem to draw the conclusions of this option. It really is quite a radical choice!

You can develop all kinds of theories about the existing structural injustices in the world. It is a fact, however, that this injustice has to do with the way our economic, political, informational, and religious life is organized.

Almost everyone is engaged in those structures. According to certain statistics forty to fifty percent of the working population is part of the bureaucracy and almost all the rest of the working population works for it, directly or indirectly.

It is difficult to expect that either of those two groups will be eager to "rock the boat." As soon and as long as the economy goes well, even trade unions have trouble keeping their members.

The change has to come from another direction, especially from those who at the moment are not part of the process: the sick, the homeless, the poor, the crippled, the marginalized, and, in many cases, the women.

That is why Jesus' option for them is very significant. So would our "option for the poor" be, if we followed his example. It would help to change the world.

Monday of the Thirty-First Week

LUKE 14:12–14

Free Service

"...you will be blessed for they have no means to repay you...."

The reign of God has to start somewhere in our lives. Today Jesus gives a hint of how to start it. The key word is not the invitation of the poor to your table, it is doing something for those who have no means to repay you. Something parents do for their children and vice versa.

Jesus suggests taking the poor up in the circle of those we serve for nothing, without expecting anything in return except—I suppose—their gratitude. It is more than rendering random acts of kindness. It is simply doing something for nothing because the person you help cannot pay you.

All of us are in situations where we can apply this reign-of-God principle—doctors and mechanics, dentists and lawyers, computer experts and shopkeepers, cleaners and engineers, babysitters and ice cream vendors.

When you meet someone who would like your service and would have difficulty paying, just say: "This time it won't cost you a cent, it's free." And when they ask you: "Why? What is the catch? What is there in it for you?" you just answer, "Luke fourteen fourteen," or something like that.

You can't render all your services free, of course. That is to say, not yet. Because if this type of royal reign service would multiply among us, it might change the whole of our world. And isn't that what Jesus intended to bring among us?

Tuesday of the Thirty-First Week

LUKE 14:15-24

Newcomers

"Go out quickly into the streets and alleys of the town and bring [them] in."

The church got emptier and emptier, first on weekdays and then even on the weekend. The heads got grayer and grayer. The voices in the choir got older and older. One day during a parish council meeting while discussing this growing emptiness in church, the council decided on a radical solution. The traditional approach for some new life would have been to invite an outsider to give a week-long mission. Those missions more often than not reach only the converted. They decided to play out Jesus' parable.

They divided the parish into blocks. They asked for volunteers who would go in groups of two to visit the families in those blocks. In homes with sick people or shut-ins they were to pray with the sick. In every home they would leave some information about the parish and the diocese. They would ask the people they visited to reconnect their life and activities to the eucharistic prayer of the community. They would ask the young people what activities they would be interested in.

They were sent out on the mission Jesus left all of us when he said: "Go in the streets and alleys of the town, open the roads and the hedgerows. Bring them in, and make sure my house is full."

It started slowly. Because of their small number they were able to reach only a few blocks. The stories they told about the contacts they had made helped encourage others to join this parish mission. Many were reached, new faces were seen, and a youth group was formed.

Wednesday of the Thirty-First Week

LUKE 14:25-33

Price to Pay

"No one who does not carry his cross and come after me can be my disciple."

Crowds of people are following Jesus. He is a celebrity by now. Some come because they want to be healed, others just to see and hear him, others again because they are really touched by what they see and hear.

At one point Luke tells us that Jesus turned around. That means he suddenly faced them. The movement around him changed. They had been following him. Now he faces them. It must have created some confusion. It is the kind of confrontation we all need.

Speaking to them and to us, Jesus says, "No one who does not carry his cross and come after me can be my disciple." In other words he speaks about the price all of us must pay to be considered one of his followers.

Does Jesus mean that we have to follow his example by being executed by those who oppose him in our world? To find the answer to this question we might ask ourselves why Jesus was crucified. One of the correct answers is that he paid in that way for our sins. In the gospels by Mark and Matthew Jesus says so himself.

There is more to the cross than that, however. In Luke's gospel the "good" murderer tells the "bad" murderer why they are hanging on the cross in Jesus' company. He says: "You have the same sentence as he did, but in our case we deserved it: we are paying for what we did. But this man has done nothing wrong." And the officer in charge of the execution confirms what the murderer said. After Jesus' death he exclaimed: "Truly, this was an upright man!" Jesus died because he lived an upright life in a crooked world. Doing that is the cross he wants us to carry.

Thursday of the Thirty-First Week

LUKE 15:1-10

Lost Coin

"...what woman with ten drachmas would not, if she lost one, light a lamp and sweep out the house...?"

Saint Gregory of Nyssa offers an explanation of the parable of the woman who lost one of her coins. His commentary (*Against Eunomius, XII*) sounds like a work of modern depth psychology. He explains that the woman in question is looking for her lost humanity. He thinks that the lost coin represents her heart and soul, and that the woman stands for all of us.

When she lights a lamp, that lamp is "without any doubt our consciousness, throwing light on our deepest depths." The lost coin can only be found in our own house, that is, in our own self.

Gregory goes even further when he adds that "The parable points at the image of our King, not yet completely lost, but hidden under the trash of our existence."

According to Gregory, Jesus is that king, the one who came to redeem us, but who in his turn has to be "redeemed" in us. If we don't find and free him, we will never be who we are supposed to be. We would be a "dead loss," a lost sheep.

That loss wouldn't only affect us. It would affect the whole of humanity, the whole of the flock. Jesus, the treasure of God's reign, is hidden in every one of us. We, too, need a lamp to light up the house, and a broom to sweep up the trash to find God's reign in us.

ORDINARY TIME

Friday of the Thirty-First Week

LUKE 16:1-8

Recycling and Waste

"There was a rich man and he had a steward who was denounced to him for being wasteful with his property."

A steward was denounced as being wasteful. His master called him and said, "What is this I hear about you? Draw me up an account of your stewardship because you are not to be my steward any longer."

In Jesus' parable the careless steward takes the accusation from his boss very seriously. He takes great care to arrange his affairs in a way that will help him get out of his difficulties. He doesn't use the most honest of methods. His boss will later call him "unjust," but he praises him at the same time for having learned his lesson and for being so "astute" as to rearrange his affairs.

If only, Jesus then sighs, the children of light would be as astute as the children of this world.

This parable takes on new significance in a time when we are accusing ourselves and one another of wasting our environment and our resources.

It will not be news to anyone that all of us could be accused of being wasteful stewards. The trash bags in front of our houses once, sometimes twice, a week give ample proof of the quantity and quality of the things we throw away, week in and week out.

The way we use and waste paper and plastic, energy and water, glass and aluminum, food and drink cry out to high heaven and ask for better management.

We have to follow the example of the steward in Jesus' parable. If not, we, too, will simply be dismissed as mere wasters of God's gifts.

Even recycling is a spiritual issue. Asceticism always was!

Saturday of the Thirty-First Week

LUKE 16:9-15

Tainted Money

"Use money, tainted as it is, to win you friends."

It is Saturday, the day many will go to shop, and we get a piece of advice from Jesus himself. He indicates to us how we should make good use of our money, adding "tainted as it is." He uses that qualifier not so much because of the unjust way in which money is sometimes earned. Even if it is earned in an upright and justifiable way it always smells because of its seductive power over us.

The advice Jesus gives is simple: "Use your money to win you friends in God's reign." The Pharisees Luke describes in our text laughed at Jesus and jeered at his advice, because—Luke adds—they loved money. How do we fare in this matter? Do we use our money like Jesus suggests?

You might check tonight. Get out your old checkbooks and read through the various entries. It is interesting, though perhaps somewhat shocking, to discover just how the money you have earned has been spent. The check entries record your vacations, travels, and various other moves. They will tell you how expensively or how cheaply you dress and how you eat.

The stubs will read like a family history book—births, deaths, and illnesses. They tell you about your tastes, habits, and interests.

They also will tell you whether and in what ways you made the friends Jesus speaks about. It might be that you need to review your budget allocations accordingly.

Monday of the Thirty-Second Week

LUKE 17:1-6

Forgiveness

"And if he is sorry forgive him...seven times a day."

When Jesus suggests that we should be willing to forgive each other up to seven times a day, he turns forgiveness into a way of life. That doesn't mean that we should take forgiveness lightly. It remains a serious issue even when it becomes our way of life.

To obtain forgiveness or amnesty in the reconciliation process in South Africa under the chairmanship of Archbishop Desmond Tutu a confession has to be made, the truth about what went wrong has to be revealed, and regret and sorrow have to be expressed. It is only when those conditions are fulfilled that forgiveness is given.

Sister Helen Prejean, who wrote the startling book *Dead Man Walking: An Eyewitness Account of the Death Penalty in the United States,* tells about a father, Lloyd Leblanc, whose seventeen-year-old son was murdered by two brothers, Patrick and Eddie Sonnier. Patrick got the death penalty.

Lloyd had told Sister Prejean that he would have been satisfied with life imprisonment for Patrick. He decided nevertheless to go to Patrick's execution, but not to see justice done or out of revenge. He hoped that Patrick would show regret and would apologize.

He was not disappointed. Before sitting down in the electric chair Patrick addressed Lloyd. He said: "Mr. Leblanc, I want to ask your forgiveness for what me and Eddie done." Lloyd Leblanc nodded his head, as a sign of the forgiveness he had already granted.

Forgiveness isn't easy, but it is the only way to overcome the past, and to bring our world together. The most difficult one to forgive is often yourself. But forgiveness is the only way to keep yourself together, enabling you to live on!

Tuesday of the Thirty-Second Week

LUKE 17:7-10

All Is Given

"We are useless servants: we have done no more than our duty."

Some years ago the film *Amadeus* was quite popular. For months people lined up in front of movie theaters all over the country to see this film, whose theme is a theological issue.

The film is about a confession. Salieri, a contemporary of Mozart and also a composer, confesses that he is probably the cause of Mozart's death. He wanted to murder him because there was something he never had understood: how was it possible that Mozart, according to Salieri a vulgar and superficial person, was able to write such beautiful music so effortlessly? All Mozart had to do was sit down and the most magnificent melodies flowed from his pen.

And he, Salieri, a serious man who had dedicated his whole life to God and lived an almost ascetic life, had such difficulty in getting music on paper.

The issue is about that total gratuitousness of God's gifts that Jesus speaks of when he says: "When you have done all you have been told to do, say, 'We are useless servants; we have done no more than our duty.'"

All we can do comes from God. All is given, everything is gratuitous. Where does the poet get his words, the painter his colors, the architect his shapes, the sculptor his forms, the doctor his healing power, the mechanic his skill, the computer programmer his creativity, and the author his inspiration, if not from God?

Even after all we might have done and all the awards we might have received, if we are honest about ourselves we will have to admit that "We are useless servants; we have done no more than our duty."

Wednesday of the Thirty-Second Week

LUKE 17:11-19

Jesus' Sensitivity

"Were not all ten made whole?"

The ten men suffering from what we call Hansen's disease—in Jesus' time an incurable skin infection—remained at a distance when they asked Jesus to be healed. He told them to go to show themselves to the priests, implying that they should start the complicated process of being declared healed. It was on their way to those priests that they were healed. Out of the ten only one came back to thank Jesus.

Learned commentators have been struggling ever since to title this miracle. Titles range from "The Ten Lepers" to "The Grateful Samaritan" to the all-inclusive "The Ten Lepers and the Grateful Samaritan."

We also could have a look at the story from Jesus' point of view. The story describes Jesus at a vulnerable moment. He seems to be upset about a lack of appreciation. The story teaches us something about his sensitivity and humanity.

Praising the one leper who came back, and blaming the others for not doing so, he shows he is hurt by their lack of gratitude. He would've liked to have been acknowledged and recognized by them as their healer.

He is one like us. All of us need the people around us to be able to be ourselves. As long as John the Baptizer was in the desert he could only hear his own echo. It was only when he came out of the desert that he became a prophet and began to understand himself and his role. It is difficult to know who you are without others. In that aspect of ourselves we need others, just like we need them in so many ways.

This is not the only time that Luke points to the very human sensitivity of Jesus. As a human being he felt the need for our appreciation and intimacy. It also means that he is able to understand our need for him.

Thursday of the Thirty-Second Week

LUKE 17:20-25

Where is God's Reign?

"No one [is] to say, it is here...there, for look the reign of God is among you."

It is with the reign of God as with the man in the old Hasidic story. He had a dream about a treasure hidden under a bridge in a far-off city he had never been to. At first he didn't pay any attention to the dream, but then he had it a second and a third time. He told his wife and they decided together that he should check it out.

After a long journey he arrived at the bridge he had seen in his dream. He recognized it immediately, and early in the morning he started to dig at the spot revealed to him in his dream. A woman came along and told him that she was surprised to see him there. She explained that she had been asked in three dreams to tell the person whom she would see digging under the bridge that he had an enormous treasure at home under his fireplace. The man stopped digging, went home, and told his wife the story. They both dug under their fireplace, and what he had looked for elsewhere he found at home.

Not all translators of Luke's gospel translate Jesus saying "The reign of God is among you" the same way. Instead of "among you," they translate "with you," or even "within you." Whatever translation you choose, Jesus says that the reign is with us and within us.

When the Nobel prize winner Elie Wiesel, a Holocaust survivor, was asked "How do you find God?" he answered, "'How do I find God?' you ask. I do not know how, but I do know where—in my fellow man" (*How Can I Find God?*).

Friday of the Thirty-Second Week

LUKE 17:26-37

Therapy

"Those who try to preserve their life will lose it."

We hear a lot about discovering yourself, about self-development, empowerment, centering prayer, mantras, self-healing, and therapy. There are all kinds of courses, exercises in self-discovery, enneagram weekends, Ignatian retreats, pray-ins, and self-discovery sessions.

Those approaches to self can be beneficial, helping us to understand that we aren't self-made and self-sufficient, and that we didn't invent ourselves.

The danger, however, is that we might withdraw from the world, and turn in on ourselves, attending to God and our inner selves only. We would like to stick to what we found in ourselves. We wouldn't like to lose it in the noise of the world around us.

There is nothing wrong in finding out that God is relating to you in a special way. It is a blessing to discover and foster this. But it would be wrong to overlook that everyone around you is in the same situation.

This insight is the ground for human equity. Like you, everyone else can pray to God: "You created my inmost self" (Ps 139:13). And the Book of Proverbs reminds us: "Rich and poor rub shoulders, Yahweh has made them both" (22:2).

The real center in your inner self will never be free from that presence and the demands of those others. Finding yourself is finding them. You can only develop yourself by "losing" your life in service to them.

Saturday of the Thirty-Second Week

LUKE 18:1-8

Pray Always

"Then he told them a parable about the need to pray continually."

To pray continually, to pray always: how is that possible? Can anyone do that? What could Jesus have meant?

Of course, he didn't mean that we should be on our knees all day praying. Even the monks in the desert in ancient times couldn't do that.

If the ideal of praying the whole day is realizable, Jesus must have been able to do it. But he, too, was not praying all the time in that formal way. How, then, did he pray all the time?

When you read the life of Jesus in any of the four gospels, it becomes obvious that Jesus had the ability to see anything that happened around him from the perspective of the reign of God. Whatever he experienced, saw, smelled, tasted, or touched betrayed the presence of that reign. It is as if he managed to look all the time through this world into that other world. Fish, snakes, foxes, sparrows, gnats, lilies, grass, mustard bushes, vines, clouds, sunsets, playing children, a found treasure, the stories and the news he heard, the rich and the poor, saints and sinners, camels, and thunderstorms—he saw them all in the context of the reign.

This is what "praying continually" means. It is the kind of attitude in which someone is simply in the presence of God constantly.

It is often called the prayer of simplicity. You need some formal prayer to reach that stage and to keep it up, but it is possible for anyone to learn to pray constantly.

Monday of the Thirty-Third Week

L U K E   1 8 : 3 5 – 4 3

Shut-in or Shut-out

"Jesus stopped and ordered them to bring the man to him."

The man was sitting at the side of the road. He was helpless in his blindness. Even when they told him that it was Jesus who was passing he felt shut out. When he shouted to draw Jesus' attention, the crowd around Jesus told him to shut up. His blindness made access impossible. Then Jesus stopped and told the people around him to bring the man to him.

Forty-three million Americans have disabilities, indicating that seventeen percent of a given parish's population will have some form of visible or invisible disability. There are 11.4 million blind and visually impaired persons in the United States alone.

According to Michael Lynch, director of the newly established Christian Institute on Disability, the church is reaching only three percent of the seventeen percent of the U.S. population that is sight-, hearing-, or physically disabled. Many church buildings and compounds are inaccessible to them. In some parishes impaired people are even told to stop complaining about this lack of access. Those called "shut-in" are often just "shut-out."

Luke relates the story of the paralytic whose friends were willing to do whatever it took—including "building modifications"—to get their friend to Jesus. Like the friends of the biblical paralytic, we must also take an active role to insure that people with disabilities are not left out of the church or its programs.

We should find out how many of our community members are impaired, for how many of them the church is inaccessible, and why. An estimate should be made of the costs of ramps, visual and audio aids, and the necessary modifications to doors and rest rooms. The parishioners should be educated and asked for their help.

And then a gospel miracle will be repeated—our way!

Tuesday of the Thirty-Third Week

LUKE 19:1–10

Jesus' Humor

"He kept trying to see Jesus, but he was too short and could not see him for the crowd, so he ran ahead and climbed a sycamore tree."

Jesus' humor often escapes us. This is because we make religion and piety such serious issues. Laughing in church seems to be somewhat uncouth, though we do it more and more.

Yet, when you read the stories about Jesus it is obvious that the crowd around him must have laughed and laughed because of his examples and metaphors. Don't you think they laughed when he compared John the Baptizer—that grim prophet dressed in the skin of a camel—with a blade of grass in the wind, and with a dandy at a royal court? And what about the beam in your own eye and the splinter in the eye of your sister or brother? Not to mention his suggestion about lighting a lamp and putting it under a bed or bucket.

Our church meetings hide the fact that the rowdy crowds around Jesus must have enjoyed his stories immensely, and that Pharisees and security guards must often have been upset when everyone around Jesus burst out in hearty and loud laughter.

Tell the story about Zacchaeus once to children, and you will see that they will be struck by the comical aspects of it: that he is a small person (all children identify with someone like that) who climbs in a tree to see Jesus (and at the same time to hide from him), who is called down to be his host. Consider the almost comical way Zacchaeus reacts to Jesus: "Look, sir, I am going to give half my property to the poor, and if I have cheated anybody I will pay him back four times the amount!" The crowd around them must have been roaring its appreciation. And Jesus looked at Zacchaeus, and said, "That is why I came!"

Wednesday of the Thirty-Third Week

LUKE 19:11-28

On Not Standing Still

"To everyone who has will be given more...[everyone] who has not will be deprived even of what he has."

At first sight this saying of Jesus seems to be unfair. Some even would say that this is exactly what happens in the world he came to replace with the reign of God. In our free trade, capitalistic, and global society the rich are getting richer and the poor poorer. Could this be the way Jesus wants things to go? The answer is obvious. So what could the meaning of his maxim be?

This parable is about using talents, and how to use them. The first two servants had used the money they got. The third one didn't, and that's why in the final instance he lost it all. Let's find some comparable examples from everyday life.

If you are a gifted tennis player and go on practicing it, you will get better and better. If you neglect your gift and never play, you will lose whatever ability you had.

If you train your body in a gym you will grow fitter, stronger, and nicer looking. If you stop doing that you will grow flabby, and in the end will lose all the strength you gained.

If you struggle to learn a foreign language like Swahili, but stop using it, its whole vocabulary gradually will be wiped away from your active memory.

If we really strive after peace and justice as Christians and Christian communities, new vistas and possibilities will open up for us. If we give up the struggle and take it easy, the reign of God will be delayed in showing itself.

Thursday of the Thirty-Third Week

LUKE 19:41–44

Shedding Tears

"...in sight of the city he shed tears over it...."

Every Christian region in the world has its religious icons. I was told that in old Poland practically every farm had a picture of Jesus sitting on a cold stone after having been scourged. When the farmers would come home from their hard work in the field they would look up at that picture and find the courage to go on.

Here in this country you find in presbyteries and homes that were decorated some years ago a painting of an old man sitting in prayer next to a table with a loaf of bread and a bread knife.

In the region I come from, in Brabant in the Netherlands, one of the customary icons in living rooms of farm houses was Jesus sitting on a hill overlooking Jerusalem, shedding tears. It showed the family Jesus' love, and even more so his humanity.

Jesus must have been a lovely person. Mothers didn't hesitate to bring their children to him, and children had no difficulties with him, either. Some people have difficulty in believing that Jesus laughed. When an artist in the 1960s drew a picture of a laughing Jesus, he caused some consternation, though Jesus once said that all those blessed will laugh (Luke 6:21).

Jesus didn't only laugh, he also wept. He wept, not because of what was going to happen to him, but because of what was going to happen to others. "If you too only had recognized on this day the way to peace!"

Friday of the Thirty-Third Week

LUKE 19:45-48

Dove Sellers

"Jesus entered the temple and began ejecting the traders."

The temple stalls Jesus knocked over were—according to an old tradition—called the "Booths of Annas." They were the property of the High Priest's family. They sold the animals needed for the temple sacrifices. Those animals had to be free from any blemish and had to pass a priestly inspection.

You could buy your animals in the open market outside the temple, but then you ran the risk of being sent back. It was far safer to buy your offering in an officially established temple stall, though the prices there were inflated. There were times that the cost of a dove in the temple was twenty-five times higher than outside (W. Barclay, *The Gospel of Luke*).

The dove sellers aren't mentioned in Luke's version of the story. In the other gospels they are mentioned. In John's gospel Jesus specifically addresses them when he says: "Take all this out of here and stop using my Father's house as a market" (John 2:16). In Mark's and Matthew's gospels he overthrows their stalls and those of the bankers.

Why did he single out those dove sellers? What about those who were selling the bigger sacrificial animals? Was it because of a story he had heard from Mary and Joseph? Did they tell him that they had offered, at his circumcision, the sacrifice of the poor (cf. Lev 5:7), two doves, and how they had been overcharged? It would be interesting to know.

Saturday of the Thirty-Third Week

LUKE 20:27–40

Afterlife

"...the dead do not marry because they can no longer die...."

One day some Sadducees confront Jesus with the question of what happens to a married person after death. They tell him a story about a woman who consecutively loses seven husbands. What is going to happen to her in paradise?

That story reminds me how, years ago, I used to bring Holy Communion to a very old widow. She lived on a farm that disappeared long ago. She was always in bed, one of those old-fashioned high wooden beds. On the wall in front of her hung a large photograph of her husband. That photo was old, too. It was yellowish and all kinds of small insects had crept in under the glass. As in many old photos, her husband looked straight into the lens of the camera, and there was no hint of a smile on his face. Taking a photo in those old days was a serious business.

The last time I brought her communion and gave her extreme unction—as it was called in those days—she pointed at the photo and said: "I am going to him." Heaven definitely meant more than that to her, yet she went to him.

Jesus would have no difficulty with that, but he said something about it that is worth reflection. "Those worthy of a place in the other world and in the resurrection from the dead, do not marry, because they can no longer die, for they are the same as the angels."

It suggests that people marry because they die. They marry because it is not good to remain alone. They marry to survive in this world, and to overcome death. They marry "until death do us part."

In the other world, there will be no death anymore, no loneliness, and no separation. The two that were together will be together again. Paradise means being all together. That widow was right, but in a different way than she thought.

Monday of the Last Week

LUKE 21 : 1 – 4

Widow

"He noticed a poverty-stricken widow."

It is reported that an elderly, partly crippled widow in the parish was dead for several days before anyone missed her. In looking through her few belongings, someone discovered her diary. Near the end of her life, as one monotonous day followed another, she wrote only three pathetic words on page after page: "No one came! NO ONE CAME!" In other words, no one noticed! Just like no one probably noticed that poor widow in the temple. His disciples didn't, but Jesus did!

For the first time in history there are today in America more people over sixty-five than there are teenagers! Increased life expectancy has brought a variety of problems: loneliness, nursing homes, and the depletion of Social Security. These problems hit women especially hard. On the average, widowhood begins at age fifty-six. Two-thirds of all widows live by themselves, and are twice as likely to be poor as elderly men.

We might wonder whether we in the church know how to deal effectively with their concerns. Does our contemporary church even notice them? The early church followed Jesus' example. From the beginning they "noticed" the widows in their midst. They faced the problem. They acknowledged that the widows were being overlooked. The disciples got together and discussed the issue (Acts 6:1–7). They chose seven of their best people and commissioned them to reorganize their service to the widows.

In his letter to all Christians—according to many the earliest writing in the New Testament—James wrote: "Pure, unspoiled religion, in the eyes of God our Father, is this: coming to the help of orphans and widows in their hardships..." (James 1:27).

Tuesday of the Last Week

LUKE 21:5–11

Hope-giving

"Master, when will this occur?"

The texts for this last week in the year are full of the symbolism, vivid images, and apocalyptic visions that Jesus used to emphasize that God will be faithful to God's people and that in the end good will overcome evil.

The world is going to change, the reign of God is at hand. "All these things you are staring at now, everything will be destroyed." Jesus warns them that even the temple they are staring at is going to disappear.

When they asked him when all this was going to happen, he doesn't give a direct answer. It isn't something that is going to happen then or there. It is happening everywhere. He tells them not to rush from place to place thinking that the end has come or is going to come.

Again and again we hear of groups who are mistaken in their belief that they know when the end will come. They have been standing with lights in their hands and in long white dresses on mountaintops, on beaches and in rain forests, after having sold everything they had, to wait for the end that didn't come in the way they thought it would. They tried to join the flight of meteors and stars, and lost themselves in their efforts.

They thought the Bible pointed at times and dates. It would happen at the re-establishment of the State of Israel (1948), the capture of old Jerusalem (1967), and at the occupation of the Golan Heights, and so on. Day after day, television preachers announce other dates, other places, other events.

It isn't going to happen like that, neither here nor there, neither at this hour nor that hour. It is happening all around us—and even within us—from moment to moment, while God's reign is growing and growing in and through everything.

Wednesday of the Last Week

LUKE 21 : 12 – 19

Your Opportunity

"...and that will be your opportunity to bear witness."

You don't have to be a Christian to know that the world as it is at this moment, can't be the right one. It might seem to be functioning for part of its population, but when we think of its global reality it is obviously unfinished. Walter Brueggemann has written that "Whether we look at the political-economic-military capacity to brutalize humanity and to terrorize the earth, or whether we look at the dysfunction of the ecosystem, dominated by greed and fear, it is abundantly clear that the world as we know it is not the one called 'good,' not the one God intended."

There is no need to strengthen this point with all kinds of statistics about the growing gap between the rich and the poor, the lack of education and health care in the greater part of the world, or the growing prison population, and so on.

You don't need much imagination to know that those who feel the need to work for justice—charged as they are by God's Spirit—will get into difficulties in the world as the world is now. Jesus makes that very clear when he says, "You will be seized and persecuted; you will be handed over...to governors for the sake of my name." And he adds, "That will be your opportunity to bear witness."

He promises that he won't leave us alone: "I myself will give an eloquence and wisdom that none of your opponents will be able to resist." "Your perseverance will win you your lives," and it can also change our world.

Thursday of the Last Week

LUKE 21:20-28

Not One-dimensional

"Watch yourselves, or your hearts will be coarsened by...the cares of life, and that day will come unexpectedly, like a trap."

Some years ago it was fashionable to call the Western world and Western humanity one-dimensional. Those who did so wanted to indicate that modern people often live as if the only thing that matters is their material welfare. They don't think of anything else. They have no further perspective on life.

They conveniently forget where they came from, and where they are headed. They live a life according to the old pagan saying *carpe diem*, which means "seize the day," enjoy it and forget about the rest.

This is a pagan approach to life, an impossible approach for a follower of Jesus. A Christian cannot forget what Jesus told us about the meaning of our lives. We don't just live for today.

Jesus speaks about our lives against a background of final things that are going to happen, when, in the end, the sun and the moon will darken, the whole of human history in the world as we know it will come to a close, and we will be swept into the world to come.

Those who believe in his words will be able to stand this changeover fearlessly. Those who never understood this dimension of our existence will be full of fear. They will not know what is happening to them.

We do: Jesus has told us. We should live each day aware of that revelation. Our acts and omissions are not just one-dimensional. They count here and in the world to come.

Friday of the Last Week

LUKE 21:29-33

Budding Trees

"Look at whatever tree, as soon as you see them bud,…you can see that summer is near."

My visitor came from that part of Africa where the trees are always green and most times even blooming full of flowers. Some trees would lose their leaves seasonally, but never all together at the same time as in the winter of the northern regions.

I fetched him from the airport in midwinter. All the trees had lost their leaves. Their branches stood naked and lonely against the blue of the sky. He looked at them, then he looked at me and said: "I had heard about it, but I did not realize that it was as bad as that."

Not knowing what he was talking about, I asked him, "What do you mean?" He answered that he heard about the effects of air pollution in America and its effects on the trees, "But," he said, "I never thought it was bad as this with all those trees dead!" I told him that they were not dead, and once home I showed him the buds still shriveled up on the branches he had thought to be dead.

It seems difficult to see the buds of the reign of God. Jesus asked us to look for them in our wintry world. Where do you see them?

The name we give to the Eucharist might give us a hint. The word for that center of our Christian life means "thanksgiving." Whenever we say a well-meant "thank you" to anyone, or when anyone says it to us, the reign of God is with us. Those words point at the buds we should be looking for. We will see them multiply and grow, because summer is near.

Saturday of the Last Week

LUKE 21:34-36

Attention

"Watch yourselves…Stay awake, praying at all times…."

The most repeated words during the celebration of the Eucharist are "The Lord be with you." They are (sometimes) said at the very beginning of Mass, before the reading of the gospel, at the beginning of the solemn Preface prayer, and just before the blessing at the end of the Eucharist. Somewhat older Catholics may still remember its Latin form, *Dominus vobiscum.*

Those words are a way of saying: "Pay attention!" Pay attention to what is going to follow. It is not only a warning; the words "The Lord be with you" also express a hope, a desire: "That the Lord may be with you!"

We all believe and know that the Lord is with us. All of us are equipped with his Spirit. That doesn't mean, however, that we are aware of this presence of the Lord in us. Some priests will change the words and say, "The Lord is with you." That is true, the Lord *is* with us, and yet, it is so often not true because of our lack of awareness.

We should be aware of Jesus' presence in us at all times, when we begin to pray, when we listen to his words, when we share his body and blood while breaking the bread and sharing the wine, and also when we are sent out in the world.

Let us pray that his presence in you and me may reveal itself in all we decide to do or not to do. And the world will be a better place for all!

Of Related Interest

God's Word Is Alive!
Entering the Sunday Readings
Alice L. Camille

Here is solid material for breaking open every reading of all three liturgical cycles, for Sundays and holy days alike. Reflection questions and points for action are included. Ideal for homilists, catechists, study groups, and those who want to delve more deeply into God's Word.
926-2, 416 pp, $19.95

The Word of the Lord
Reflections on the Sunday Readings
Philip J. McBrien

Summarizes the three Sunday readings and ties them together in a single theme. Excellent for homilists, Scripture study groups, and for personal meditation.
Year A: 659-X, 160 pp, $9.95
Year B: 700-6, 184 pp, $9.95
Year C: 729-4, 168 pp, $9.95

A World of Stories for Preachers and Teachers
*and all who love stories that move and challenge
William J. Bausch

These tales (over 350 of them!) aim to nudge, provoke, and stimulate the reader and listener, to resonate with the human condition, as did the stories of Jesus. Intended for preachers, storytellers, teachers, and for every person seeking to gain or impart wisdom.
919-X, 544 pp, $29.95

A User-Friendly Parish
Becoming a More Welcoming Community
Judith Ann Kollar

This handy guide for parish leaders, ministers, and committee members emphasizes the "sign value" of clear information about parish staff functions and committees. It offers communication and organizational tips as well as advice for solving or preventing problem situations.
937-8, 80 pp, $7.95

Available at religious bookstores or from:

TWENTY-THIRD PUBLICATIONS

P.O. BOX 180 • 185 WILLOW ST. • MYSTIC, CT 06355 • 1-860-536-2611 • 1-800-321-0411 • FAX 1-800-572-0788

Call for a free catalog